Impact of Healthcare Informatics on Quality of Patient Care and Health Services

D0140783

Impact of Healthcare Informatics on Quality of Patient Care and Health Services

DIVYA SRINIVASAN

CRC Press
Taylor & Francis Group
Boca Raton London New York

CRC Press is an imprint of the
Taylor & Francis Group, an **informa** business

A PRODUCTIVITY PRESS BOOK

CRC Press
Taylor & Francis Group
6000 Broken Sound Parkway NW, Suite 300
Boca Raton, FL 33487-2742

© 2013 by Taylor & Francis Group, LLC
CRC Press is an imprint of Taylor & Francis Group, an Informa business

No claim to original U.S. Government works

Printed in the United States of America on acid-free paper
Version Date: 2012928

International Standard Book Number: 978-1-4665-0487-5 (Paperback)

This book contains information obtained from authentic and highly regarded sources. Reasonable efforts have been made to publish reliable data and information, but the author and publisher cannot assume responsibility for the validity of all materials or the consequences of their use. The authors and publishers have attempted to trace the copyright holders of all material reproduced in this publication and apologize to copyright holders if permission to publish in this form has not been obtained. If any copyright material has not been acknowledged please write and let us know so we may rectify in any future reprint.

Except as permitted under U.S. Copyright Law, no part of this book may be reprinted, reproduced, transmitted, or utilized in any form by any electronic, mechanical, or other means, now known or hereafter invented, including photocopying, microfilming, and recording, or in any information storage or retrieval system, without written permission from the publishers.

For permission to photocopy or use material electronically from this work, please access www.copyright.com (http://www.copyright.com/) or contact the Copyright Clearance Center, Inc. (CCC), 222 Rosewood Drive, Danvers, MA 01923, 978-750-8400. CCC is a not-for-profit organization that provides licenses and registration for a variety of users. For organizations that have been granted a photocopy license by the CCC, a separate system of payment has been arranged.

Trademark Notice: Product or corporate names may be trademarks or registered trademarks, and are used only for identification and explanation without intent to infringe.

Library of Congress Cataloging-in-Publication Data

Srinivasan, Divya, 1988-
    Impact of healthcare informatics on quality of patient care and health services / Divya Srinivasan.
       p. ; cm.
    Includes bibliographical references and index.
    ISBN 978-1-4665-0487-5 (alk. paper)
    I. Title.
    [DNLM: 1. Medical Informatics--United States. 2. Electronic Health Records--United States. 3. Quality of Health Care--United States. 4. Telemedicine--United States. W 26.5]

610.285--dc23   2012038889

Visit the Taylor & Francis Web site at
http://www.taylorandfrancis.com

and the CRC Press Web site at
http://www.crcpress.com

This book is dedicated to my loving parents,
who have guided me and given me the courage to pursue my dreams.

Contents

Introduction xi

1 HIPAA: Intent versus Actuality of the Law in Upholding the Privacy of Health Records 1
    Overview 1
    Introduction 2
        How Did HIPAA Make the Policy Window? 3
    The Public Choice Theory.. 4
    Stakeholder Analysis 6
        Stakeholder #1: Congress and Its Impact on HIPAA's Formation 6
        Stakeholder #2: Hospital and Provider Organization Staff (Physicians, Nurses, and Assistants) 7
        Stakeholder #3: The Patient and Consumer of the Healthcare Markets 9
        Stakeholder #4: Insurance Companies/Third-Party Providers.................10
        Stakeholder #5: The Researcher 10
    Policy Analysis: The Past, Present, and Future of HIPAA 12
    Conclusion...13

2 Organizational Culture Differences in Incorporation of Health Information Technology (HIT) across Healthcare Providers 15
    Overview 15
    Introduction 15
    Organizational Culture Driven by a Hospital's Mission and Values................18
    Managerial and Employee Ethic and Compensation: Impact on Organizational Culture...20
    Training and the Impact of Training on Quality of Care across Hospitals...................... 23
    Cultural Competence of a Hospital 25
    Goal-Oriented Behavior of a Hospital with Technology 28
    Policy Implications and Conclusions...31

3 An Overview of How Health Information Technology Will Make a Mark on Hospital Financing..35
    Overview 35
    Introduction 35
    Supply Side of Healthcare 37

Demand Side of Healthcare 39
Structure of Hospitals and Their Financing Mechanisms 39
Mergers and Acquisitions of Hospitals 42
Tax Exempt or Tax Paying Status of the Hospitals 44
Management of Hospitals: Is There an Impact on Healthcare Financing? 45
Possibilities in Technological Changes in the Healthcare Setting 46
Conclusions and Policy Implications 48

4   Funding Electronic Medical Records: Reality or Illusion? A Cost-Benefit
    Analysis **51**
    Overview 51
    Introduction 51
    Background Factors 52
    Policy Analysis 54
    Cost, Benefits, and Constraints 55
    Conclusion 61

5   Impact of Organizational Behavior Characteristics on Usage of a Healthcare
    Provider's Health Information Technology (HIT) Services **63**
    Overview 63
    Introduction 63
    Past Literature 65
    Methods 66
        Descriptive and Inferential Statistics 66
        Logistic Regression Methods 71
        Model 1: Outcomes: Differences in HIT Usage across Organizational
        Providers and Characteristics 71
        Model 2: Installing a New or Replacing an Old EMR within an Organization 72
        Model 3: Likelihood of E-Billing and Electronic Claims 74
        Model 4: Electronic Prescriptions 76
    Interaction Term 78
    Robust and Reliable Outcomes Check 82
    Policy Analysis and Implications 82
    Limitations of the Study 84

6   Quality of Care and the Patient **85**
    Overview 85
    Past Literature on Quality of Care 85
    Data Source 87
    Methodology 87
    Variables 87
    Descriptive and Inferential Statistics 88
        I: Quality of Care 88
        II: Quality of Service Based on Medical Errors, Time Issues, and Arising
        Communication Problems 88
        III: Computing Discrete Change Based on Technology Use 90
    Limitations 93
    Conclusion 93

7 **Physicians and Perceptions on HIT Medical Malpractice Lawsuits: Can Physicians Reduce Their Chances by Using Health Information Technology?**..........97
   Overview 97
   Introduction 97
   Studies on Malpractice Concerns.. 98
   Focus of the Chapter... 100
      Analysis 101
      Outcomes of Medical Malpractice Perceptions 102
      Hypothesis for This Theoretical Model 106
   Overall Outcomes for the Models...106
   Policy Implications and Conclusion 108

8 **Community Impacts from the Detection of Bioterrorism Using EMRs** 111
   Overview 111
   Introduction 111
   Literature Review..112
   Financial Issues for the Nation Regarding Bioterrorism............................ 114
   Policy Implications/Analysis 117
   Conclusion..118

9 **Health Informatics and the New Direction of Healthcare: Mobile Health, PHRs, Mobile Health Apps, and More**.. 119
   Overview 119
   Introduction 119

Bibliography...131
Index 141

Introduction

In the year 2012, healthcare has been a fairly controversial issue for the United States, as state, federal, and local policies continuously debate big buzzwords like autonomy, leadership, regulation, and their presence in citizens' lives. What many healthcare professionals do not realize is that **healthcare information technology**, or **HIT**, usage in healthcare settings has been one of the few long-standing issues that has been supported by presidents of *both political parties* because of its pivotal role in improving healthcare quality, cost, effectiveness, and efficiency. HIT will work toward not only touching the lives of many and, possibly, saving lives in the process, but also affecting subcultures, groups, organizations, and more granular levels of society. HIT is, therefore, one type of information technology that could lift barriers between the patient and physician, patients to each other, physicians and governments, and, on a global level, could impact electronic government and intergovernment initiatives.

While many books propose topics that explain HIT in some regard, this book proposes an interesting and extremely important objective—to engage the reader in a discussion of HIT in the United States in an unbiased, research-centric manner, with a focus on various facets that will be grouped into two parts. *Impact of Healthcare Information on Quality of Patient Care and Health Services* takes an integrated approach, looking at different types of organizations, such as non-profit hospitals, for-profit hospitals, community health centers, and government hospitals, and, by doing so, provides a comparative perspective of how different organizations (specific to the United States) tend to adapt and use technology differently. For this reason, it is emphasized that there is really no "one size fits all" approach to HIT adoption, implementation, and meaningful use, but rather there needs to be efforts to help different organizations with their weaknesses and fortify strengths in technology adoption. Currently, the government approach targets all organizations at the same time and is trying to propose change on this macro level. Rather, this book emphasizes the importance in understanding that organizational level and microeconomic differences in order to produce change on a domestic level and, possibly someday, a global level as well.

The first part of the book (Chapters 1 to 4) will cover the basics on HIT and how the HITECH Act (Health Information Technology for Economic and Clinical Health, 2009) and HIPAA (The Health Insurance Portability and Accountability Act, 1996) will be implementing serious changes for stakeholders of organizations that propose to get on the HIT bandwagon. It also targets these key organizational culture factors that differentiate organizations, management changes from HIT, hospital financing changes that will take (and have taken) effect, a cost–benefit analysis of electronic medical records (EMRs), and numerous organizational behavior changes stimulated by HIT. The second part of the book (Chapters 5 to 9) focuses on the broader community: the patient, the physician, government, and how the impacts of HIT will be felt on each of these, as well as in the aggregate, as they all work together to create a strong HIT infrastructure. These chapters will cover quality of care and cost impacts on the patient from HIT, changes for patients of varying socioeconomic statuses (including Medicare and Medicaid populations), physician perceptions of HIT and medical malpractice lawsuits from use of HIT, bioterrorism and use of EMRs, and finally a discussion about mobile health and how a new growing mobile health generation will change the face of healthcare as we know it.

Let's begin with a quick 60-second overview of how all of this came together. When did the first health information technology first spring up?[*,†,‡,§] While the concept of informatics for health research was established globally after the end of World War II, the U.S. began using the first digital computers for health research on dental care for the National Bureau of Standards and the United States Air Force. Not until the 1960s was the use of the computer for generalizing human behavior based on demographic characteristics as well as the use of larger sample sizes, statistical analysis, and subgroup sampling methodologies. Through the introduction of a machine for similar purposes as the electronic medical record (EMR) today, computers were being used for the purposes of automating health checkups. This idea was established by a physician in the research department of Kaiser Permanente in the 1960s. Disappointingly, the mainstream usage of EMRS did not come about till one to two decades later, and even that did not have much of a presence besides in government hospitals, such as the Veterans Administration (VA). The boom in EMRs in the late 1990s and now in the 21st century has been a silo effect from other industries that began to adopt technologies, which trickled down to healthcare organizations, which have been slower to adopt health information technology (HIT or health IT).

Next, let's discuss some of the theories that apply to technology penetration, adoption, and use in healthcare organizations, some of which are scattered throughout the book as well. The table below demonstrates some of these theories, which will be expanded on as you begin reading.

Some of these theories provide the roots for how these issues came about. As the topics are covered more in detail, we will go back to these theories to demonstrate how the topic came to full fruition. It will be easier to move forward to discuss healthcare and what changes to health reform holds for the future if we have this foundation.

To begin, Chapter 1 explores HIPPA (the Health Information Portability and Privacy Act), which has important implications for the adoption and expansion of HIT. It also provides a foundation for why HIT is becoming the path for the future of medical and health services.

---

[*] "The History of Health Informatics." *Health Informatics, Nursing Informatics and Health Information Management Degrees.* University of Illinois at Chicago.

[†] November, Joseph. (2012). *Biomedical Computing: Digitizing Life in the United States.* Baltimore: Johns Hopkins University Press.

[‡] Collen, Morris F. (2006). *A History of Medical Informatics in the United States, 1950 to 1990.* Bethesda, MD: American Medical Informatics Association.

[§] Collen, M. F. (2006). Fifty years in medical informatics. Yearbook of Medical Informatics, 174–179.

Chapter	Theory
HIPPA and the HITECH Act: The mainstream trend toward HIT adoption across the United States	Electronic government (E-government) initiatives, legislation stakeholder analysis
Organizational culture	Deal and Kenney (2000) Organization-wide cultures that affect adoption Hofstede's cultural dimensions theory
Hospital financing	Supply and demand of EMRs and technology at hospitals The Capital Asset Pricing Model and arbitrage pricing theory
Cost–benefit analysis of EMRs	Theory of valuing the costs and benefits
Patient quality of care and cost	Marketing theories; patient satisfaction and meeting higher standards for care
HIT usage across providers	Usage of EMRs; organizational culture, capital, coordination systems
Physician perceptions of HIT	Physician education, training, and attitudes; reasons for inertia to technology, malpractice risks
Bioterrorism and EMRs	Emergency preparedness; using technology to improve public health surveillance techniques
Mobile health culture and innovation	Patient connectedness to healthcare; patient self help; techniques for prevention of illness

Chapter 1

HIPAA: Intent versus Actuality of the Law in Upholding the Privacy of Health Records

Overview

Whether you are for it or against it, the new healthcare reform law and its many provisions have pushed health information technology (HIT) into the forefront, kindling hope for a brighter tomorrow. Goals of higher life expectancies, lower rates of medical errors, fairer standards of pricing, and greater transparency of information may be achieved for all through HIT. Yet, the controversy and backlash that has been received about healthcare reform should not taint how individuals—patients, physicians, lawmakers, researchers, health professionals, and more—view health information technology. The use of HIT is a step in the right direction for the future, as many other industries (not to mention countries) have already gone electronic. And, while some provisions of the healthcare reform law, the PPACA (Patient Protection and Affordable Care Act), are yet to be debated and unraveled, health information technology is definitely not going to disappear during this period; rather, its effects are only going to be felt more and more on America's economy and impacting physicians, patients, providers, health insurance carriers, and, of course, academics and policymakers. For this reason, it is time to analyze a culmination of topics that aggregate the effects of HIT, rather than taking a look at them separately and as mutually independent.

This book covers a specific corner of the healthcare reform initiative, regardless of the individual mandates' impacts (or what was lack thereof during prehealth reform periods), which is Title II of the Health Information Privacy and Accountability Act (HIPAA). HIPAA is the confidentiality clause for patients, so this chapter will provide a strong platform for how using electronic medical records systems in hospital settings will impact privacy and confidentiality regulations and safe record keeping for patients. HIPAA has impacts on every level (the local, state, and federal level), which is why HIPAA is being covered first before discussion of HIT's impact on the organization. By providing a clearer picture of how policymakers framed HIPAA, the perceived benefits of HIT should shine through.

The idea is to analyze the stakeholders that took part in the framing and planning of the law and are impacted parties from the increased regulation over privacy and confidentiality stipulations in using healthcare technology. This chapter is broken down into sections including: the introduction and policy window* that brought HIPAA to the forefront, theoretical underpinnings to explain the nature of the law, stakeholder analysis from the bill's formation and impacts, and, finally, how this is all currently impacting and projected to impact the United States and the world in the future.

Introduction

There has been an important emphasis on the movement toward greater security and privacy in health informatics through the Health Information Privacy and Accountability Act, or HIPAA. It is an interesting law that has been around before and, after the passage of the new healthcare reform law, or the Patient Protection and Affordability Act (PPACA), which is why it has evolved through the process of healthcare reform. It is an important law that has been around since 1996, before the passage of the new healthcare reform law. HIPAA has been updated multiple times in history, especially during the HITECH Act of 2008 and the Patient Protection and Affordability Act (PPACA) of 2009. The focus on HIT has brought up new questions about healthcare IT privacy standards, and has led to the new additions in HIPAA that will be discussed. Some of the stakeholders involved in the process include those who shaped the law, such as Congress and legislative bodies tied to it, the physician implementing HIPAA in his or her hospital or practice, the patients who must comply and understand their new privacy regulations, the third-party payers and insurance providers, and the researchers, who impact and are impacted by the law.

Looking briefly at the basics of HIPAA, it was introduced as a bipartisan bill by Senators Edward Kennedy and Nancy Kassebaum in order to address the issues of healthcare portability, privacy, and confidentiality in its Title I through Title V as well as healthcare information technology as part of Title VIII. It was passed in 1996 by Congress; however, Congress quickly washed its hands of the responsibilities of framing the law. Rather, the Department of Health and Human Services (DHHS) and Office of Civil Rights (OCR) took on the responsibility of defining it. In general, the field of healthcare information management takes time, resources, capital, and compliance from various stakeholders. Thus, through the changes and new requirements of HIPAA, there has been a widespread revamp of the enforcement of healthcare technology concerns and it relies on the various parties to transition properly. Enforcement and interpretation of HIPAA occurs through the OCR of the DHHS. A civil money penalty of between $100 and $25,000 annually can be implemented for HIPAA violations by the Secretary of Health and Human Services, so there are steep penalties for not complying with HIT regulations in HIPAA, for the organizations, consultants, and physicians as well as the patients involved.

After the Affordable Care Act and healthcare reform changes of 2009–2011, some major steps in the process of using health IT have been created. One of them is the process of making sure health plans comply with the regulations and operating rules for each of the HIPAA covered transactions where the patient, physician, and insurance companies may have a stake. Next, a unique, standard Health Plan Identifier (HPID) will be set in place that will require compliance by three stakeholders: staff, physicians, and clinicians, and, again, the health insurance companies as well

---

* Kingdon, W. John and James A. Thurber. (2010). *Agendas, Alternatives, and Public Policies*. Boston: Longman, pp. 273.

as developers of health technology who will need to create databases to document the ID numbers of each patient. Another addition is the inclusion of a standard set of operating rules for electronic funds transfer (EFT), electronic remittance advice (ERA), and claims attachments. This is very important for various stakeholders, such as the insurance companies, patients, and the physician.

The Center for Medicaid and Medicare Services (CMS) has specified the entities that are required to comply and be covered with HIPAA. These include healthcare providers, such as doctors' offices and hospitals, healthcare plan providers, and the health insurance companies. Companies who provide services on behalf of covered entities also are affected by HIPAA, as well as vendors who sell products to the healthcare industry. This may add a whole new dimension to how insurance companies will impact their patients (depending on whether HIPAA turns out to be beneficial) by making insurance companies more efficient, or if it slows down the claims process, especially for claims that may be based on government insurance plans, such as Medicare or Medicaid. This book focuses on Title II, which discusses health reform from fraud and abuse of patients' confidential records.

How Did HIPAA Make the Policy Window?

While it was signed into law in 1996, HIPAA did not become popular and was not taken seriously until the early 2000s. Why is this? Because the policy window for health reform began simultaneously, in the early 2000s, with state reform from Massachusetts and when the executive branch initiated a greater focus on health reform issues. The major push for HIPAA was concurrent with the big push toward health information technology, with subsidized services and aid from the government to promote the investment in HIT. This led to the necessity for a secure system with strong protocol in place and a higher standard for privacy and confidentiality for the patient.

Interestingly enough, other influences, such as the focus on the banking industry collapse, deregulation of and changes to the airlines, deregulation of the FDA (Food and Drug Administration), and more, actually led to the necessity of a new mechanism in place to regulate the healthcare system. The major crisis that seems to have led to healthcare reform is the costs of healthcare on both the federal deficit and at the individual level during a recessionary climate. Because of the U.S. financial meltdown, which began in 2006, there has been a push for transparency in the determination of healthcare premiums and costs of health insurance, as well as a domino effect for greater ethical provisions in every industry, both healthcare and nonhealthcare related, which has driven the importance of HIPAA. These two factors, as well as the backdrop of the other economic problems, such as increasing unemployment, have led the country into a state of healthcare reform, investment in healthcare technology, and an electronic medical record system across the board for premium hospitals. Along with this comes hope for new jobs in the field, as well as a more ethical way to conduct the healthcare business and improve the status of health overall. Running parallel, there is a need for strong healthcare ethical regulations to prevent the release, tampering, and misuse of the public's confidential information.

Another possibility for why the topic of healthcare privacy reform reached the policy window is that the executive branch of the government pushed very resiliently in the direction of healthcare. It did not get distracted by other economic pressures and problems that could have diverted its focus, which has occurred in other administrations; rather, beginning with some pushes from President George W. Bush toward electronic medical records in the hospital setting, and now President Obama's strong resolve in bringing the subject of healthcare to the forefront, the subject of fully implementing HIPAA has reached fruition in the policy window. The movement from a pluralist to a public choice theory (Kingdon, 2002), as well as a greater emphasis on the policy sciences, has been the fundamentals shaping how stakeholders influence HIPAA and how HIPAA in turn has impacted its original stakeholders. The most plausible scenario is that a strong push from the executive branch and the backdrop of a double dip recession where change was a necessity, rather than a luxury, has together united to cause the growth in the formation and need for HIPAA.

The Public Choice Theory

The effects of HIPAA and its impact on various stakeholder groups will be forthcoming, but first it is important to understand the theory behind the fundamentals in shaping this specific law. The theory, in this case, pulls from mixed methods of multiple major theories, though the focus will be placed on the public choice theory. Primary emphasis is on the public choice theory by Kingdon (2002) because of the way healthcare has been formed, especially under the grounds of fragmented groups, all fighting for a greater government presence in healthcare. There also has been a shift toward a public system with an easier exchange of information and ideas of what healthcare plans can be purchased. This should be much more transparent compared to the current system, which has been entirely employer-run or income-based. The policy sciences play a large role in shaping the importance of technology in the changes to healthcare reform, so it has some impacts on HIPAA as well, though it influences the researcher stakeholder group the most.

There has been a transition from a pluralist theory to a public choice theory in healthcare. The public choice theory proposed by Schneider and Ingram (1997) has some major takeaways and applications to HIPAA, though there are some criticism and counters that can be made to their perspectives. The pluralist theory revolved around the notion of elected elites and institutions playing an important role in democracy, as well as the role of the "invisible hand" and "free markets" (p. 14) in healthcare. This moved, in the early twenty-first century, to the need for implementing corrections to the way the healthcare system was running from its original self-correcting stance. A new notion of collectivity and how it is used to "aggregate" individual preferences in health plans becomes prevalent during healthcare reform. This translates into the satisfaction and welfare of health for the public good. The idea that preferences should be aggregated and that more people should be required to buy healthcare with tighter government regulations on how the plans are sold is counter to the free markets theory and is treated with cynicism in their book. Yet, this idea may be a fresh start from the direction pluralism was heading for so many decades in U.S. healthcare. Thus, the public choice theory, formed through HIPAA's generation, is the first time individuals are making their own healthcare decisions, especially with changes to the health records and an infrastructure that is being remodeled. As a contrast to the pluralist view of an active citizenship, there is actually more bounded rationality* during healthcare reform, which leaves many citizens confused and unsure of the new transition that is being set forth. Bounded rationality, a concept by Herbert Simon, discussed a mismatch between the information, incentives, and opportunities of a decision with the "bounds" placed on the decision by the environment. The bounds on the decision may limit the rationality or utility maximization of the decision. An example is purchasing health insurance, which may be limited by an individual's place of work, health conditions, lifestyle, income, and other factors as well as uncertainties in the insurance plan itself such as penalties, deadlines, and rate hikes, that take effect from a certain date (during health reform).

---

* Simon, Herbert. (1991). Bounded Rationality and Organizational Learning. *Organization Science* 2 (1): 125–134. doi:10.1287/orsc.2.1.125.

Rather than wait to receive all relevant information, individuals may panic and not make the most utility maximizing decision, limited by such environmental constraints.

The point that Schneider and Ingram make is to be wary of the public choice theory, because of the presence of so many fragmented groups and their power play. In these policy decisions, they state that at least two groups always lose for one groups' personal victory. An example of this will be portrayed by the stakeholders analyzed in the pages to follow. While patient advocacy groups face the benefits of HIPAA through secure data and privacy considerations, physicians now require better auditing standards and quality control to care for electronic data storage. Taking this one step farther, it also should be noted that probability and perception of an individual's decision, or risk analysis, makes him or her value his/her judgment and interest in a situation. So, if an individual or a stakeholder group's perception of the healthcare market is not entirely impacted by the passage of HIPAA, they may not see a need to review the law more deeply or get involved in supporting or discussing it. This, as the authors point out, is a more realistic perspective than the pluralist theory.

Yet, at the same time there are some obvious pitfalls in the pluralist theory that Schneider and Ingram propose. Because groups begin to receive more power from the government, such as researchers, lobbyists, and the executive branch, they begin to organize and expand so that healthcare reaches its policy window. This is even more interesting considering HIPAA had already been created, but had not been able to stand on its own in policy debates until major healthcare reform discussions and legislation of 2009 and 2010. There is also a sense of rational choice theory for HIPAA legislation because of the gradual nature of the law's formation and implementation. It was very much an incremental process rather than a spontaneous transition, though as policy sciences theory supports, the technology has helped in the quicker transformation of HIPAA from its theoretical beginnings to its applied current state.

Analyzing HIPAA through the public choice theory lens leads one to believe that government is ineffective and unclear of its interpretation and vision of the law; therefore, the law is open to interpretation, rather than held together by certain principles. While Congress's role and the state's role (which will be discussed next) are apathetic at best, it is interesting to see how they have had a role in changing individuals' lives as well as the infrastructure of healthcare. While it may seem inefficient as a whole, once Title II of the law is closely analyzed, it is actually clear that there is room for growth in the area, as well as a place for new jobs and roles within the industry as well as new outcomes, especially a higher standard of quality care and cost effectiveness for the public as a whole. These effects stem partly from HIPAA regulations, making one think that the government's role in HIPAA, using the public choice theory, cannot be all that ineffective as Schneider and Ingram claim, especially when long-term consequences from HIPPA prove beneficial.

Another important criticism of the public choice theory is its collective action and free rider problem. Those who are unhealthy and have health insurance will be driving up the cost of healthcare even more, therefore, a burden on other healthy people's health plans. Yet, HIPAA should, in the long term, produce a more efficient mechanism that will engage more individuals and keep individuals from getting too sick through early detection and prevention of illness and disease. HIPAA provides a gateway to better healthcare through its structured data entry and trend toward use of electronic medical records that are private and confidential, so that patients need not worry that their records at the doctor's office will be easily accessible to anyone. HIPAA also allows privacy between physicians and hospitals and a stronger coordination system so that records can be easily managed and accessible between communities, states, and across larger regions in a timely manner. Physicians also will be required to keep accountable records of their claims, billing, patients, and accounts. This again will impact patients through cost effectiveness and quality of care if physicians are keeping track of their fees, charges, and standards of care. At the same time, patients also may be held accountable for misusing emergency rooms and not getting preventive care if there is an electronic system in place. HIPAA also works to change earlier concerns for those who want to attend a Community Health Center clinic for a preventive care problem, but are worried they will need to redo massive stacks of paperwork, be denied healthcare coverage, or whose paperwork will not be kept private from employers or others who may discriminate due to a preexisting condition.

One last criticism I have of Schneider and Ingram is the assumption they make in their theory that humans are all rational beings. Some individuals panic more than others, and some may feel the need for their records to be more rigidly secured than others. Viewing insurance companies as profit maximizers rather than as rational beings changes their goals and may put pressure on them if they are unable to use patient data to their benefit to sell plans, especially under HIPAA. It may mean that HIPAA impacts them from a political and economic angle that could hurt their ability to do business, possibly driving up costs even more. An analysis of the major stakeholder groups involved will be discussed more in detail next.

Stakeholder Analysis

Stakeholder #1: Congress and Its Impact on HIPAA's Formation

HIPAA was lobbied by various healthcare organizations and presented from healthcare technology firms and groups to gain more access to resources as well as gain political coverage. It also was brought to the forefront by the executive branch in numerous administrations, including Presidents Clinton, Bush, and Obama. However, once the issue's policy window opened up, it was no longer in the lobbyist's hands to control; Congress is the body that controls the votes on major decisions and their formation into laws. So, it was time for Congress to take charge. Congress will be the first to be discussed in its importance and impact on the formation of HIPAA because it has been widely debated on what kind of impact Congress had on the law.

Looking at the impacts of the policy through the eyes of Congress is complicated, to say the least. The stakeholders who now see healthcare reform in their policy window must act quickly to adjust and transition so that too much inertia does not prevent the law from being implemented. Yet, when the HIPAA law was presented to Congress, even the 24-month period provided to develop the national standards for the law were not enough. Congress had no answers. Also, initially, it was in Congress's hands to provide protection against inappropriate use of protected health information (PHI). Thus, because Congress failed to develop the standards for HIPAA, the responsibility fell to the DHHS that now monitors HIPAA compliance (O'Herrin, Fost, and Kudsk, 2004, 772).

The change in shaping of the law from a legislative branch of government to governmental subunits may have impacted both the motives for the act and the amount of interest and support for parts of the act, based on political, economic, and financial concerns. It is said that these impacts will run deeper for business and government within the healthcare industry than for the public. With such an extensive set of rules and possible loopholes to the rules, could it be that the main focus of the law is to provide businesses easier access to the public's data rather than actually privatizing the data and securing it (Annas, 2003)?

Also, HIPAA has changed many times since its initial creation and has been seen as a misuse and "a profit center" for the private sector including lawyers, lobbyists, technology vendors, consultants, and many others. The flurry of economic activity is nice, but dollars spent on HIPAA compliance may not go to treating sick children or keeping prescription costs down for seniors right away. Until enough research is conducted on HIPAA's benefits to the American public, the public should continue to demand "demonstrable improvements in their privacy for this cost" (The HIPAA Privacy Regulation, 2003). This is because, in the short run, implementation of the new law will definitely be an expensive venture, have impacts on the markets (may even slow them down), and produce complications in the purchase of insurance and access to prescriptions, as discussed in a report by Privacilla.org, titled HIPAA Privacy One Year Later: Prognosis . . . Negative!.

This organization also analyzes how Congress should first "capture" the concept of privacy before it gets the wheels of HIPAA regulation spinning. It is very important to clarify the definition of privacy, as various rule-making bodies may categorize an issue as a privacy issue differently from other organizations. The difference is especially present when a governmental organization discusses privacy versus a private organization. The report states that this leaves Americans also at a loss on what angles and perspective of privacy that the law is actually targeting. This fundamental flaw could mean that once again, policymakers will be spending money and issuing "costly regulations" on consumers without being on the same page with Congress on what programs are going to be important to HIPAA and what goals and objectives HIPAA will be trying to reach with benchmarks of progress.

Congress has been criticized, time and again, for its lack of decisiveness in public policy matters. In the case of healthcare, Congress provided extensions for compliance to HIPAA, rather than providing incentive or penalties for lack of compliance in order to speed up the implementation of the law. In 2004, Congress granted a one-year extension to smaller plans until April 2005 and a further 12-month extension also may be provided. This questions Congress's credibility. Congress has gotten a bad reputation for trying to keep an impartial political face so that it doesn't develop enemies. Take the case of the origination of HIPAA, where Congress completely loosened the reigns and handed it over to DHHS. From that point forward, if any conflict arose, it was not Congress's fault anymore, and the DHHS would be held responsible. At the same time, if the law was working according to plan, the credit still goes to the members of Congress for having passed the law. DHHS has to bend over backwards in order to please constituents, without Congress having to lift a finger.

Recommendations for HIPAA came from DHHS during a politically heated time. In a sense, it was controlled by the winner of the Clinton versus Dole election. This was because the winner of the election could "veto any privacy legislation coming from Congress after the HHS had issued its recommendations" (The HIPAA Privacy Regulation, 2003). Rather than HIPAA being a combination of consensus from both federal law and executive mandate, HIPAA emerged from politically chaotic times and evolved during various election cycles. Candidates chose to use HIPAA as an interesting tool for bolstering their own political stances, so it may question the true ideals of HIPAA to some extent.

Stakeholder #2: Hospital and Provider Organization Staff (Physicians, Nurses, and Assistants)

This stakeholder group is important because of the way it impacts and has been impacted by HIPAA. Those handling electronic records and hospital records—staff, doctors, and trained personnel within the hospital/agency—are the ones implementing HIPAA and impacted by HIPAA's creation and they are invaluable in ensuring that its outcomes are beneficial to the public.

The members of this group are going to be responsible for the specific privacy regulations of HIPAA because they will need to create a new infrastructure to manage risk and security/privacy considerations. This could mean altering the current organizational behavior to a top-down or bottom-up style of management through initiation of training programs, constant goal setting, and measurement of HIPAA on healthcare quality. Yet, there are difficulties here. The first is being able to designate and delegate proper tasks in the roles of administrative, physical, and technical safeguards. The other major difficulty is actually filling the role and carrying it out correctly while also not duplicating efforts. Tracking efforts tend to be duplicated, so investing in technology to handle these data is important. At the same time, the technology can have its own issues if it's not backed up securely, therefore, many issues hinge on this. This has been a major concern because patients who attend multiple locations are hoping there will not be duplicated payments and costs for care at each location. Rather, health information technology should speed up the process while also lowering the cost by providing networks and channels to electronically send the data in a secure manner. For this reason, it is a must that the stakeholder group of physicians and healthcare worker personnel take great care not to allow errors and data entry issues to slip through the cracks as data entry can mean the difference between patient's wait time, cost of care, and quality of care (Kilbridge, 2003, 23).

Another big issue is being able to reduce use of confidential information identification (typically the first and last name) in the office or clinic or hospital setting. This is a concern with HIPAA because this can initiate major malpractice cases filed on the grounds of selling or providing confidential information to third-party providers (Kilbridge, 2003, 25). Another major responsibility of this stakeholder group is having strong antivirus software and user id and password management systems and the ability to track down where a patient is at any given point, and not misusing this knowledge (Kilbridge, 2003, 28). Another responsibility of the healthcare provider stakeholder group is management of the organizations that fund the hospitals, otherwise known as financial management. This includes the "business associates" who bind the doctors to HIPAA privacy practices and who are in charge of putting together the hospital directories. It also includes those leading, sponsoring, and fundraising for the hospitals, such as the MBAs, CEOs, marketing teams, and more. *The New England Journal of Medicine* discussed how the American Hospital Association in 2000 estimated the average cost of compliance per hospital to be anywhere from $670,000 to $3.7 million in total, a significant amount more than the 2003 projections (Kilbridge, 2003, 1424). Hence, costs also have increased dramatically and will continue to increase from the addition of HIPAA laws to hospital practices and the bureaucratic concerns involved.

Teaching hospitals also have a major issue in compliance and privacy issues. This is because they have the largest number of in-training nursing and medical students who are allowed to access the minimum amount of the information necessary to expand their knowledge. But, if there was a scandal, staff in the hospital would get the blame for not providing the level of training and using the correct protocol in the field. This was present pre-HIPAA, but will be enforced much more strongly post-HIPAA because of the level of importance placed on privacy, integrity, and confidentiality. There are contradictory findings present from physician's use of HIPAA. Physicians from numerous health affairs journals have stated that HIPAA as a whole and provisions in it don't really accomplish anything on impacting confidentiality of information; yet, some specific requirements may be improving privacy protection, especially from an organizational standpoint (Slutsman, et al., 2005, 839–840). For now, it seems as though it is merely looked upon as the minimum standard, as providers are only doing as little as they can to get away with compliance, especially in smaller clinics where compliance initiatives are expensive and difficult. HIPAA also is not enforced across the board and is only required for certain care providers in the primary care services. Some oral, mental, and behavioral services may not be required to comply with these requirements. Therefore, the question remains: Is HIPAA actually beneficial to the public or is it going to greatly change the organizational framework of healthcare?

Stakeholder #3: The Patient and Consumer of the Healthcare Markets

The next major stakeholder group is the patient. Studies differ between adults and adolescents/minors, and by the condition the patients may have because this will impact usage of healthcare providers and, thus, HIPAA compliance.

Through the passage of HIPAA, patients now have the right to decide how their information is listed. While they do not have control over distribution, which is where the other stakeholder groups (such as the hospital management) comes into play, their choices impact the level of confidentiality they have at every stage of their life, be it during temporary or chronic illness, disease, injury, sickness, birth, and death (Kilbridge, 2003, 1424). The patient's main stake in HIPAA is to ensure efficiency and effectiveness in healthcare, and improved healthcare standards for both the markets that sell insurance plans, medications and drugs, as well as provide better healthcare outcomes of quality and cost effectiveness to consumers. These goals are tough to evaluate in the short run, though in the long run it will be more likely to see if HIPAA has presented the consumer with a higher level of satisfaction.

State law defines the legal rights of children and their parents, and state law continues to govern parental rights of access to a child and, more controversially, a minor's medical record. So, concerns about privacy can prevent adolescents from seeking care that has become a problematic issue (English and Carol, 2004, 80). When states are unclear or silent, it is the professional's judgment call that puts quite a burden on the physician and related stakeholder group (p. 83). One of the major areas where confidentiality impacts adolescents is when millions of them seek family planning services and sexually transmitted disease (STD) screening. This is where it is tough to draw the line between necessitating parental involvement or regulation, especially if states do not provide strong guidelines. On the other hand, children become an issue because a physician can deny parents access to their child's medical records if the physician has reasonable cause to believe that access is likely to cause "substantial harm." This can be in cases of physical violence by the parent against the child.

The same rather polemic standards affect mental health regulations, with Montana being the example. For example, psychotherapy notes in Montana are treated differently than other records under HIPAA. Some psychiatry and mental health treatment regulation standards are not treated the same way in HIPAA as other types of medical treatment, such as substance abuse, so it is up to the state to determine how these medical records are kept private and the level of restrictions on patient confidentiality. This shows that HIPAA needs to define the fine lines on what healthcare programs the state controls and which community programs and services it cannot control, because this could make the difference in whether patients will or will not seek these early prevention programs. This could also have impacts on the state and the community's budget based on the role they have in decision making for private and public programs for the community.

Interestingly, both HIPAA and FERPA (the Family Education Rights and Privacy Act) address the concept of patient directory information, but use opposite approaches when it comes to students. FERPA provides for opt-out and HIPAA requires opt-in. College students/young adult patients on college campuses have the issue that some of their records are controlled by FERPA.

The issue also depends on how much personally identified information is present. For example, some Student Health Centers are controlled under FERPA, not HIPAA. More gap analysis is being done to determine whether FERPA and HIPAA regulations are a duplicated effort and what roles need to be designated specifically to one or the other. One study by the University of Alabama at Birmingham was conducted that appointed committees to study, across campus, self-assessment for compliance tools and will be providing results once a longer time frame has passed.

In general, evidence and data currently suggests that patients are the major stakeholder group that HIPAA was created to support, but has not necessarily been catered to. This may be just a short-term effect, so it will take time for the long-run conclusions to be made.

Stakeholder #4: Insurance Companies/Third-Party Providers

Third-party payers are the next major stakeholder group because they are the intermediary between the patient and physician. This group consists of insurance companies that help subsidize the cost of healthcare for the patients, which can be in the form of employer-funded or government-subsidized plans, including Medicare, Medicaid, Tricare, PPO, and HMO plans, and more. This group has had one of the hardest times in adjusting to the HIPAA law, especially the magnitude of the law in coordination with healthcare reform. As of January 2003, only 9% of the nearly 500 major provider organizations felt they had achieved the full standard of compliance to HIPAA regulations (Kilbridge, 2003, 1424).

Here is where the physician and intermediary group have some aligned and some conflicting interests. Prior to HIPAA, insurance providers could use patient information, bought from hospitals and care providers, to find the most cost-effective treatments and insurance plans, as well as learn about preexisting conditions that could discriminate against the consumer. This provided power in the insurance providers' hands in the markets, just as the pluralist theory would denote. However, under HIPAA, patient information is supposed to be secure, and discriminating based on preexisting conditions is against the law, so insurance providers will be audited and regulated to ensure that they are handling consumer information with a high level of security. Yet, in reality, poorly functioning healthcare markets allow third-party payers themselves to oversee choices that patients would otherwise make in confidential consultation with their doctors. Possible solutions to this would be involving auditors and governance over the providers to ensure they are not misusing data and selling it for their own profit. Some say, to ensure that HIPAA works correctly, the answer is to transform the tax policy, by enhancing government entitlements, and restoring a discipline in the healthcare markets. This will provide a safety net from cheating or gaming the system and making additional profit from unfair use of patient information (The HIPAA Privacy Regulation, 2003). Currently, there also is lack of a penalty system that will punish insurance companies for interpreting HIPAA the way they want to interpret it. This can be problematic because of loopholes again that may allow insurance providers, healthcare providers, and the very powerful pharmaceutical industry to work together to game the system.

Stakeholder #5: The Researcher

Researchers drive a lot of decision making for policies, which can also influence lobbyists, professionals, Congress, and policymakers. HIPAA effects research funding and the ability to conduct research as well as the new policy topics for research. As more researchers move into top policy spots in politics, such as seats in Congress and the executive branch, it influences the way research boards review new research projects and the research that is considered timely and important.

For researchers, HIPAA can be a double-edged sword. Some researchers are not covered by HIPAA and do not need to follow its intricate protocol. Yet, those who are covered feel that they are overwhelmingly inhibited by the scrutiny that HIPAA places on medical record and database research. Ethical considerations in healthcare research are paramount, and current HIPAA implementation strategies increase workload for the Health Security Council and researchers, and increase the dropout rate for proposed studies when investigators are unable or unwilling to meet the regulatory requirements. The policy science theory plays an important role in linking the role of research to HIPAA. The theory demonstrates that the policy sciences provide an evidence-based methodology for providing data to fit policy decisions, and the importance of the researcher in being objective for this role.

While Schneider and Ingram (1997) didn't discuss the sides of technology and the policy sciences that are newly emerging, such as plagiarism, they did mention the old-fashioned idea of researchers as manipulators. They have the ability to take whatever they want into consideration, and team up with the rich and the powerful by bolstering them with facts to earn the federal and state aid. However, this cynical perspective must be taken with a grain of salt. Today, there has been change due to a higher level of research ethics and protocol expected during every research study, and the importance that research plays in linking all the disciplines to each other. Research also has a standard across the world and sparks competition across nations to develop stronger, better results that have a high level of external validity. Basically, it must be generalizable across large units. This is not touched on by Schneider and Ingram and deserves note here. From what research has been done so far, it is unclear whether and to what degree the new HIPAA requirements add to protection of privacy for patients (O'Herrin, Fost, and Kudsk, 2004). Many academic studies, especially meta-analysis, try to decode this, but it may be that the law is too recent to measure the impact on protection of privacy. Yet, the presence of HIPAA has opened up new areas of research, from research on the impacts of HIPAA on health outcomes for patients and efficiency of techniques in healthcare to cost-based studies that measure how HIPAA impacts patients' costs, providers' costs, and insurance companies' costs due to higher levels of regulation.

The HIPAA rule has been seen to reduce the number of patients in outcomes research, defined as research done to identify "the end results of particular health care practices and interventions" by the Agency for Health Research and Quality (AHRQ). However, it also may be introducing selection bias into data collection for patient registries. A study on HIPAA and its impacts on health outcomes research took 1,221 patients with acute coronary syndrome during a pre-HIPAA time frame, and compared the effect on the patients' post-HIPAA period. Consent for follow-up in studies decreased from 96% in the pre-HIPAA period to 34.0% in the post-HIPAA period (Armstrong et al., 2005, 1125–1129). This could mean that patients felt unsure about their information being held private and confidential, and were less willing to participate in follow-ups, post-HIPAA. Also, looking at impacts of patient satisfaction with HIPAA, a national survey of clinical scientists showed that only a quarter perceived that the rule has enhanced participants' confidentiality and privacy. The HIPAA Privacy Rule is also perceived to have a fairly significant negative influence on the conduct of human subjects' health research. This can add uncertainty, cost, and delay to the efficiency and effectiveness of HIPAA's usage.

Looking at how the law as a whole has been viewed by researchers is politically debated. A conservative approach to the law is that adding stringent regulations can only be a hindrance to health research, and will prevent better findings from occurring. A liberal approach states that this level of scrutiny is required to see quality of care improvements in the long run. A high level of rigor in the epidemiological, health services, and environmental and occupational health research archives will be important in a broader sense as well, looking from a pharmaceutical standpoint as a higher level of rigor will be important when marketing the efficacy of medical equipment and medical technology that will be used.

Policy Analysis: The Past, Present, and Future of HIPAA

Studies show that initially as HIPAA has been introduced, a disconnect is present in the level of information that these various stakeholders have concerning the law, its stringency, and its importance and rulings on decision making. This can be a difficult process to straighten out, especially as these groups are stuck in the pre-HIPAA era and must transition into the new rules.

One study in the state of Nebraska analyzed 25 health board/facility oversight managers and 20 health professional association directors, and noticed that these directors were not on the same page on requirements and understanding of privacy and security issues important to creating a new and improved health information exchange (HIE) with a new approach to how the markets would conduct business. Many of top officials and managers were not clear about the federal agenda and purpose, as well as the national initiatives present (Cox, 2004). Both need to be in line for HIPAA regulations to have beneficial effect. Rural states face the most challenges to complying. Tracy Christerepho (2005) discusses this in his book. A total of 308 physicians from West Virginia participated in a survey to assess their HIPAA awareness levels. They also were provided with free training. The respondents were to provide the major barriers they thought were present in handling compliance to HIPAA. The conclusions were that there was vagueness and confusion in knowledge of the regulations.

Practitioners also have developed close relationships to state-elected officials. Defining that fine line between the information they can provide to these state officials and that which they cannot is very important. There may be a lot of pressure to satisfy the state officials' expectations, which may differ from that of the expectations of HIPAA. Healthcare has become such a widely debated field that state professionals must be on top of their game in order to answer in an educated manner about the reform law and HIPAA as well. Yet, there is a lack of transparency and in-depth coverage of the HIPAA law, so it is difficult for them to glean what they need to, especially from a management front. This is also a big concern for the relationship between practitioners and the media. Insurance is a highly connected industry to healthcare and the media tries to gain as much information as possible about the impacts of HIPAA on insurance as well as insurance companies' take and influence on HIPAA. The media tends to provide a blurry analysis of the HIPAA law, especially during its beginnings when a lot of the initial pitfalls and problems of the law were being straightened out. This can cause a reduction in consumer confidence. Thus, these stakeholder groups are closely intertwined, and it is important for information to be transparently passing from the governing bodies that are passing the laws to the providers implementing them and the patients using them. This will reduce the spotlight on the issues that are showing up and being exacerbated by the media, while also showing that progress is being made as the healthcare reform law unravels.

Looking beyond a domestic angle, the growth of medical tourism also can be reason to believe in the importance of HIPAA and how it ties to some of the fundamentals of the American dream and American values. HIPAA serves as checks and balances and a regulatory mechanism within healthcare to ensure that rights of Americans are not violated. In aligning with other nations that have lower healthcare costs and trying to reduce the numbers of patients leaving the United States for medical tourism each year, the United States has adopted this new standard of healthcare ethics and privacy. While America has prided itself on having some of the best doctors, nurses, healthcare professionals, and healthcare research in the world, the rest of the world, especially parts of Singapore, Thailand, and India have become the new destinations for medical research and medical care due to cost effectiveness and health informatics. If all goes well, this will be held as a pedestal and model for other nations, and improve its level of quality of care and being a leg up on medical tourism destinations that provide cost effectiveness, but lower levels of quality care rigor. HIPAA provides a check on health insurance companies also, as a new layer of regulation to ensure that there is not unfair distribution of individuals' information and rights. Such a high level of confidentiality, if carried out properly, will give the United States a cutting edge reason to market itself. It also will provide a redemption for the prescription drug abuse scandals and pharmaceutical scams that have repeatedly occurred in this country if the technology and HIPAA can together work to reduce fraud in the industry.

Conclusion

For a long time, the pluralist theory has been at work in the healthcare field. Without strong governing forces in the healthcare industry, the consumer had the responsibility to purchase a healthcare plan if that was in their interests and budget. But, in an age where the world is more connected and diseases and illnesses spread quickly, the United States has finally decided to move in the direction of the public choice theory in healthcare policy. In order to correct stark disparities among individuals who are receiving healthcare coverage and better healthcare overall, healthcare reform has worked to develop a new framework that will promote cheaper, better, and more rigorous standards for the healthcare industry to impact patient quality of care and cost effectiveness. These standards are known as HIPAA.

HIPAA has been brought into the policy window by numerous stakeholder groups, including the Department of Health and Human Services, Congress, physicians and healthcare providers, the American people and users of healthcare, insurance companies, and researchers. They are all simultaneously impacted by HIPAA regulations and use HIPAA in different and sometimes similar ways. It is yet to be understood how drastically HIPAA will impact the patients because it was originally created to change the healthcare climate and markets for exchanging healthcare plans, drugs, and more. The effect will differ across the short run, and long-run consequences quite significantly, as research has shown, due to stigma against change and lack of incentive to transition into the new rules.

As long as there is transparency and clarity on what the law is upholding and the exact effect it means to have on each stakeholder group it is impacting, there will be success. Yet, as history has shown, there has been a disconnect between what the law was originally crafted to do and how it has been interpreted, as well as gray areas about many of the different provisions it imposes. This is also because healthcare is a very complicated industry with multiple subunits. It is going to be important to clear up a lot of the issues that have come up so that progress can be made toward a stronger healthcare framework. Otherwise, loopholes and shortcuts will revert the healthcare status back to how it originally was, and only be a large financial sap on funds for the government, industry, and the individual. As the United States has moved toward a higher standard of technological change and improvements to its healthcare structure, it will undergo some turmoil initially as has been seen. Hopefully, it will surface victoriously in its efforts through strong collaboration and coordination networks between stakeholder groups and by providing clarity on the true intent and goals of HIPAA's enforcement and implementation.

Chapter 2

Organizational Culture Differences in Incorporation of Health Information Technology (HIT) across Healthcare Providers

Overview

Healthcare reform in 2009 placed a focus on increasing HIT adoption for healthcare providers through government funding. Nonprofit, for-profit, and government hospitals and health centers tend to be driven by a few core competencies that define their organizational culture: (1) mission statements, management, and compensation of employees; (2) training of staff; and (3) goal-oriented behavior. These factors will likely impact the ability for an organization to adopt and implement health information technology (HIT), which should translate into lower costs and higher quality of care, yet organizations are not adopting HIT. An abundance of literature has discussed how organizations internally differ in their organizational culture, but literature doesn't expand on how these differences vary across providers, and how they impact the variation in HIT adoption. This chapter will address gaps in the literature and provide policy analysis that can abound by internalizing HIT as a part of the organizational culture across healthcare providers.

Introduction

With the backdrop of healthcare reform, the Health Information Technology for Economic and Clinical Health (HITECH) Act, and economic changes introducing new technologies into the workforce, hospitals have transformed rapidly in the past 15 to 20 years. Through the HITECH Act, which is legislation that was passed through the American Recovery and Reinvestment Act of 2008 and 2009, all hospitals are required to have fully functioning electronic medical record systems, preferably within the next decade, and available funding to provide subsidies to purchase the technology. The reason for this mandated change is simple. Not only has basic technology, such as x-ray machines, helped improve diagnosis, but large-scale infrastructural technologies, such as electronic medical records (EMRs), have revolutionized the organizational structure and dynamics in hospitals. How? The use of HIT has shown to produce gains in efficiency and effectiveness through better communication channels between the patient, provider, and any intermediary networks. It is proposed that HIT will cut costs in the long term, for the provider and the patient, though it may be expensive initially to adopt and implement. Redundancies in repetitive testing and paperwork also are avoided through the use of electronic records, billing, and prescribing.

Yet, one cannot assume that implementation of technology will be constant across various types of hospitals. Rather, there is good chance that for-profit hospitals actually are incentivized differently in their technology adoption process than not-for-profit hospitals. Some general terminology that must be noted are examples of HIT, which in this context will primarily include electronic medical records and electronic functioning of the various departments of hospitals, including e-billing, e-prescribing, electronic lab results, and telemedicine. The different stages of technology usage are interesting and important as well, as for-profit hospitals, not-for-profit hospitals, and government-owned hospitals will each see their needs being met at different stages of technology adoption and implementation and derive efficiency from technology differently. The three main stages of technology usage are, in order from beginning to completion, (1) technology adoption, (2) technology implementation, and (3) "meaningful use" of the technology, which is defined as finally using technology in every dimension of the hospital's services—a term that is portrayed by the HIMSS (Healthcare Information and Management Systems Society) Adoption Model. We will analyze the figure more in detail in the following chapters. Meaningful use is the ultimate goal for all hospitals to achieve in the end of their technology adoption and diffusion phases, as reported by the Center for Medicare and Medicare, DHHS (Department of Health and Human Services), and the Affordable Care Act of 2009.

Thus, the case in point for this chapter may seem blurred by the many dimensions and elements in the analysis, but it is fairly simple. The research question in this chapter is asking how organizational culture that allows adoption and implementation of HIT varies across different health providers, including nonprofit hospitals, for-profit hospitals, and government-owned hospitals (also known as community health centers). The variation in the organizational culture of these types of health providers cause variation in each one's ability to adopt and implement HIT at different rates and stages and further impacts the healthcare playing field, as some organizations may adopt more quickly and others may lag behind in the process. This chapter will assume that all healthcare providers have access to sources of funding for the technology. The reason for this assumption is that the HITECH Act provides reimbursement to hospitals and clinics (especially those with high levels of Medicaid patients), in order to provide a more even playing field for both high capital and low capital hospitals to adopt electronic medical records. But, technology adoption has been seen to occur at varying levels and speeds.

While some hospitals (the majority of which are for-profit) have achieved nearly complete technology implementation and meaningful use status, other hospitals, such as nonprofits, especially lower budget and those with a high volume of low income patients, are still stagnating at the technology adoption phase and are unable to produce technological efficiencies.

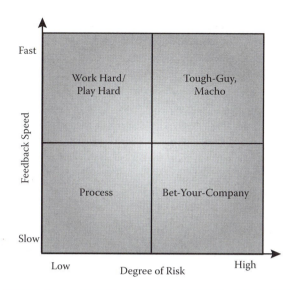

Figure 2.1 Deal and Kennedy's culture types.

There are a number of theories that relate to this subject, including technology adoption,[*,†] technology acceptance models,[‡,§] and some organizational behavior theories that were developed. Max Weber (known as a principal architect of modern social science), who spoke about the relationship between rational organizations and links to charismatic leadership; Hofstede's (Dutch researcher) cultural dimensions theory, which discusses the dimensions of culture and subculture in an organization; and, most importantly, Deal and Kennedy's recent Theory on Culture (Figure 2.1), are examples of theories for this topic that will together form an important foundation for the subject of technology implementation across many structures. Deal and Kennedy (2000) differentiate across organizations, rather than within, which is what their book on corporate culture discusses (Deal and Kennedy, 2000). Figure 2.1 simplifies the information on Deal and Kennedy's theory.

The process culture that Figure 2.1 defines would best describe a government hospital, with high levels of bureaucracy, low risk behavior, and low speed of execution in technology adoption. A nonprofit hospital could be in a number of these categories, depending on how rigorous its culture is, and how incentivized and goal-oriented it is in achieving low costs as well as high quality of patient care. For this reason, nonprofits, which are behaving like for-profits, typically large nonprofit conglomerates that have potential to grow as quickly and as large as many of the for-profits, may have the work hard/play hard culture or the tough guy/macho culture shown. This could end up in quick and efficient technology adoption as well as beneficial technology implementation and meaningful use at a fast pace, or it could end up in a much slower technology adoption with inefficient and ineffective technology adoption outcomes. The latter describes the "bet your

[*] Beal, George M., Everett M. Rogers, and Joe M. Bohlen (1957) "Validity of the concept of stages in the adoption process." Rural Sociology 22(2):166–168.

[†] Rogers, Everett M. (1962). Diffusion of Innovations, Glencoe: Free Press.

[‡] Davis, F. D.; Bagozzi, R. P.; Warshaw, P. R. (1989), "User acceptance of computer technology: A comparison of two theoretical models", Management Science 35: 982–1003.

[§] Davis, F. D. (1989), "Perceived usefulness, perceived ease of use, and user acceptance of information technology", MIS Quarterly 13(3): 319–340.

company standard (Figure 2.1)" category, which still involves high risk (the high level of capital and resources required to invest in expensive technologies), with low levels of feedback and outcomes. On the other hand, for-profit hospitals have an "in it to win it" attitude, at the intersection of the "work hard/play hard" culture and the "tough guy/macho" outcome philosophy. As will be described next, these structures have different organizational characteristics that will differentiate their behavior to adopt technologies.

My hypothesis is that this phenomenon of variation across providers in their ability to adopt technology is *not* random, rather, to explain the variation in the speed of technology implementation across a for-profit versus a not-for-profit hospital, there are specific organizational characteristics: ownership, management incentives, training of staff, cultural competence, mission statements, and goal-setting behavior. Taking just this handful of characteristics, it is interesting to analyze the differences in organizational culture between a not-for-profit hospital and a for-profit hospital as well as government hospitals. Some examples also will be provided of hospitals today that have achieved efficiency and effectiveness in using technology versus those that have lagged behind.

Organizational Culture Driven by a Hospital's Mission and Values

First of all, what is the mission of a hospital and how does it relate to the organizational culture of a hospital? The mission of a hospital can be defined as the guidelines of what the hospital represents, in terms of what its focuses are and how these focuses impact health outcomes. Some examples of mission statements are shown in Table 2.1

How does a hospital's mission drive its goals, especially when its goals, with emphasis from CDC (Center for Disease Control), CMS (Center for Medicare and Medicaid Services), and DHHS, are to fully incorporate technology into the hospital setting within the next decade? The missions of not-for-profit, for-profit, and government hospitals can have major differences that may or may not be very noticeable to the naked eye.

An interesting feature about the mission of a hospital is that it represents the contributing factor to the agenda, planning and progression, and some would say, the success of the organization. An article by Desmidt and Heene (2007) brought up a valid point. They state that the organization's management, as well as its members, are equally responsible in carrying it forward and sticking with the mission of the hospital such that they are achieving results close to its mission. The analysis of the organization's members has not been done before, and at this Flemish hospital, discussed in the journal article, it was a fresh perspective on the importance of a mission statement. What the article finds is that the management is much more positive and driven toward the mission statement than staff, which creates a cultural divide as well as a barrier in driving improvements in healthcare. More so, these results will be important when technology is introduced if it is included as part of the mission statement in driving value added to the organization.

How members and the managers perceive the organization's technology together will impact how quickly and how easily the organization embraces new technological development and runs with it. This leads to a new question: Should all hospitals universally within the United States make revisions to their mission statement to show that they will make the effort to adopt, implement, and meaningfully use technology? Would having this as part of the mission statement have an impact on management, members of the organization, or both? Or would no effect be driven by this inclusion in the mission statement? The answer to this question depends on two very

Table 2.1   Examples of Mission Statements

Hospital	Type	Mission Statement
INOVA Health Systems	Not-for-profit	The mission of the Inova Health System is to improve the health of the diverse community we serve through excellence in patient care, education, and research.
Kaiser Permanente	Both for-profit and not-for-profit entity	Kaiser Permanente exists to provide affordable, high quality healthcare services to improve the health of our members and the communities we serve.
Arlington Free Clinic	Community health center/government funded	Arlington Free Clinic provides free, high-quality medical care to low-income, uninsured Arlington County adults through the generosity of private donations and volunteers.
Community Health Systems	For-profit	The consolidated organization owns and leases community hospitals that offer quality, cost-effective healthcare including a range of inpatient medical and surgical services, outpatient treatment, and skilled nursing care.

important characteristics in organizational culture: time and spatial constraints. Based on the short run, the mission of the organization may be to boost technology adoption and use, whereas by the long run, the mission may change to more effectively using technology such that it drives cost effectiveness, quality care, and innovation as well. It should be driving positive change and successes while also lowering negative consequences and misconceptions about technology in the long run. Yet time plays an important role in the big picture that workers and management take toward their own jobs and how they perceive the mission impacting their position's salaries, perks, and incentives to succeed.

Spatial constraints are equally interesting, though not addressed by Desmidt and Heene (2007), because hospitals surrounded by very productive and mission-driven hospitals may mimic that behavior as well. Further analysis is necessary to test whether hospitals strive closer to their mission if other hospitals are doing the same or if there is no impact of their surroundings on their accountability to their mission statement. The government could have some interesting and controversial push back from requiring technology to be a goal in all hospital providers' mission statements. But, while there is controversy over most regulations, it may also drive a greater achievement and goal-oriented behavior that could be beneficial to most organizations. The closest to this requirement is the current impact of IRS guidelines requiring all nonprofits to document their community outreach and community benefit in their Schedule H tax forms as part of the PPACA (Patient Protection and Affordable Care Act). This is not specific to requiring health information technology to be displayed on tax forms. Possibly requiring this would be an interesting and important policy that could impact how organizations perceive HIT.

Managerial and Employee Ethic and Compensation: Impact on Organizational Culture

The stark financial differences between a not-for-profit and for-profit is in compensation, stock ownership, and benefits at many levels. First, take the case of payment to managerial-level staff, which drives the organization, both from providing capital and investments in the organization and seeing returns from the organization's success. Roomkin and Weisbord (1999) find that the top two executive jobs in for-profits are better paid and have higher bonuses than those of the not-for-profit sector, but brings up a less obvious point: Hospitals that are of a for-profit status also have better incentive structures, such that they can easily monitor and reward staff based on efficiency, effectiveness, and good work. Performance reviews are frequent and provide incentive to staff to produce results, much as the theory identified by Deal and Kennedy.

Roomkin and Weisbord's thoughts may seem controversial, as for-profits have gotten a lot of bad press for their squandering of money and high CEO bonuses when they are supposed to be providing patients with care and services. Yet, their assumptions outline that there could be a reciprocal relationship in why specific managerial employees decide to work for a not-for-profit or a for-profit organization. They point out that not only is the organization's mission aligning with the manager, but the manager finds advantages out of working for that type of institution and, for this reason, accepts the position, and lowers the supply price for that position. This chapter is driven from theory on organizational behavior and systematic differences between organizations and their managers. Yet, once technology is added to this equation, there may be even more to consider on incentives for a manager to take a position at a specific type of hospital. Whereas not-for-profits do not always have the means to incorporate health information technology, once they do, there seems to be greater outcomes from it. Many managers may see hospitals with technology as a high risk or low risk environment, and then choose to fill that position on the basis of whether or not the hospital has a medical malpractice policy and how high premiums are in that state. This is a very controversial topic as well, and may have policy implications on the kind of personnel willing to work at a certain kind of health organization. The ethical nature of the organization is definitely at play when management incentive structures are involved, which impacts the reputation of the organization. The difficulty is defining the line between an organization that is being cutting edge in technology, such as highly innovative, while also producing low risk to its patients, with a low level of medical malpractice lawsuits filed. Only time will tell, as research has not demonstrated a clear relationship between technology and its impacts on medical malpractice in organizations today.

On the other hand, while for-profits have the capital, they may be working purely on efficiency that is based on results and goal attainment, so the management may be well trained and more incentive-based on doing well and working on performing along with the technology. This differentiation is something that is *not* pointed out by Roomkin and Weisbord (1999, 773). Rather, they point out that the expected utilities for management at either organization would be equal in both a not-for-profit and for-profit in their impact on income and work effort. What they miss is that, specific to hospitals and the future of health information technology, there will be different maximizations of utility due to adoption and implementation as well as "meaningful use," the criteria that identifies what the hospitals must do to evidence how they are using their HIT. The level of utility maximization of HIT may be just Stage 1 or 2 on the HIMSS Adoption Model for a small nonprofit, whereas for-profit hospitals strive for the highest stage of adoption and utility maximization, purely on the basis of need, incentives, and interest in HIT.

Roomkin and Weisbord also point out that the variance for for-profit managers' bonuses is also greater than not-for-profits, regardless of manager level. This is key, as this can be applied to the hospital industry as well. It is acceptable to assume that variance and, unlike Roomkin and Weisbord's hypothesis, expected utility also will be greater at for-profit hospitals than not-for-profits. This is an important component that impacts organizational culture because these variances will generate a varying degree of cultural flow and cultural acceptance. Also, the high variance in bonuses and compensation to managers may cause them to focus more on employee satisfaction than on patient satisfaction; there may be a focus on performance of the employee that is supposed to lead to better quality of care for the patient. On the other hand, for not-for-profits, it is assumed that all the benefit will go directly to the patient and that the management is only paid so much because the infrastructure and patient are already bearing the fruits of investment made to the firm. The two authors note that the not-for-profit incentive plans are vague and have a much higher likelihood of stating that the incentive plans are based on "other" criteria, not necessarily related to employee perks. This supplements the hypothesis on for-profit management have a more direct impact on employees through a defined employee incentive structure compared to non-profit management structures.

The next study looks specifically at some not for-profits' CEOs in Ontario to identify whether CEO compensation is related to hospital financial performance. Contradictory to how a nonprofit is believed to work, it was found that there was a continued "upward trend in salaries" even during times of financial underperformance by the hospital (Reiter et al., 2009). This finding shows that some not-for-profits from this case may be acting much like for-profits. While the Ontario example may not be exactly applicable to the U.S. healthcare system today, it is still relevant in analyzing trends in time.

As the United States undertakes healthcare reform, it will be interesting to see whether efficiency is driving reduced costs to the firm and higher pay for top executives, or if performance actually reduces in the short run due to instability, but pay for executives continues to climb. This would mean that performance is no longer a driver of compensation because compensation is exogenous and continues to adjust itself even in tough times so that management personnel always win—until they are audited, at least. This cynical view could mean that not-for-profits and for-profits alike have upper executives that are highly compensated and these institutions act similarly in pay structures from a top-down approach, though the bottom of the pyramid may have more volunteers and low-paid physicians at the not-for-profits. As the demand for physicians will be growing and supply continues to fall, only time will tell whether the not-for-profit behavior will soon come to mimic the for-profit behavior in performance, incentive, and achievement standards.

Next, a paper by Weisbrod, Wolf, and Bird (1993) discusses the voluntary nature of jobs in not-for-profit hospitals. How volunteers decide on where to work is an important decision that may be rooted in organizational culture. The article found that volunteers do not view all hospitals alike when deciding to volunteer, which is an important part of the theory that hospitals with new technologies also will impact who chooses to volunteer. The study incorporated some interesting characteristics, such as ownership status of the hospital, the volunteer's own religion, political identity, age and years of education, to identify how likely they are to choose a specific organization. Interestingly, about 54% chose not-for-profits of a government or private nature, whereas only 1% chose a for-profit institution. The remainder had no particular preference. The study can carefully be applied to an analysis of the industry, 20 years later, when technology is an integral part of a hospital. While some volunteers who are older would prefer to work at a less advanced organization that may still use paper records, an older, possibly more educated person may be interested in looking at organizations that invest in technology. At the same time, a religiously inclined and politically conservative person may shun technology, especially use of technology for the purpose of child birth or abortion, so they may choose against volunteering where technology is present in the hospital services industry. The only component that this paper did not point out is the effect of volunteer labor; while volunteer labor may be extremely useful at smaller not-for-profit clinics and/or federal clinics, a large for-profit firm may not need or use volunteer labor. This also could make a significant impact on the study. Whether or not volunteer labor impacts quality of care is debatable. "Teasing out," or defining and controlling (in a statistical manner) for the volunteer labor hours as a proportion of the hours going toward paid labor/management, is neither a simple nor easily definable task. For this reason, another study by Puffer and Mendel (1995) that carefully researches individual attitudes, motives, and performance in volunteering at the United Way can be analyzed. People may actually internalize the culture they see in an organization and carry that with them to another organization, which is an important point that is very important in the case of volunteers who have diversified backgrounds (Puffer and Mendel, 1995, 361). The article analyzes two major types of culture: self-centered, ego-centric values and altruistic socio-centric culture (p. 361). Interdependence and team work as well as a more sociocentric workplace contributed to volunteers with better performance and interest in serving not-for-profit hospital entities. What is interesting about this article is that, in the light of hospitals with health information technology, it would be interesting to measure whether volunteers who use technology currently in their workplace are better able to understand the use of technology at hospitals and can be of greater use for their voluntary tasks due to this enhanced set of skills.

Next, looking at the difference in attitude between paid and volunteer workers in a study by Laio-Troth (2001) may be interesting as it provides a window into the incentives people have in working in any type of organization as well as reasons for choosing a specific type of organization. This paper takes a look at workers in similar jobs in the hospital in order to identify how their own inherent values, attitudes, and mission impact organizational culture and justice. The findings show that the individuals who worked for pay versus worked as volunteers were not very different in logic. What is missing in this study is the presence of hierarchy between paid employees, as there is no mention of this and whether there was variation between the levels of paid employees. New components that could be added to the study are presence of this hierarchy to both the workers as well as volunteers, as volunteers who have experience may still have greater intangible benefits, such as networking and knowledge base, versus those who are new volunteers. The next point is that of comparing hospital-wide characteristics such as these across hospitals. An interesting study would look at the difference in paid and unpaid workers across government hospitals, for-profits, and not-for-profits, and see if they are all similar or differ drastically because of the premium for-profits provide to their workers, based on job performance, bonuses, and more. The diversity of skills and culture brought by employees to the hospital, that Laio Troth (2001) brings up briefly, is also going to differ across the type of hospital, so this could be studied in greater detail as well (424).

Attitudes toward organizational culture from physicians and nurses are another important component of management besides just looking at compensation and individual beliefs toward community benefit. A study on how open a hospital's personnel are toward change shows that hospitals that have more collaborative techniques and tend to be democratic and less hierarchical had employees with positive attitudes toward change (Seren, 2007). This could be interesting because many hospitals going through mergers, especially for-profits buying out not-for-profits, have the collaborative strategies, but should have a more democratic approach in order to allow for an easy path toward change.

Another group of studies analyzing smaller, cash-poor rural hospitals showed that organizational characteristics such as market power, ownership, and size had a hefty impact on rural hospitals (Scott et al., 2003; Horwitz and Nichols, 2009). Hospital revenue growth in this study was supposed to be more likely at for-profit hospitals than those in less competitive atmospheres. Regarding this subject, there has been work in the past. From a socioeconomic and cultural perspective, there have been studies that show that competitive atmospheres and rising prices in a vicinity cause changes in the behavior and pricing models of various hospitals, including not-for-profits, but have no effect on government hospitals. The government hospital category is inclusive of rural hospitals as well (Horwitz and Nichols, 2009). Yet, this study indicates that a policy initiative to increase rural hospital profitability would be to decrease competition in the areas.

This may be a contradiction to the idea of organizational culture and the stimuli that organizational culture has on the atmosphere, especially a competitive one, in driving affordability and improved care. Rather than decrease profitability, internal organizational culture characteristics and impacts of government and state aid are a key component that the study did not take into consideration. There is little impact on government healthcare organizations from a highly profitable hospital setting as a backdrop, so it will be interesting to see if government hospitals and for-profit hospitals produce the same amount of progress through technology. Rural hospitals will be provided government reimbursement for resources for which for-profit hospitals have the capital to afford, so there should not be very stark differences in the vantage point in which they see themselves, but instead there will be differences in their outlook; motivation to adopt, implement, and meaningfully use technology; and, finally, how results-oriented the organization is. What creates variability across the two types of organizations also could be their staff and their staff's training. Because staff is not provided the same level of reimbursement at each organization, they may not be as incentivized to perform and use new technology and drive savings in cost and care.

Training and the Impact of Training on Quality of Care across Hospitals

Some may wonder how training could be a form of organizational culture. Within a hospital that is changing at a dynamic pace based on technology infusion, it is important to train the staff, administration, and management. However, there may be different types of training specific to different kinds of organizations. Some organizations may require a heavier emphasis on training on certain departments in HIT, such as electronic billing. For example, nonprofits with large Medicaid and Medicare clientele will have complicated e-billing systems and will require greater training on this than a for-profit that has mainly pay out-of-pocket or private insurance billing.

Also, during the twenty-first century, the patient mix is much more diverse in almost all hospital settings, which will cause an emphasis on cultural training, again based on the organization. More patients are culturally diverse, especially in America, and making sure that staff can easily incorporate cultural differences into their own activities and interactions with patients is pivotal. Thus, training can be defined in different ways, but for the purposes of this section, training is the process of educating staff on handling a new organizational culture that involves technology, while also incorporating the needs of different patient ethnic cultures, with translators and technological improvements in cultural context incorporated in their information management. It is a complicated balance because new technology, especially electronic medical records, has translator systems to understand non-English-speaking patients and providing a better understanding of health needs in different ethnic and racial groups. However, sometimes these translators can be extremely literal in nature and must be used with caution. Some prior research covers many different aspects of the community through the incorporation of cultural competence, health literacy, and training for technology in the hospital setting. But, a major component is lacking—understanding the differences across various hospitals, with a comparison and contrast of how these different kinds of hospitals use training to become more culturally tolerant and technologically savvy.

While community health-center clinics and free clinics tend to have a very diverse patient mix as compared to larger for-profits and not-for-profits, their staff lacks cultural training as well as technological training, a big pitfall in meaningfully using technology and also being able to understand the patients' needs and concerns. Here, technology and communication will be going hand-in-hand as the new century begins, because technology plays such a large role in predicting outcomes and answering questions that patients have. For doctors, choosing a prescription medication or good cure to a condition can be now done at the click of a button on an EMR, but priority must remain on a patient's cultural and ethnic background and context, because these issues could impact what medication, treatment, or health-related outcome the patient is most comfortable with accepting. The most obvious example of this is a devout Catholic woman who has just gotten married, and wants to ask her doctor for the best family planning advice, but does not accept the usage of birth control pills due to religious reasons. The doctor should take this into account as one method that is not likely to answer the patient's questions, and reroute her to other available forms of family planning, such as counseling or the Billings Ovulation Method,* which may be better options. Especially during healthcare reform, such topics are controversial, and the common misconception is that technology will be more of a handicap in limiting options for patients; however, it may actually help coordinate and connect as well as provide quick references for those who need them, if used correctly. For this reason, training is again of utmost importance and must not be taken as something that can be standardized across organizations, but should be tailored to the organization's needs.

Looking at the literature, there are some basic categories that have been researched. Some speak directly about the training required in specific forms of technology adoption, including the computerized physician order entry system (CPOE), electronic medical records, Six Sigma, or patient safety training and adoption strategies that have allowed for better adaptation to a technological culture within the hospital setting.

A paper that does discuss strategies for properly diffusing technology within a hospital is by Ford et al. (2010). They demonstrate how health information technology can be "meaningfully used," which can be defined as actually being in a state of activity within the hospital, be it through interaction with patient, use by the doctor, or to facilitate any provider's access to records and proper usage of data between healthcare management within or connected to the hospital. Rather than lie on a shelf and catch dust, the technology is providing support to the personnel, regardless of its outcomes, and how useful it may be. This has some relation to training as well because training is one of the most important features in providing support to the staff on learning techniques and providing ease of access to the health informatics. Yet, many of these papers do not look to the core of how technology may be able to sync or may be shattering the possibility of integrating culture into the medical profession and drawing conclusions on the impact of training on the quality of care to the patient.

---

* Teaching the Billings Ovulation Method, Dr E. L. Billings AM, MB BS, DCH (London), 2001.

Cultural Competence of a Hospital

Next, discussion of cultural competence and cultural training within and across the different hospital settings is a subject of interest. This is necessary to understand what factors most impact the cultural climate within a hospital and ease the transition into it. Cultural competence is defined by Betancourt, Green, and Carillo (2002, 5) as the "ability to provide patients with diverse values, beliefs, and behaviors, including tailoring delivery to meet patients' social, cultural, and linguistic needs." The purpose of measuring and proliferating cultural competence within a hospital is to enhance acceptance and attract a larger patient base, while also hoping to improve the quality of care for new groups of patients. While some components of this discussion, such as studying cultural competence within hospitals, has had a fair amount of past research, doing a comparison across hospitals to see how they compare in terms of their cultural competence may be an interesting further frame of study. This is to identify the pitfalls and strengths that various kinds of hospitals have to provide care and patient satisfaction. Also, they may have a deeper motive—to analyze whether cultural competence plays a role on the patient base that comes to a for-profit versus a not-for-profit versus a government hospital—because patients feel more comfortable attending one type of hospital over another based on their cultural needs and concerns.

Betancourt, Green, and Carillo (2002, 6) identify some of the most difficult barriers to the hospital setting in terms of cultural abilities. Some of these include (1) presence or lack of a diversified workforce, (2) "systems of care" to meet patients concerns, and (3) communication skills and cultural interaction between patient and provider. The study provides insight from some academic and government hospitals that were visited, which provided information on the cultural battles faced. The various sites visited had a new added curriculum component—to provide cultural training to staff—in order to see how the staff was utilizing this cultural education and its impact on any quality of patient care measures. The Mexican Health Project and the Sunset Park Family Health Center, set up in the 1990s, were a few dated examples of integration and cultural literacy efforts to make immigrant groups feel more comfortable accessing healthcare services. Mostly, examples of integration efforts include having translator and linguistic services, trying to train staff on cultural needs, and introducing more ethnically diverse staff that had prior knowledge of languages spoken at the clinics in order to better communicate with patients. Other more "systemic," or system-wide, efforts include greater research and data collection on needs of populations and groups of populations that were culturally bound, conducting community health needs assessments that analyzed concerns and issues in the communities with a cultural focus, and providing health materials in both the language of the immigrant population as well as in English. The health literacy efforts noted were of importance and have become even more important today. The report is slightly outdated in that it doesn't report on electronic health usage and how important this will be in providing help to English as a second language (ESL) patients. The Internet provides information in other languages that may help break down some of the barriers, if there is ease of access for patients.

The Delmarva Foundation report, written in 2002, is behind many of the technological improvements that have occurred and may have changed the systemic, cultural, and clinical changes within the healthcare framework. There has been a new focus on electronic health and electronic governance, which has had diversity incorporated through social networking and health forums online, that provides patients with group discussions and blogs of advice, specific to cultural enclaves, and for those who need effective, culturally competent solutions. Advice is readily available on many electronic sources, such as www.WebMD.com. More representatives at the congressional, federal, state, and local level are of diverse backgrounds and represent community efforts from an integrative approach on acceptance of linguistic, ethnic, racial, religious, and gender differences, and are making this a bigger part of their agendas as communities are expanding.

Another article that focused primarily on mental health shows how cultural competence must be worked into a system's development in reducing mental health disparities (Harper et al., 2006). What it doesn't discuss is the importance of achieving this from a grassroots level. What needs to occur is the simultaneous training of staff at every level, from the most recent hires and most basic administrative positions to those at the highest echelons. Nobody should be considered above or beyond the need to become culturally aware and should take training on cultural differences, especially because the world is changing at a rapid pace and globalization has made such a mark on an evolving world. Some of the article's focus is on making culture a context or backdrop for conducting healthcare and providing services (Harper et al., 2006). Yet, by limiting culture to just being a context or setting for healthcare services, it is just as wheels are to the car rather than the engine that drives many healthcare decisions. Culture can be a defining factor for the decisions of a patient, as patients will receive healthcare based on what degree they are integrated in their own sociocultural identity. Therefore, being not only culturally aware, but treating culture as a driver for health quality improvement outcomes is essential, as healthcare is defined to some extent by immigrant niches, cultural communities, cultural values, and identification with morals, and/or lack thereof of these characteristics. For an atheist, for example, he or she may not identify with any religion, any cultural background, or specific religious or ethnic system. But, his or her American (or other national and/or political identity) values may still shape health literacy and impact access to preventive care and affordability of services.

Another report discusses where to look for cultural competence within an organization, or proxies for culture competence factors. Some of these include "organizational values, governance, planning and monitoring excellence, communication, staff development, organizational infrastructure, and services/interventions" (The Lewin Group, 2002). Each factor is then described in more detail. While all of these components definitely must have a degree of cultural competence, the outcomes are based on evidence in three separate categories: the organizational perspectives, client perspectives, and community perspectives. What is lacking is the way that the interaction occurs across and between these different categories. Aren't these factors shaped by each other? Isn't how the community perceives its providers as culturally competent as important as how the providers view the community in terms of its cultural breakdown? Aren't how providers interact with each other, through collaboration networks, especially what services they provide, just as important as how providers envision their patient mix?

With the HITECH Act and changes to information technology adoption and integration in healthcare, there is definite need to see how organizations implement technology and what their cultural attitudes, norms, and acceptance toward technology is. Technology and culture are more intertwined than meets the eye because of the spatial- and time-oriented characteristics that define a community and which may define a patient mix attending a hospital. From the patients' perspective, it is important to be able to access their own health information through technology (smart phones, apps on Ipads, or use of the Internet), finding information on health providers in the area, as well as access to preventive care at health service organizations with their language, religious, and cultural needs in mind. From a provider perspective, it is about knowing the cultural setting as well as patient's needs and identifying what treatment is right for the patient as well as technology that will improve or exacerbate a patient's condition (The Lewin Group, 2002).

One of the reasons why this topic has not been researched thoroughly is that many of the variables involved in analyzing cultural competence are socioeconomic variables that are complicated to measure. As a report by DHHS discussed back in 2002, there is not much empirical support

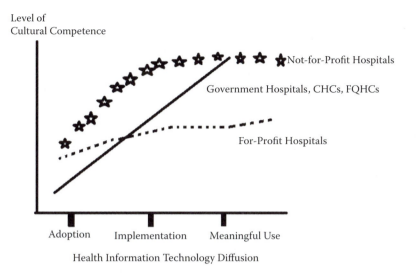

Figure 2.2   Stages of HIT Diffusion and Impacts on Cultural Competence.

to analyze and operationalize the link between health disparities across ethnic and racial backgrounds and how they are impacted by cultural competence of a hospital and/or a healthcare provider. As communication between physicians and patients may be improved, this is not enough to show the presence of a relationship between cultural competence and health disparities, be it linear or otherwise. This only makes the case of technology more interesting. It could be possible that technology will standardize any differences that once came up between physicians in how they treat patients, especially as technology has translation mechanisms and e-health provides patients and physicians with better outlets to reinforce what treatments or interventions may be necessary for any given health condition. Thus, technology in this sense could either empower or could disempower the physician. It also has a consequence on the patient, as patients have better ways to analyze a hospital based on remarks made on the hospital, comments, blogs about a provider or insurance carrier, and greater portals to engage in discussion and communication regarding a hospital's quality of care, efficiency, and effectiveness.

One more interesting component of a hospital's cultural competence besides driving health literacy for the patient and the physician is its ability to shape a hospital's mission. As a hospital's mission may differ, cultural competence may be the one factor that will standardize the differences between treatment of diverse patients across hospitals. If all hospitals are to create an environment of cultural acceptance, their mission must be driven by a high level of cultural competence as well as cultural training sessions (The Lewin Group, 2002).

As Figure 2.2 demonstrates, not-for-profit hospitals may begin the highest in cultural competence because historically they have undergone several levels of regulation to ensure they meet cultural benchmarks. Government hospitals show the most growth in technology as their patient mix will be most affected through technology implementation all the way until meaningful use of technology is to occur. While they start off at a lower point due to how much more diverse they are, they will catch up to not-for-profits, though it's difficult to predict which will show the most cultural knowledge and growth. More than likely, technology will standardize levels of cultural competence among government hospitals and not-for-profits once they are both meaningfully using the technology. Governments undergo the highest level of rigor from adoption to implementation of technology regulations, therefore, their approach is more linear in technology implementation and cultural competence because they have the greatest impetus to achieve these standards. For-profits will show the least growth as their goals and incentives align least with adding cultural experiences to the hospital setting, and their patients may be choosing their hospitals more carefully, such that they have a preconceived notion of what the hospital will be like and whether or not it has the level of cultural competence for which they are looking. Typically these will be people of affluent classes that can afford for-profit hospital services and are not looking to see much change in cultural competence from the introduction in technology.

Also, for a for-profit firm, cash flow creation is tantamount in driving healthcare services; their main goal is to derive the gains in their stock ownership and profits. The not-for-profits, on the other hand, are working for the community benefit and to fulfill a charitable purpose, so while they do gain some tax benefits from being a charitable organization, their organizational culture should offer a different perspective. Not-for-profits can be in different forms, either privately run or owned in part by the government. Government hospitals include community health centers and federally qualified health centers that have unique underlying factors on their internal and external development. Government programs also tend to be in the form of pilot projects and pilot programs, which test out various new features, such as technological innovation, cultural training sessions, and other additives to the hospitals or clinics, and thus many of these studies are not as well documented or researched. Roger (2003) has an interesting technology diffusion model that can be expanded on, by showing three different lines of technology diffusion, depending on the organization.

Goal-Oriented Behavior of a Hospital with Technology

Why is goal-oriented behavior such a driver of organizational culture in hospitals with technology? Examples of goal-oriented behavior include community health needs assessments; adoption models for technology, such as the HIMSS Adoption Model, which measures how much progress has been made; the hiring of consultants solely for the purpose of analyzing the firm's competitiveness; and more.

While examples in the literature lack taking organizational culture into account for technological implementation, there have been studies on quality improvement (QI) and quality management tactics, which analyze how an organization drives affordability and high standards of care through better implementation strategies. While the success rate of these QI programs have not been high (about 40% at best (Huq and Martin, 2000)), comparisons can be made of QI programs and technology implementation programs, which need better structure to properly conduct and make effective for the future.

An interesting article by Prince (1998) identifies community hospitals and then indexes them based on their adaptability to new technology and keeping up with the most current changes in technology. The technology present at a hospital is used to predict the bond ratings and the profitability through operating revenue of a nonprofit hospital. This is fairly important from a financing perspective of a nonprofit, as the largest part of investment in the organization is derived from municipal bonds and bond ratings. How effectively they utilize technology and begin to make progress could mean a better bond rating and better flow of capital into their coffers. These are links many hospitals are not making to technology. They simply see it as a hindrance and costly expense to their organizational dynamic, rather than a tool for progress and driver for success. They should take better note, so that nonprofits see technology as reducing risk on their bond ratings, which could drive down the amount they pay on interest to finance their hospital structures.

Another interesting proxy for the ability of hospitals to be climbing the ranks of hospital readiness and HIT efficacy could be the number of beds in the hospital, because the number of beds may represent achievement, as demonstrated by HIMSS Analytics findings. It could be because a larger hospital typically has larger investment and capital potential, or it could be that hospitals with a greater number of beds are under greater pressure to implement technology from the government. For example, HIMSS Analytics (2012) reports suggests that "60 percent of hospitals with more than 500 beds reported being ready or most likely to achieve Stage One, but by comparison, only 20 percent of hospitals with under 100 beds were ready or most likely to achieve Stage One."

Yet, there are exceptions to the stereotypical boundaries of progress that researchers tend to set around achievement differences between nonprofit and for-profit hospitals. For example, Citizens Memorial Hospital (CMH) in Bolivar, Missouri, and Stanford Hospital and Clinics in Palo Alto, California, deliver care in a paperless manner, readily sharing clinical information across healthcare providers and using electronic collaboration networks. CMH was the first rural hospital to achieve stage 7 in the HIMSS Analytics Model for completely electronic use. What did they do differently? This could be an excellent case study, because it could be one of multiple reasons. The area itself is surrounded by an extremely affluent set of neighborhoods, so it could be that donors were helpful in pushing the hospital along, and charity care doctors were abundant. But, most likely is the presence of competition in such a market, where the rural hospitals see the kind of care being provided around them, and realize that they need to stay connected to these other hospitals, and the best way to do this is to go electronic and speak the same language as their affluent counterparts. This worked the way they wanted it to, if not better for the case of Citizens Memorial. Funding in California at a state level did not undergo as harsh of cuts as many other parts of the nation, so rural hospitals may be at less of a risk there. Recovery Act Funding, likewise, provided quite a few hospitals with options on providing care to the underserved. Of the $121 million provided to community health centers (CHCs) toward HIT development (adoption and implementation of certified EHRs) all over the nation, the states fared differently in making use of the opportunities(Data from HHS.gov*). For example, $0 were awarded toward HIT for Montana, compared to $7,994,894 awarded to HIT at Texas CHCs. This may have to do with the larger volume of CHCs per state and the focus these CHCs are placing on technology versus development of other parts of their infrastructure.

Another goal-setting characteristic that is quite interesting is analyzing the priorities of hospitals and how they use the funding and aid they receive from state and federal grants and subsidies to enhance their services. Table 2.2 shows a comparison of a few states, including New York and California (which are affluent in nature), and Ohio, Oklahoma, and Texas (which can be argued to be affluent, but with pockets of high poverty zones) and lists a comparison of their resource use. Granted, political culture and autonomy may play a role in shaping where changes and developments are made, depending on the opposition, inclination, and perspective of the state and local officials toward HIT.

Prioritizing of such investments is a struggle, when comparing the have and have-not hospitals. As stated before, some government hospitals have large amounts of aid and donorship and are at a good place, such that they can afford to put more resources toward infrastructure and efficiency gains. Others may barely have the infrastructure or staff to support patients and, therefore,

---

* http://www.hhs.gov/recovery/programs/hrsa/index.html

Table 2.2   Health Information Technology Funds by State in FY 2011

State	New Access Point Services	Increased Demand for Services	Capital Improvement Construction Program	Facility Investment Construction Program	Health Information Technology Awards Round 1 & 2	Total
California	$15,600,000	$48,274,320	$109,264,437	$65,600,989	$24,499,751	$263,239,497
New York	$7,068,705	$19,778,572	$53,452,437	$15,561,175	$7,102,697	$102,963,586
Texas	$14,272,127	$20,201,876	$44,576,879	$37,347,795	$7,994,894	$124,393,571
Oklahoma	$6,362,316	$8,070,049	$21,283,725	$24,849,555	$0	$60,565,645
Ohio	$7,800,000	$3,250,205	$7,818,390	$14,813,647	$0	$33,682,242

cannot afford to put money toward new technologies. The stark difference between California, which received a grand total of $24 million in investment toward HIT, compared to Oklahoma and Ohio receiving $0, is shocking and perplexing, and shows that there is still much to be done between states to get every healthcare provider caught up to a basic standard of quality care and technology usage to derive better results.

Currently, only about 1.1% of the more than 5,000 U.S. hospitals in the HIMSS Analytics database have reached stage 7 status of meaningful use of technology achievement. The basic parameters to receive the HIMSS Stage 7 award is that an organization "must have a complete electronic health record (EHR) system, including computerized physician order entry, physician and nursing documentation, closed loop medication administration, clinical decision support, ancillary systems, a data warehouse, and the ability to exchange information with other healthcare systems" (HIMSS Analytics, 2012).

Collaboration is also a subcategory of performance and goal-setting standards. It becomes both an internal goal such that there is better collaboration within the organization's teams and departments, and an external goal in developing outreach networks and having members of the board who are interested in connecting with other organizations and linking similar interests. This is key, otherwise resources are wasted. The mission at the end of the day is helping as many patients as possible with the least amount of resources wasted, least amount of costs, and least amount of time consumed. Rather than just serving their own needs and trying to use predatory pricing in the markets, these organizations that have an affluent status should be making efforts to tie themselves with other organizations.

This is not necessarily the same as mergers and acquisitions. Predatory pricing could be one of the reasons many smaller not-for-profit hospitals and government hospitals do not survive, and mergers and acquisitions are the other reason that these clinics or providers that are serving rural or underserved populations shut down. On the other hand, collaboration networks will allow for the right patient base to get care, especially preventive care, which is one that is most lacking in indigent and impoverished neighborhoods today, and this way less emergency room and hospital visits that are unwarranted will take place on taxpayer money. This cost shifting is a problematic outcome because the middle and upper classes end up paying for the high levels of expenses that poor patients cannot afford and make use of their Medicaid or welfare status to help leverage care. Then the cost gets placed on the government that shifts the cost to the taxpayer to help pay for the health insurance and healthcare, and this has been the cycle of damage that continues to burn a hole in the wallets of citizens and the government today.

Other forms of collaboration that are key to include would be collaboration across hospitals, interaction across hospitals and clinics, and interactions across physician networks. This would reduce information asymmetry about services provided, resources present, and more. It also can be an important marketing tool needed to analyze whether patients' needs are being met in the area that the clinic or hospital is serving versus the patient having to travel outside of the locale to get care. It would be helpful to inculcate better values in the hospital management and/or provider's mind of the business, marketing, and geographic research to meet the needs of populations in the area, which would prevent a squandering of resources on similar issues within this area. Diversifying various services with networks of care makes more sense than the current situation, where primary care physicians end up in affluent neighborhoods and it is mostly hospitals and concierge medicine present in its low income neighbors, which can be a drain on our current healthcare system. For this reason, community health needs assessments have become an important addition to the IRS requirements for nonprofit hospitals, and county needs will be identified by the hospital personnel. Then an implementation strategy will be created to represent how the needs will be targeted and taken care of and which collaborative organizations will participate in the process. This also can prevent squandering of technology investments if all the organizations are connected and can easily transfer records, information, e-billing, e-prescriptions, lab results, and more. Ethics and privacy will be better upheld as well if all the organizations are uniformly using the same technology rather than the current mishmash of some being paper and some electronic.

Policy Implications and Conclusions

This analysis brought up new and important points about the inclusion of technology in the field of organizational behavior across various healthcare providers. The literature so far has not suggested much on the lines of how technology impacts nonprofits and for-profits differently and doing comparisons on technology implementation across health providers. The importance of this data could help these organizations thrive and grow together rather than at different speeds, which will narrow barriers in providing health to the community. The importance of this topic can be felt across health information technology, economics, the life sciences, and even financing and other systems that help fund the changes in this transformation. For this reason, the impact of such a study is not only far reaching, but interdisciplinary and effective across multiple bodies of literature. It is relevant today during healthcare reform and will become more relevant as technology becomes the language of the future for communities both domestically and internationally.

Some policy suggestions for improving the inertia toward adopting HIT for organizations include:

- Inclusion of HIT in organization's mission statement
- Improving training of staff in cultural competence issues
- Using Webinars on training for HIT by being affiliated with trade organizations that provide this help
- Increasing transparency of goals of the organization as well as management incentives toward HIT by providing greater awareness of the impact of HIT to organizations

Better collaboration and bureaucratic initiatives to increase HIT involvement in every level, as well as providing incentives to adopt, will allow for a more efficient use of resources, time, and energy spent on HIT.

The economic, financial, and sociocultural structure of the hospital is defined by how successful a hospital is in instituting its different cultural features, including the hospital's mission, management and incentives, cultural training, and goal-oriented behavior. Beginning with comparisons across these different characteristics, it can be seen how the ownership and type of hospital will impact the organizational culture of the institution. This literature has yet to be uncovered, as most published information on the subject does not do comparisons across these institutions, rather, they analyze the organization from within. However, cross hospital comparisons are necessary to understand what drives cultural change. Relevance in this chapter stems from the focus on technological change comparisons across providers, as a good deal of research has not yet shed light on these differences and its impact on the stages of technology diffusion: implementation, adoption, and usage.

Technology integration at hospitals has occurred at a much slower rate for the healthcare industry, thus trying to pick apart this phenomenon is important to improve the efficiency of the system. Important policy implications will become more prevalent as technology integration unravels. Some policy solutions to the current problems with technology integration will include understanding health information technology as being utilized at different rates and for different purposes at each organization based on how goal-oriented the organization is, what its mission is, management incentives are, and other characteristics. By recognizing these differences, there could be greater benefit derived by focusing on plugging the gaps for each organization individually rather than a focus on collective change. For example, electronic billing may be more prevalent at for-profits due to the sheer complicatedness of the process at nonprofits. Therefore, electronic billing may require more training sessions and efficiency. On the other hand, electronic prescriptions may be utilized more by community health centers, as government mandated prescriptions, due to new e-government regulations, are a better way to handle the system.

Another policy conclusion from this chapter is to look at these organizations in their stakeholder dynamics and see how their management may be constraining or easing regulations to integrate technology. Also, state and federal regulations may be impacting how funds and resources are being utilized by various organizations, so comparisons across states may not be as valid as comparing organizations of a similar regional or state regulation background. Finally, from a broader picture, volunteering and community benefit may be defined very differently in different regions, and this can be standardized by IRS guidelines that include health information guidelines in the mission statement of an organization. This may be of great interest to organizations that want to provide a technologically savvy persona. Also, better collaboratives that address needs across the region and are ensuring that services are not being duplicated in regions where they are of low need, is of extreme importance. The use of information technology to provide streamlined databases and connectivity between organizations is key in facilitating better marketing of services and better organizational collaboratives that address what has been done and what needs to occur to provide better healthcare to each pocket of the community, including those diseases and health conditions of very high risk all the way to conditions of low to no risk. This would be an effective way to bridge the gaps that are faced by populations with high emergency center inpatient care that could be avoided.

Finally, policy implications are still evolving and for this reason, there is no reason to believe that technology integration is not occurring. Rather, it has been a slow and steady process, so it is best to continue research and have a wing of the organization that is participating in research and development on the subject, such that the organization is getting feedback on how they are doing at technology adoption and implementation. Without this, there is no way to know whether the organization has showed some change and which departments are lagging behind and need more help. Continued research will allow for high-impact, timely solutions to the healthcare information technology needs of the community organizations and how they can be tailored to the organizations' current needs, resources, and abilities.

Chapter 3

An Overview of How Health Information Technology Will Make a Mark on Hospital Financing

Overview

Important differences between the financing structures of not-for-profit hospitals and for-profit hospitals lead them to be equipped differently in their services, use of capital, and mission to provide quality healthcare while cutting costs. The new dimension to this dynamic is the introduction of health information technology (HIT) to hospitals, such as electronic medical records, during this period of healthcare reform. It is possible that HIT could help or hinder, depending on the type of hospital, ease of usage, prediction of its return on investment, and more. The technological performance at a hospital can be based on how easily hospitals will be able to finance and incorporate technology in their infrastructure. For this reason, a study on the literature of health information technology and its impact on some of the important features that contribute to hospital financing, including tax exempt or tax paying status of a hospital, ownership, management, and compensation, as well as mergers and acquisitions, is key to the study of different types of hospitals and their ability to adjust to technological change.

Introduction

As the U.S. healthcare system and its ability to be financed have controversial and questionable elements that have driven an era of reform, the field of healthcare has introduced technology, such as electronic medical records, electronic billing, electronic prescribing, and more, into the mix to produce efficiency and effectiveness. The question is: Who will be impacted? This is dual ended;

both the hospital and the patients who attend will see impacts, but this chapter will focus primarily on the hospital side and how technology impacts a hospital's finances.

Through healthcare reform in the United States, there will be changes to the way the public and private sector in healthcare is run because technology does not just impact healthcare in general, but it impacts various healthcare providers, especially different hospitals in different ways, in how hospital financing occurs and will occur in the future. First, the discussion will engage in defining the supply and demand side of healthcare economics with changes that must be made to incorporate HIT. Then, the discussion will be on the healthcare financing mechanisms of the different kinds of hospitals (not-for-profit, for-profit, and government hospitals) and what drives differences among them. Finally, with the addition of technology in the twenty-first century healthcare finance equation, the structure of healthcare finance in each hospital setting will be envisioned in a new light. An in-depth policy analysis and impacts of technology on healthcare finance will then ensue, to wrap up the findings from this field and tie the field's many components together.

This research analyzes the impact of introducing health information technology to not-for-profit and for-profit hospitals' financing structure, respectively. Because of the differences in how each type of healthcare provider finances its organization, the hypothesis for why technology impacts each financial structure differently involves various possibilities: differing management and mission characteristics of the organization, investment and debt of the organization, and the impact of mergers and acquisitions. There are possible reasons why health information technology adoption will occur in different time frames and may be slower or faster at some hospitals than others, reaping profits for some hospitals while possibly causing skyrocketing prices at others.

First, a brief summary of health economics and the supply and demand sides of the hospital market. Looking at healthcare broadly, in determining whether it should be considered a "luxury" or a "necessity," Getzen (2000, 268) states diplomatically that it depends. His paper provides an economic model of how groups will have enough within-group variation for their income elasticities to differ substantially, making health insurance more of a luxury for some and a necessity for others. Specifying the exact unit of analysis is key to the study, because the individual will be risk averse, whereas markets and firms will engage in risk pooling and riskier behaviors. The use of multilevel decision modeling is interesting. He points out that while an individual's income rises, on average, it will see less need for health insurance, making the income elasticity negative or near zero. The national averages for demand for health insurance change substantially when the income changes, since this is an aggregate. This causes the national averages to have positive income elasticity. Another interesting point he brings forward is that of the behavior of group means versus the individual mean. The two are not alike, he notes, and lays out assumptions for the multilevel model. Yet, one of his basic assumptions is that "the primary purpose of insurance is to make sure that $dp/d\ x < 1$." This assumes p is the health insurance premium and x is the expenditures. This could be misconstrued because the premium to expenditure ratio can be less than or equal to 1 in order to satisfy the customer, again depending on the specific needs of the customer: income elasticity, level of sickness or health condition(s), and more. As long as they are not paying a higher premium than the amount of expenditures, the ratio should still be satisfied, but the author should not rule out the likelihood that the percentage that the premium is of the base level of expenditures will differ based on preexisting conditions, a chronic disease, and/or how the premium is set by the various health insurance providers. What the author does not mention is that he is assuming a normal distribution when, actually, the distribution will have unequal variances and heteroskedasticity across people and more than likely not a normal distribution. This is because healthcare is vast and the number of problems people have in some subfields of healthcare, such as postacute care (typically taken care of by for-profit hospitals), radiology, and other fields of specialization, are much greater than others. For example, the premiums paid by those with gynecological problems will be much higher and a greater percentage of these people will have other related expenditures for side effects to treatments of such problems.

Also, typically, those with lack of access to preventive care facilities may need greater levels of care, paying high premiums that are still only a small portion of the true expenditures, a high level of risk and debt that is passed off to the health insurance provider and/or a government program, such as Medicare or Medicaid, to even out. This caveat deserves mention, especially today, when nearly 87 million, or 30%, of the U.S. population is on a federal welfare health insurance program (Census Bureau, 2010). When analyzing healthcare finance, a micro and macro perspective with a strong justification for the unit of analysis has become more and more important in the economic analysis of healthcare (Getzen, 2000). But, the point that could be debated from his paper today is that "boundaries of transactions [bounding patients by a provider network]" rather than geography are what determine cost (p. 267). Actually, geography plays an extremely important role today on the healthcare provided to communities, especially when looking at the density of populations and the percentage of the population in rural versus urban areas. Rather than just being bound by the providers in a network, healthcare information technology, an important new dimension to healthcare financing, has created collaboration and coordination networks that expand the ability for providers to connect with each other and also lower the transaction cost as well as provisions to provide services. This can be an important variable that needs to be held constant when economically analyzing the impact of HIT on financing a hospital.

From both a micro and macro perspective, the individual and the community are affected by provider networks and now can get access to care even if they are in rural, impoverished, or far-reaching networks. Through the electronic age, technology is mobile as are providers who can go to the patient's location to provide services. Examples of this today include the Amish populations and Native Americans, who are provided care through mobile vans, which will come to them if they are unable to access care. While this analysis of a micro and macro infrastructure is important in economic analysis of healthcare going forward, it is important to include the integration of technology and its ability to change connectivity in healthcare, possibly reducing costs in the long run on the micro and macro level. The "allocation" of total expenditures across individuals can be defined as: $ai = xi/X$ in Getzen's article, but this allocation will change according to the technology integration component on the micro and macro level. There will be increasing costs as the burden of technology expenses is placed on the taxpayer and/or patients (at least initially) who are being served at technology-rich hospitals and, thus, easing the burden from those who don't have to pay at centers without technology. In the long run, though, those at technology-rich hospitals will be able to recover the costs and may even save money because of improved functionality at these institutions. Technology will reduce the cost to individuals (in the long run) through a reduction in extraneous costs, lab tests, and improvements in preventive care techniques; however, in the short run, it may increase the cost to the infrastructure of health providers and drive up initial costs to the patient. For this reason, it is important to explore how healthcare financing occurs at various hospitals today, and how it may change through the era of technology.

Supply Side of Healthcare

The supply side economics of this chapter will discuss the provider's perspectives on cost, financing, and the decision-making processes that are in the healthcare provider's best interests, while keeping its mission in mind. The mission of a not-for-profit is to support the best interests of the community, while the mission of a for-profit is driven by stakeholder compensation. The mission of a government hospital will be funding within the coffers of the government to impact those most in need of subsidized healthcare. While quite a stab has been taken at analyzing within group differences of the hospitals, there has been much less research on comparison across hospital settings, especially since the advent of advanced technology across not-for-profit and for-profit hospitals. This comparison is key to the body of scholarship because it will help implement programs and policies that will specifically cater to better financing strategies unique to not-for-profits in incorporating high capital health information technology, which may differ from the methods used by for-profits. For example, a for-profit hospital may have plenty of capital or require only a smaller loan to finance the new technological changes to its hospital, whereas not-for-profit hospitals may have a higher debt to asset ratio, and require high interest loans in order to finance the purchase of technology. This and more examples will be explained in greater detail. The literature so far has captured some differences between these types of hospitals, namely the financing structure and tax exempt status, as well as CEO compensation and incentives of employees, but literature does not incorporate differences in these features for technology-rich, not-for-profit and for-profit hospitals. A few differences include how technology will be incorporated as a sunk cost, the amount of capital to drive the funding of technological improvements in hospitals, the compensation changes that will occur through technology improvements, and the decisions to merge with other organizations in order to get hands on the capital rich improvements in technology. These assumptions will be looked at more closely once the financing mechanism is presented in greater detail below.

Ellis and McGuire (1999) identify a free rider effect, which is based on the theory behind how hospitals can seek out reimbursements and aid for their spending. New trends in hospitals show that they base their quality of care, services, and cost per patient on reimbursement mechanisms from the state and federal government. It is in the hospitals' power to decide which patients' conditions should be accepted at the hospital, especially if it impacts the amount of market share the hospital has in the industry or the region. The investment in new and better hospital services also is impacted by a hospital's motives, capital, and organizational management. Again, technology can play a greater role in changing the dynamics of intensity of services provided, regardless of the size and market share of the hospital; therefore, discussion that can shed light on technology will be key for the future of healthcare services.

The reimbursement of hospitals and federally run health providers both will be impacted, though those hospitals with larger percentages of disadvantaged patients on a welfare plan, such as Medicare or Medicaid, may be likely to gain greater reimbursement for health information technology investments. This is part of the Health Information Technology for Clinical and Economic Health Act (HITECH Act). This provides incentives to organizations with lower capital to invest in technologies that can improve productivity, growth and efficiency, and effectiveness going forward. An important take away from the article is that length of stay "has actually increased for short stayers" making hospitals more competitive in attracting profitable, short-stay patients based on a model of moral hazard, selection, and private style effects (Ellis and McGuire, 1999, 274). This could get worse, as the health information technology structure may allow for easier possibilities for selection of patients with less severe conditions, though ethics laws, such as HIPAA (Health Information Portability and Accountability Act), are trying to prevent the manipulation of technology for such purposes.

Demand Side of Healthcare

This chapter does not focus in on the demand side of health economics as a direct effect. Rather, the chapter defines the direct impact of HIT systems on healthcare finance at various hospitals that will impact the patient *indirectly* through reductions in cost and improved quality of care. Because of the patient mix that is typical of for-profit versus not-for-profit hospitals as well as the government hospital patient mix, the patient is definitely impacted by changes to technology, but the impact is not measured here because the focus is on healthcare providers—the hospitals, specifically—and their networks.

With that being said, a brief outline of the supply side of health economics introduces the concept of moral hazard problems of hospitals. It is interesting to consider what incentives people have in purchasing health insurance and engaging in preventative healthcare, based on income elasticity, access to care, and access and affordability of coverage. Herring (2005) contrasts the absolute versus relative costs of healthcare. Their model looks at the purchase of premiums occurring when the reservation price, or out of pocket expenses, is greater than the amount paid in premiums, for any risk averse utility maximizer. Due to "diminishing marginal utility of wealth," the prospect of receiving unanticipated charity care seems better than the need to be covered by insurance. From his analysis, Herring notes that the "low-income, uninsured pay about one-third of the total medical care they received," while the uninsured in higher income groups pay for nearly half of all the care with which they are provided (231). What is strong about Herring's approach is his "access to care" measure, which takes into account the reason for access to care issues, especially to determine if difficulty in financial barriers to care existed due to lack of access to a charity care center, which includes hospitals, clinics, and federally funded community health centers. He then makes an important point, which is that, during healthcare reform, there may be a switch by current low-income groups from a private healthcare provider to charity care due to the financial ease of community health centers based on moral hazard (231). For this reason, a mandate of all people to be carrying health insurance, or possibly a lack thereof, is key to the discussion of how expensive financing technology at hospitals will be. It could inflate prices at hospitals if there is still a large uninsured population and the cost of technology is not spread out across organizations. Yet, if the mandate for required insurance for all occurs, technology implementation will be much cheaper as costs get spread over a large populous.

Finally, hospitals must have a patient-centric focus because this drives the demand side discussion of financing of hospitals. The patient should be the most important focus because consumers should be the driving force for better output for hospitals as well as be the focus of the organization's efforts. However, not surprisingly, evidence does not support this. Quality of care and cost for patients are of optimum importance, but competition has driven prices up and led to debate on how to provide better quality and lower costs to the patients of the U.S. healthcare system.

Structure of Hospitals and Their Financing Mechanisms

Three types of hospitals exist today: government hospitals, not-for-profit hospitals, and for-profit hospitals. However, they are constantly changing and competing in their characteristics, quality of care, and services provided. The majority of the 500,000+ hospitals today, or 60 to 70%, is not-for-profit, whereas the other 35% are split between for-profit and government-run hospitals. These numbers have changed, and tend to rise and fall based on the boom and bust cycles of the economy, making them difficult to predict, but variable on many factors. A few major components that set the three types of hospitals apart from each other are mergers and acquisitions, the treatments and services provided, hospital ownership and taxation status, and, finally, management characteristics that include the role of hierarchy and employee–employer relations and incentives to work.

While some studies analyze the financing mechanisms and differences in longevity and market share capacity and expansion, others cover the effects of multiple providers, such as the number of for-profits and not-for-profits as well as HMOs (health maintenance organizations) within a vicinity, on the providers' behavior in the market. From a study by Horwitz and Nichols (2009) that used a survey provided to the AHA (American Hospital Association) and analyzed services provided and the ownership characteristics between hospitals, there is evidence to believe that not-for-profits change their behavior based on the surrounding majority of organizations present. In regions where for-profits dominated the landscape, the not-for-profits in those areas tended to compete by providing more profitable services (mimicking the for-profit behavior) in order to stay competitive and pick up the share of the services in which for-profits were not participating. Examples of such services include home health, nursing, and more. This assumes that for-profits behave in a cherry-picking manner, such that they do not want to provide services that may be unprofitable or likely to be unreimbursed. This means that, based on this study, not-for-profits do change behavior based on the behavior and services provided by organizations around them. It was found that there was little difference between for-profit and government hospitals, even when surrounded by a for-profit-dominated region that was selling extremely profitable services (Horwitz and Nichols, 2009, 935). The only assumption that was not covered in this paper was that of the difference in maximizing utility between these institutions, including how they perceive the rational choice model and/or bounded rationality. It's plausible that differences in the services provided by not-for-profits and for-profits are driven by what the patient wants rather than what the hospital wants to provide because the patient may choose to go to a nonprofit over a for-profit for religious (affiliation) reasons, ease of access, or provider networks. The fact that patients take an interest in the provider they choose, yet have limited options or are limited through options provided online, is much less studied, and an important ideology because today there are many tools available to the patient, including the Internet and other networking opportunities, to learn about the provider. They also can learn whether or not the provider can offer the patients what they want in terms of quality of care, cost, or choice of specialty services, outpatient services, and more.

While it may be assumed that nonprofits work in a "profit sharing" way, such that the profits they earn will be used to subsidize community benefits as well as better quality of services, it is plausible that the actual intent is not occurring and that profits are misused by managers in the overarching scheme of things. The breakdown of mismanagement of funds will be discussed later. So, this creates a further dichotomy between the kinds of hospitals present, albeit "cash-rich hospitals" that actually may engage in greater arbitrage, which accounts for a large portion of their borrowing abilities versus "cash-poor hospitals" whose debt has little impact on their own borrowing abilities (Gentry, 2002, 850). This was an interesting article that further points out endogenous factors that have been missed in articles that discuss price-raising behavior. It also brings out the importance of accounting versus economic profits at hospitals that are glaringly different and analyzed separately. Accounting costs are a relative price ratio of patients being "charged" a fee versus patients paying completely at cost. The difference in these patients is dependent on how much aid and reimbursement the hospital gets from them based on Medicare, Medicaid, or private insurance and other factors. Danzon (1988, 30) notes that accounting costs are just "the price to cost-paying patients" rather than a measure of economic costs. Yet, price discrimination between cost paying and charged patients is limited by the Medicare formula to reimburse hospitals based on the ratio of their Medicare charges to private patient costs.

This difference in accounting and economic profits is an interesting one. Once implementation of technology is considered, there will be large-scale changes in evaluating the economic profits compared to accounting costs for hospitals. Sunk costs[x], though theoretically not included in economic costs, make a great deal of difference as time goes by, and will need to be modeled into the equation of how hospitals are financing investments. A comparison of sunk costs between different kinds of hospitals may be difficult to do because the costs of health information technology will be subsidized by the government for those hospitals with a larger welfare patient base versus those with smaller groups of healthcare subsidized patients (through the HITECH Act as part of the PPACA (Patient Protection and Affordable Care Act) and healthcare reform initiatives). Yet, sunk costs are never included in economic costs, whereas prospective costs will be included. Technology will be considered both sunk and prospective costs, depending on when it is implemented and what kind of technology it is, so this will need to be defined more clearly going forward in adding to the literature.

The Capital Asset Pricing Model and Arbitrage Pricing Theory models are important in supporting the Sloan et al. (1988) work on cost of equity and debt in not-for-profit and for-profit hospitals. Due to high levels of undiversifiable risk for investors, the article discusses the very high appreciable rate of return on equity capital charged by investors. The reason that the hospital industry cannot diversify risk is that government policies have a big role in shaping the debt-to-equity ratios in hospitals, based primarily on reimbursement policies for for-profit hospitals and bond issuance for not-for-profits (Sloan et al., 1988, 42-43). This government impact has grown today, as the Healthcare Reform legislation is only going to take on a new dimension of healthcare financing. The creation of health information exchanges that will allow for patients to compare government-subsidized pricing of various healthcare plans in an open forum will speak volumes to the shaping of debt-to-equity ratios of hospitals as well as reimbursement of hospitals as these new health information exchange (HIE) plans emerge as competitors to what is already present.

Currently, another big issue is that of "managed care organizations" that some say have resulted in the burden on public hospitals to take on the charity care patients that private hospitals refuse to accept (Currie and Fahr, 2004). The reasoning is actually contradictory to the cherry-picking conclusion. Instead, the authors are interpreting this as due to higher HMO penetration, for-profits are driven out of the market, not necessarily impacting the patients they choose to serve (p. 440).

So the difficult undertaking of comparing hospitals by their treatment of patients and any discrimination present is done by an article (Lindrooth, 2007, 354) analyzing the differences in religious nonprofits versus secular for-profit institutions. This study analyzes hospice care to see whether hospitals respond differently, based on ownership type, in the form of "LOS" or length of stay provided, due to reimbursement in Medicare dues. For-profits were found in the study to be less likely to admit patients with shorter and less profitable length of stays. Some characteristics found to be used to "choose" the patient, and in turn profitability, in for-profit hospitals were "primary diagnoses, recent curative care, and age of the patient." Something that is not noted by this study is the idea that many of those who have a disease of this kind and attend a not-for-profit or for-profit may be self-selecting the hospital based on their own geographical region, income level, or social networks. Possibly they are inclined to attend the institution with a friend or family member over one to which they have been referred. This concept of referral networks and patient reference to an institution is an interesting one that is difficult, but important to analyze. Also, recent articles published have noted that for-profits tend to "offer cardiac and diagnostic services, while their nonprofit counterparts often provide more less-profitable services, such as trauma centers, burn centers, and alcohol- and drug-treatment programs".*

Similarly, the CBO (Congressional Budget Office) conducted a 2006 analysis of the 1,000 nonprofit and for-profit hospitals in five states, finding that nonprofit hospitals were more likely to provide uncompensated care based on the share of operating expenses to this purpose, compared to for-profit hospitals. These differences in services provided as well as behavior by nonprofits mimicking for-profits have great impact on financing technology within the larger scheme of the hospital. As hospital financing will need to incorporate costs of technology, those hospitals with a greater demand for acute and profitable services may be ahead of the curve by exploring with new technology and, though initially may find some barriers to implementation, will succeed and begin to make progress. On the other hand, hospitals slow to adopt will take time to understand the technology, especially if their services involve little technology and are more preventive care associated. Government hospitals and community health centers may not require an electronic format for everything they do, and it may actually cause prices to rise and efficiency to lower if they are not planning to train staff quickly and proficiently on new technology. In the end, this will lead to even greater differences across hospitals and impact coordination networks and communication between them as some will be electronic and others may not be, and the marginal revenue may be lower than the marginal cost across all hospitals, causing a deadweight loss to society as a whole.

Mergers and Acquisitions of Hospitals

Because of the stark differences in the hospital mission, setting, care, and financing mechanisms of the different kinds of hospitals, mergers and acquisitions of not-for-profit hospitals by for-profits and vice versa may seem counterintuitive. Yet, a new trend in the hospital industry that has been seen to occur is the mergers and acquisition process of capital-heavy for-profit hospitals buying up the not-for-profits to gain market share and market power. This may not seem intuitive in impacting the financing structure of hospitals or related to HIT changes in the infrastructure of the hospital. Yet, it is a buying out process and impacts organizational behavior tremendously, while also contributing to organizational culture shifts in adaption to new technology when HIT is thrown into the mergers and acquisitions process.

The way that hospitals work is similar to the general infrastructure of all not-for-profit and for-profit organizations, so when a for-profit wants to merge or acquire a not-for-profit, the proceedings are typically situation based (case by case). Usually, a not-for-profit that wants to be acquired is in some need of being acquired; either it is too far in debt or sees some advantage of being bought out. This being said, the major purpose of the acquisition/merger is for a for-profit to expand its reach and a not-for-profit to be somewhat "saved" from bankruptcy or a diminishing status. While all not-for-profits began as for-profits, they are mainly differentiated from for-profits through their tax exempt status. Thus, the acquiring for-profit firm has one of two choices: (1) the for-profit can either keep the not-for-profit as a similar entity that is still working toward community benefit and charity care and have that as one free-standing component to its organization, or (2) it can convert all the not-for-profit's assets and debt onto its own balance sheet and income statement such that it gains the investments and firm's rights.

---

* (http://www.usatoday.com/money/industries/health/2010-07-13-hospitalmergers13_CV_N.htm).

One study analyzing the impacts of the merger and acquisition (M&A) process takes a look at pricing behavior and does a comparison of for-profit and not-for-profit trends in pricing over time. It uses cross-sectional data from California to show that prices have been driven upward in nonprofit markets. In this study on quality of care, a comparison of smaller versus larger hospitals was done, and showed that, before and after the Medicare Prospective Payment System (PPS), the smaller hospitals did not have as good quality of care and had lower prices than large hospitals. Looking at how they calculated mergers, there may be some inaccuracies. When mergers occur, the prices and price structure may not be changed immediately; hence, a lagged effect must be noted, which Keeler et al. (1999) fail to note in their equation. One major effect from mergers and acquisitions is noted by Keeler et al. as diseconomies of scale (instead of economies of scale, which is a reduction in cost with an increase in profit), but they leave out two other advantages of M&As: economies of scope (through greater efficiency in demand) and the information asymmetry this has overcome. While Keeler et al. find that nonprofit hospital mergers actually lead to diseconomies of scale and higher prices, it may be that their equations do not account for the time lag where hospitals are adjusting their infrastructure to the new prices. They mention that larger hospitals currently have higher costs due to "diseconomies of scale, offering a more sophisticated high tech product, or having sicker patients (75)." The variation across specialty care services in hospitals that is present due to technology is another field that is lacking research today, possibly based on the newness of the field and entry barriers to it.

Today, M&As of hospitals are a growing trend. Examples include, but are not limited to:

1. LifePoint Hospitals, encompassing nearly 48 hospitals in 17 states, which bought out Clark Regional Medical Center in Winchester, Kentucky
2. Community Health Systems, which owns, operates, or leases 122 hospitals in 29 states, is purchasing Bluefield Regional Medical Center and Marion Regional Healthcare System
3. Ardent Health Services, which owns eight hospitals and is buying Forum Health, a three-hospital system in Youngstown, Ohio

This new trend of for-profits buying not-for-profits is a fairly recent one, and could have interesting implications because of the use of technology that will now be required across the board, in all organizations. It also could be a culture clash between organizations that merge that are not on the same trajectory or stage in technology adoption.

Another big theme in the twenty-first century is the comparison of top-down and bottom-up management of hospitals, both under the light of M&As as well as just organizational culture within one organization. Kaiser Permanente is a great example of a not-for-profit health organization network that has a combination of top-down and bottom-up management because parts of its healthcare infrastructure, such as the hospital systems and health plan, is run as a not-for-profit, making it well known as one of the largest health networks. On the other hand, the independent Kaiser Permanente Medical Group is a for-profit entity, reimbursed by the Kaiser Foundation Health Plan. The medical groups are physician-owned, and provide and arrange for services and care for the nonprofit Kaiser's members in each Kaiser region. What's interesting about this model is that the not-for-profit is incentivized to do well for community benefit, but also in order to support and ensure progress in the for-profit sector. So, there is a double-edged sword here—the fact that the Kaiser health plans and hospitals impact its medical group's funding may be why it chooses to set goals and improve its care and revenues, so that the for-profit sector doesn't go under, or fall into debt or financial instability. While highly controversial, hospitals are moving in this direction today, and technology may only be providing ease of connectivity between organizations, such as Kaiser, and across provider networks or their joining bodies as well. This, of course, has the caveat: The organization has to take the initiatives to adopt technology as a joint effort or else there will not be consistency.

Tax Exempt or Tax Paying Status of the Hospitals

One of the basic differences between for-profit and not-for-profit hospitals is that for-profit hospitals do not get the same tax exemptions. This is supposed to provide not-for-profits a benefit as they engage the community in charity care, sliding scale fees, and other packages to help those who cannot afford healthcare, who are typically a larger proportion of their patient mix in comparison to for-profits. Looking closely at not-for-profits and the literature that is written on them provides a heavy analysis of the flaws and benefits of the way not-for-profits are currently structured and what can be done to better them. On the other hand, for-profits are able to generate profit through the issuance of stockholder equity, which has been seen to change their focus on the way the hospital is run and the care delivered to patients as well. Because there have been trends in the not-for-profit sector of not using their tax exempt status toward community benefit and societal contribution, there have been more studies published on how not-for-profits may be operating differently today than the original intent, for better or for worse. The question of whether the organization is operating as a for-profit or not-for-profit can be whether they operate this way as a moral obligation or if they are doing it purely for both financial reasons and financial gains. This question comes up time and again in various pieces of literature though continues to be an anomaly.

One of the older papers from the late twentieth century covers the competition in the healthcare market, and the most pivotal factor in the not-for-profit provider market: the tax-exempt municipal bond (Grossman et al., 1993). This is the single, largest, "long-term" source of financing for not-for-profits, making it the lifeline, to some extent, in the existence of not for-profits in the United States. Yet, the fact is that these bonds are provided in a two-fold mechanism: whereas financing authorities that are part of state and local governments issue the bonds, the source of the bonds arises from investment banks that finance and sell the bonds. The competition in the markets is what drives the bond market and financing of not for-profits. The literature takes the basics of the bond market and analyzes how the source of competition from various government authorities impacts the market of the municipal bonds, with specifics on the source of capital also being measured which has previously not been done (Bernet, Carpenter, and Saunders, 2011). A study by Bernet et al. is of a principal–agent model, where the yield earned is the investor's, or agent's, prediction of the return from the hospital's growth over time, and the principal is the hospital getting the "true interest rate cost." The study is conducted as a regression model. The economic language of the paper details the information asymmetry that exists in the bond market, and the best way to reduce it. The market for state-wide authority bonds is more transparent, reducing information asymmetry and, in turn, keeping interest rates down as investors feel more secure about these investments (Bernet et al., 2011, 68).

A component that will need to be included going forward in such studies is that the return on investment that investors see will be dependent on capital already present in the hospitals, and this capital can be impacted by state and federal government-backed subsidies for technology and infrastructure improvements that are likely to take hold. Through the HITECH Act, the financing of hospitals will change in terms of the return on investment and changes in short- and long-term costs within a hospital, based on their meaningful use of electronic medical records and health information technology. So, in this discussion, one of two things may occur: (1) return on investment will either increase or decrease based on how the investors predict the technology to impact a hospital, or (2) loans and bonds will be provided on a higher or lower yield, again being impacted by predictions of how technology will stimulate or slow down a hospital's performance.

Yet, ensuring that the hospitals are really achieving proper implementation of the technology with the investment incentives of the technology is going to be important. The comparisons of the frontrunner in the field who is best able to adopt and implement the technology versus those who are squandering the incentives will be a useful tool in analyzing where greater impacts need to be made between for-profits, not-for-profits, and government-run hospitals. Bernet et al. (2011) also doesn't discuss the state authorities' oversight on health information technology, and the change in perspective that investors may have in hospitals, once they see hospitals building onto the health-care market through investments in technology. It could have either positive or negative impacts and this can be estimated based on how elastic the demand for the technology is in the hospital. As a general rule, the elasticity of demand and supply would both increase, and, as currently predicted, return on investment should be high enough for investors to charge lower rates to hospitals that show an interest in implementing technology as well as quicker results in improvements in quality of care and cost, based on proper adoption and implementation that varies by type of health provider.

Looking at the tax-paying status of for-profit hospitals, efforts to implement health information technology will be an interesting proxy for growth in high technology services, such as radiology, nanotechnology, cardiology, and areas of science requiring electronic imaging and electronics. Hospitals may be more likely to adopt the technology based on higher capital investment ability *or* if they are tax exempt, they may be willing to pump in more into their infrastructure because they don't pay taxes on gains they reap.

Management of Hospitals: Is There an Impact on Healthcare Financing?

Next, the analysis shifts from the institutional components to the staff and management of hospitals. This is an interesting one, as physician compensation and CEO compensation are big issues today, when fraud and scandals of misused funds in most organizations have shot up sharply.

Preyra and Pink (2001) have done a study on compensation of CEOs using a principal–agent model. These numbers are based on a model of not-for-profit and for-profit hospital firms' CEOs in Ontario.

What is problematic to this model is the co-linearity that may exist in surplus and service through corporate philanthropy for for-profits. Preyra and Pink (2000) demonstrate that the non-profit will have weaker relationships between pay and performance because there is a more even "distribution of executive effort across all specified tasks" (513). On the other hand, for a for-profit, the variance of the financial performance measure will play an important role in calculating how the surplus and service are distributed. The specific component that this model was missing was an analysis of those organizations that have components of both nonprofits and for-profits.

Also, there should be determinations of how their performance is measured, especially with how much impact M&As have on today's hospitals. The model illustrates that CEOs of proprietary firms will be rewarded for the risk-taking nature of their firms because these CEOs have a higher "degree of income uncertainty" (521). The study shows that calculated differences were found in not-for-profit managers' earnings, which were about half of what for-profit managers made. However, the authors provide another point in that monopsony power in the market also can play a role in how much the organizations are funded. For the Ontario case specifically, a large percentage of hospital expenditures are government funded, and as a result will have an impact on salaries of managers and heads of these facilities. While the United States may provide a comparative perspective, the government does not play as large a role in the hospital sector as in the Ontario case, so the results of this study must be judged accordingly. On the other hand, during healthcare reform, with greater government influence on healthcare, the government funding and incentive provisions will continue to have an effect on the changing financing climate of hospitals and the way their compensation plans are put together.

Other principal-agent model papers, such as Laffont and Martimont (2001), revised by Yaesoubi and Roberts (2011), also identify important conclusions. Yet, some flaws exist to these models, as they do not account for the various competing interventions, surgeries, and clinical practices as well as aid from government reimbursements in technological change that could be present for a single condition or multiple conditions. Being able to measure the capacity of patients impacted also is not to be seen in the literature. Principal-agent models up to this point do not analyze how agents will foresee the growth in hospitals going forward, especially since the Center for Medicaid and Medicare Services is providing reimbursement potential for hospitals that adopt technology and meaningfully use it. There could be a drastic impact on how much return on investment hospitals project as well as how much short-term or long-term debt may be presented and initially taken on. The differences between debt on the hospital when technology, which is a large investment of capital, is initially adopted versus over time as it begins to show productivity or lack thereof, are going to be important features that impact the structure of healthcare finance in hospitals. The presence of HIT in health economics is going to play an important role going forward and needs to be researched and analyzed in greater detail.

Possibilities in Technological Changes in the Healthcare Setting

From a policy perspective, the most important update to the literature on healthcare financing is going to be inclusion of healthcare information technology into the infrastructure. This field not only impacts the supply and demand of technology, but also other sectors, such as the employment of physicians and new healthcare professionals, management of the organization as a whole, decisions to merge with other organizations, the cost-benefit analysis of the organization, and, most importantly, providing better quality of care and cost to patients.

A paper on physician integration by McCullough and Snir (2010) is one of the most recent examples of publications in the realm of economics that distinguishes the role of health information technology. Today, the adoption and integration of HIT is a complicated issue, as it is supported by state and government aid and laws that govern the subsidized cost of HIT to various firms.

The article discusses a theory of how integration of HIT impacts the technological demand in hospitals. It is a principal-agent model, with the endogenous variable being the integration of technology and the exogenous variable being the physician's outside opportunities. The interesting component of HIT integration is that of the differences in horizontal and vertical integration in the industry. McCullough and Snir in 2001 found nearly 69% of the hospitals show some form of vertical integration, which is an upward trend since the 1990s. The change from horizontal to vertical integration is interesting considering how mergers and acquisitions have impacted the hospital industry today. There could be a possibility that horizontal and vertical integration are occurring together rather than separately, especially as new types of industries are being brought together. In this case, technology and healthcare are merging, bringing about horizontal and vertical ties between industries and operations.

A variety of other topics on HIT integration include incentive agreements to ensure compliance of health information adoption and implementation strategies and more. Yet, the model is not complete because the way that physician incentive is measured does not incorporate federal aid, a large portion of the 2009 PPACA, which the Center for Medicare and Medicaid Services has decided will go toward hospitals that meet a certain patient threshold for Medicaid/Medicare patients. Nonprofits see greater benefits from physician integration according to the study because physicians use what profits are left over toward the benefit of the community, though this is more vaguely specified from the study. At the same time, for-profits may use their profits toward more training and hiring programs to ensure the technology is controlled and consulted, possibly from adoption models that track the progress of technology from within. Yet, not enough information on this is specified from any studies thus far to really provide conclusive evidence.

A part that is lacking in the literature on this subject remains the measurement of what stage an organization is at in implementing technology. While adoption model systems exist that rank the organization according to a stage-by-stage process, the research and academic literature on the subject is nonexistent. Rather than classifying technology as a dummy variable that is or is not present in the hospital setting, a mechanism to portray the level of implementation must be developed, be it by interacting a dummy variable with a continuous variable that measures exact level of technology implementation, or by creating a freestanding continuous variable that is in itself a measure of percentage of adoption and/or percentage of meaningfully using the technology, with a weighting of the type of healthcare provider. Each provider may have a different rate of usage of technology based on its unique characteristics. The reason for the need for a weighting mechanism is that the organizations with greater reimbursement opportunities for federal aid may be complying and adopting more quickly than those that do not meet incentive criteria to get access to financial aid to invest in the HIT. A lagged effect also is important in analyzing prospective improvements, organizational effects, and more.

Other parts of the field that were pointed out through the McCullugh and Sair piece are: lack of analysis on how the principal-agent model has changed (if any change) through the course of technology, how mergers and acquisitions have changed (if any change), how the heart of hospital financing has changed in a broad sense (if any change), how compensation and reimbursement both of hospitals and the management and staff of hospitals have changed, and the economics, specifically demand and supply elasticities of HIT based on income elasticities of the hospital. These characteristics also are based on the specific type of institution, be it a for-profit, not-for-profit, or government hospital, and research is lacking in pointing out cross-institutional variation in these various features and their components.

The case of government hospitals is the most interesting, including community health center clinics and federally qualified health centers, because these institutions are either provided pilot programs to test how HIT impacts them, or are reimbursed on their Medicare and Medicaid financing. So, capital is not necessarily a problem for smaller clinics, yet, what is a problem is efficiency in training the staff and providing support to doctors who may need greater time in learning the technology and using it on a regular basis. For this undertaking, especially for charity care specialists, is a big investment of energy, time, and resources, and it may be more difficult to incentivize such hospitals to make progress with technology. Also, patients may not be able to connect with doctors who have this technology because many indigent patients themselves don't have access to the Internet or other storage input sources that may be linking the patient with the doctor in using health information technology. Again, this is an information asymmetry problem that stems from income inequality.

Looking at technology introduction in the not-for-profit and for-profit markets, there may be the case of greater bounded rationality because patients may see technologically advanced hospitals as better serving their needs. Another behavior may be that while HIPAA and other ethical considerations prevent hospitals from viewing demographics of a patient, there are loopholes to this, which can impact the behavior of not-for-profits and for-profits that have technology and want to "select" which types of patients will be the most profitable to them, or reimbursement worthy. Thus, looking at the Currie and Fahr (2004) piece once again, things may change drastically in areas where HMOs are penetrating the market and for-profits have or do not have technology. The consequences could be of a greater cherry-picking nature in favor of profiting the for-profit hospitals, or it could ensue that enough not-for-profits have introduced technology such that there is a level playing field and patients are not impacted by cherry-picking behavior, because hospitals are able to be efficient regardless of how sick the patient is. At the same time, there may be greater advancements in the security of records and inability for organizations to hack into the patient confidential information, so there is also the possibility that less cherry-picking behavior will occur. While some of these ideas may seem cynical, it is worth giving some thought to how technology may have indirect or direct negative consequences just as it has positive consequences to the financing of a hospital.

Conclusions and Policy Implications

These topics cover just the surface of the differences between not-for-profit and for-profit hospitals. The comparison, with a take on HIT, is not yet heavily studied, but it is an important discussion that deserves greater economic modeling and work as well as inclusion of new innovations and changes taking place during the twenty-first century. The application of technology to hospitals has already created much change both within the hospitals and across various kinds of hospitals. The already complex process of hospital financing is only going to grow more complicated as the financing of hospitals changes, for the investors, for the hospital management, and for the patient, with the introduction of technology. Policy analysis will be done through a new light, with hopefully more benefits through technological efficiency and effectiveness. However, it cannot be forgotten that these changes are going to be slow-moving and possibly staggered based on how quickly the hospital can adapt to changes. Some hospitals, possibly not-for-profits, will be working toward greater profits and cost cutting, which may initiate them to implement and adopt technology much faster. At the same time, reimbursement of hospitals for technology use is mainly going to impact government hospitals and hospitals with a large Medicare and Medicaid patient base, so they are on a heightened time frame to quickly install and use the technology to demonstrate change through pilot programs and research grants. This also could mean a changing dynamic in the number of welfare recipient patients who are recruited to attend for-profits because for-profits may want a larger chunk of the government reimbursement monies to adopt and meaningfully use technology so that higher profits are created in the long run. For-profits seem least likely to take the lead on these initiatives because they are least impacted by reimbursement policies. Yet, if stockholders see technology as the most likely to revolutionize healthcare and be a profit center, services may have a strong technology focus and for-profits may outshine the others in growth and productivity. As there is not a lot of data or implications in this field so far and much of it will be based on standards that are constantly being toyed with by government and nongovernment agencies right now, it is a good field to begin speculation and creation of various mechanisms to analyze and model the interactions of the various issues in the field.

The field of healthcare finance has been studied rigorously over the past 30 years, though changes will be occurring as the healthcare reform legislation hits the United States. Comparisons across countries and also trends within the country over time are important to note, to see what has influenced the growth and development of hospitals. The history of healthcare finance is a long and interesting one. It all began with the evolution of fringe benefit inducements through employer-covered medical insurance in WWII, and then government fee-for-service reimbursement in the 1960s, where almost 90% of the population was covered by some form of insurance. Then, from the 1970s through the 1990s, an era of wariness of government spending and cost cutting began in order to limit the amount of Medicaid reimbursement. Both the inpatient and outpatient reimbursements were curbed so that they were based on the category of patient condition, such as a diagnostic-related group (DRG) or discharge diagnosis and ambulatory payment category. While aging of the American workforce and employer-funded plans have grown out of proportion and exacerbating the problem, by the 2000s, it has become very difficult to curb the amount spent on healthcare. The annual spending was in the $5,000 range per person by 2002, and has increased more today. The question becomes how to cut spending and still improve quality of care and efficiency in the hospital setting. One of the long-winded solutions for this became the introduction of HIT and how it can impact cost savings, quality care improvements, and drive the economy toward progress. There are many patient-centric elements that healthcare finance impacts, and some of these elements are not presented in this chapter. Yet, this paper represents the necessary improvements in the field that will integrate technology and healthcare financing, with a focus on the organizational structure of a hospital, as there are unique characteristics of each that will allow for tailor-made solutions to each institution's ability to incorporate technology.

From research in the field, it seems likely that the goals and incentives of various not-for-profits and for-profits drive their behavior, though over time and spatial variations, there has been a changing dynamic to how institutions act. While the subject needs to be researched more specifically across various types of institutions, it also must be devised such that technology integration is not seen as a constant across institutions; rather, it is an important variable that impacts changes in healthcare and is impacted by investments of capital and organizational behavior characteristics, respectively. Some of the defining organizational characteristics are, but are not limited to: financing mechanisms for the institutions, capital present, stockholder premium from decisions, employee compensation, hierarchies within the institutions, mergers and acquisitions across the hospital systems, the boom and busts of the economy, geographic and spatial diversification, patient mix, organizational culture, and much more.

Chapter 4

Funding Electronic Medical Records: Reality or Illusion? A Cost-Benefit Analysis

Overview

Electronic medical records (EMRs) are the beacon of hope in providing twenty-first century healthcare solutions for the public. Some of the benefits include reducing mortality rates through earlier detection of problems, improved patient quality of care and service, better communication from physicians to patients, and more economical financing and efficiency through electronic billing, some of which are achievable in the short run and others that will be achieved in the long run. Then, what remains in implementing this progressive system? It is a lack of financial resources, especially for smaller organizations, that allows for the adoption of healthcare information technology (HIT) to occur. Unless there is greater incentive to adopt through both financial and management support, there will be no drive toward accelerating the implementation. By finding out what more the government, government organizations, and market forces can do in bringing down prices and costs of adoption of EMRs, especially to smaller clinics that have low capital, there can be visions toward a nation that is completely electronic in its healthcare infrastructure.

Introduction

As mentioned before, the American Recovery and Reinvestment Act (ARRA) and the HITECH (Health Information Technology for Economic and Clinical Health) Act of 2009 were passed to ensure that efficient and economical adoption of healthcare information technology is occurring and the technology could be more rapidly implemented nationwide. As a part of this procedure, new government incentives also have been used to weaken the financial barriers present in adoption of the expensive electronic medical record systems, especially for providers that cater to Medicaid and Medicare patients.

Through research, financial barriers have been suggested as symbolizing one of the most prevalent problems in adoption of the EMR systems, so by studying this problem in greater detail and identifying a cost-benefit evaluation of the process of adoption of the equipment, more insight can be shed on how to ease the monetary concerns present. Also, studying the lack of financial resources required in adopting the technology can serve a dual purpose of analyzing past problems and flaws and pushing for feedback on changes necessary in making adopting more viable in the future, possibly through government and outside monetary funding. To better provide EMR and EHR (electronic health record) investors with financial incentives, there must be strategic financial aid provided by the government so that both small and large companies may have the resources and ability to invest and jump on board with the technology. This will create a standardized system across the country and improve coordination across healthcare providers if they are all consistently working with electronic medical records. Providing analysis of how government incentives can make a difference in ameliorating needs of healthcare vendors, organizations, businesses, and hospitals may allow for greater policy interventions in the transition from paper-based to a completely electronic medical record system in the United States.

Background Factors

Over the past few years, there has been quite a bit of light shed on "healthcare reform" as the citizens of America have been demanding changes to the current healthcare system. Yet, introduced even earlier to this were changes in the fusion of healthcare and technology that began in President George W. Bush's term and has continued and been built more upon during President Obama's term. The HITECH Act has a distinct focus on an electronic medical record system and movement away from a paper-based system. The obvious reasons to make this transition a reality is that as technology is the fiber of most organizations, healthcare-related organizations and hospitals may be more efficient through an electronic mechanism, rapidly able to coordinate documents and transmit information, conduct electronic payment methods, electronic research, and have technical, qualitative, and bureaucratic efficiencies. As Michael Porter (2009, 110–111) concluded, EMRs are not going to be cost effective and justified unless they provide a value-based, goal-improving coordination across all healthcare organizations and providers, which paper-based systems aren't currently doing, and providing better outcome measurement and updates to regular information in a real-time manner. From a societal point of view, the need for electronic medical records has been evident, producing large-scale problems, such as the detection and surveillance of anthrax all the way to detecting smaller issues, such as the common cold or flu. However, the bigger issue is what needs to be present to ease the adoption of EMRs.

Studies have shown that contrary to popular belief, it is not just that organizations are uninterested or lazy in switching over to such a system; rather, it is the lack of financial resources to adopt such expensive systems. Government funding has increased, now at $27 billion in grants to organizations that need help adopting the systems. Government agencies also work toward funding research and quality studies to assess the impact of healthcare technology. One such organization, the Agency for Healthcare Research and Quality (AHRQ), has contributed $50 million already in funding grants to both organizations and research efforts in HIT (Burton et al., 2004). Currently, penalties are in place and further developing for small businesses if they do not show their switchover efforts to EMRs by 2015. This does not mean the government has not done enough to provide funding and resources. However, nationwide, there has not been enough of a push toward small businesses moving to an electronic setup through constant reviewing, auditing, and surveillance of healthcare organizations with paper-based systems. Marketing, educational training, and advertising for movement in this direction has not been proportional to the changes and penalties that have been set, meaning many organizations have not seen the seriousness or relevance of the matter. Yet, studies, such as *Rethinking Medical Professionalism* by David Mechanic (2008), discuss how EMRs have been seen as a new culture among physicians, creating both a higher level of care, but also greater expectations on the physician to deliver the best results of a professional nature from better note-taking in ambulatory and emergency care. Hence, it is important to create a bandwagon effect and urge more hospitals to make the transition.

Looking at how it has played out for different sectors of organizations and physicians provides insight into the factors that are of importance when choosing whether to utilize EMRs. For example, a study of Indiana family care physicians done by Loomis et al. (2002) identified what characteristics of EMR users differed from nonusers, and they found that non-EMR users were not convinced that EMRs could facilitate accuracy and lower errors, and they felt that EMRs did not provide enough confidentiality. The characteristic that both the nonusers and users agreed on was the cost of the technology. The study suggests use of EMRs to be centered on urban areas and supporting hospitals that could afford it. More than 80% of family physicians in this study would be inclined to switch over if they pay no more than $5,000 for the EMR technology and no more than $100 a month for updates, a fix of technical difficulties, and of follow-up problems (Loomis et al., 2002). Currently this criteria is almost impossible to meet. Greiger, Cohen, and Krusch (2007) also did a study to analyze the return on investment of EMRs with the idea that there was a changing climate in the regional health information infrastructure, seen from examples like California and Indiana. Examples by them also included loss of paper medical records in New Orleans after weather calamities, such as hurricanes, flooding, etc., have occurred. They point out that an electronic documentation system would be backed up and better coordinated with departments all over the nation, possibly someday the globe, so that some, if not all, of the documentation could be recovered in the event of a calamity. Geiger, Cohen, and Krusch target their study and findings toward ambulatory offices that are closely linked to hospitals, which may not be completely applicable to all organizations, but their findings on cost-benefit analysis will be discussed later. A study by DesRoches et al. (2008) showed that the percent of physicians with a fully functional and adopted electronic medical record systems was estimated to be about 4%, whereas those having a basic system was around 13%, with the majority of these being part of hospitals, medical centers, and in the western region of the United States, again fortifying the studies done in California. Evidence from these articles points to the same underlying idea: It is a political issue, and a heightened political priority for many of the Democratic states over Republican states as Democratic states tend to be more open-minded and accepting of healthcare reform, transitions toward electronic medical records, and healthcare information exchanges across networks. Again, this study showed that 66% of those surveyed listed "capital costs" as being the no. 1 problem in adopting electronic medical records (Greiger, Cohen, and Krusch 2007).

Another interesting point made by Greiger, Cohen, and Krusch (2007) is that the adoption of EMRs didn't differ among those providers that had a majority of Medicaid-receiving patients, minority patients, and uninsured patients. The government has been trying to focus on organizations with a large Medicare and/or Medicaid base because these organizations don't typically have as much funding enabling them to transition to an electronic system. The Center for Medicare and Medicaid Services (CMS) introduced new rules and regulations in 2009 expanding government aid toward Medicare/Medicaid patient-centered organizations (typically having a cutoff of 30% of either welfare program patients) that want to adopt, but don't have the means. An issue noted in many studies is how the transition to EMRs will impact smaller hospitals with disabled, chronically diseased, and handicapped patients. The question is: Will this kind of patient base dissuade going electronic because it may be too expensive in the short term, through e-billing and the necessity for greater electronic paraphernalia as costs for patients with these kinds of problems who seek constant treatment? Will it incur more losses now that patients have electronic means to test themselves with the emergence of personal health records, e-mail communication, phone applications, and more that can check patient well being, such as blood pressure and other stats? Or will EMRs be worthwhile because they coordinate care all over, as noted by Burton et al. (2004)? They bring up two important points: the possibility of the presence of a common health record across the nation, such as the Continuity of Care Record to facilitate care, and also the possibility of payment to afford the EMRs. For example, they point out that "Medicare beneficiaries with five or more chronic conditions fill an average of 48 prescriptions, see 15 different doctors, and receive almost 16 home health visits during one year." Therefore, this study evaluates EHRs' ability to coordinate care, especially for patients who frequently need to visit the hospital, and see if it will expedite and facilitate their needs or have negative effects. The importance of privacy and confidentiality rules also must be kept in focus as this remains a major area of contention and debate in the backdrop of whether or not to use EMRs.

Policy Analysis

While there are other reasons why organizations and individuals have been slow to adopt EMRs, because the leading factor in most studies is financial barriers, deciphering how to improve adoption rates of EMRs from a financial standpoint will be the policy problem to tackle in order to see improvements in EMRs. Possible alternatives to actually adopting EMRs will be fading out over time as this is a government-mandated project within the PPACA (Patient Protection and Affordable Care Act). The possibility of penalties has already been put forth by the government as well as advantages—in the form of grants and monetary incentives—to those who are early adopters. In the long run, most likely between the next five years and a decade, it will be mandatory to be meaningfully using the technology, thus EMR will no longer be a choice.

Hence, in terms of possible policy alternatives for improving financial incentives to EMR adoption and usage across organizations, one possibility is standardizing the equipment so that there is only one brand or one kind sold and heavily subsidized, making it standard for everyone. This may have several weaknesses and/or advantages. Another alternative would be keeping the status quo as it is now and allowing competition in the market of EMR adoption so that the market will determine the price of the equipment and the best rate that organizations may get. The government may play a role here in providing aid to organizations with underprivileged patients who may need heavier funding to afford EMRs. An even stricter alternative that has not been taken into consideration, but could work, would be to not only financially penalize physicians not adopting EMRs, but not allowing them to practice medicine unless they have one. For all new physicians starting their own practices there would be no option whether they want to keep paper records or move to electronic, from day 1 when they opened their practice. This might force a lot of organizations to realize the importance of the issue and begin training toward the new system so they will be adjusted to it before it's too late. New budding physicians that have just entered the field would jump on board as well with the system right away if this was the case. This could be compared to CPAs who have seen the transition to online payroll and tax software systems that have become a must today, even in college classes where students learn the ins and outs of these systems before they graduate. It also would make sense to have more professionals auditing these systems, which has been talked about as an emerging professional need for health professionals. Marketing of EMRs would have different strategies based on how EMRs are developed on the market.

Regional governance councils, also known as health information exchanges, allow for a better trade of healthcare products and plans as well as EHR equipment. They provide a fair assessment of rates and price ranges to allow for fair competition in the market place. This is where the current status of the nation is in terms of healthcare and movement toward more exchanges and more trade with government subsidized plans, and assistance is the most likely direction of the future in ameliorating high-cost structures related to EMRs. These different ideas can be assessed based on their advantages and disadvantages, either from past examples or from hypothetical assessment if they haven't as yet been instituted.

A final idea that might benefit the process of adoption of EMRs in a smoother and less expensive fashion is having consultants assess the organizations that are transitioning into an electronic system with what is known as an EMR adoption model system. An example can be provided by HIMSS (Healthcare Information Management Systems Society) analytics who have created an adoption model ranking system. This system actually assesses the stage at which an organization has adopted and continually checks on the adoption speed of the organization to see what can be facilitated and which wing is lagging behind in meaningfully using and adopting the technology. For example, if the radiology department of a clinic is having problems and is still not using the EMRs or has come across problems, it will be analyzed and have more training sessions to catch up the personnel to other parts of the clinic that have smoothly transitioned into the adoption process.

Cost, Benefits, and Constraints

Before analyzing the financial EMR suggestions to see if they are worthy of instituting or furthering, it is best to look at basic costs of EMRs and analyze what the estimates are. This will make it easier to impact the financial system and target factors that will lower costs. Mechanic (2008) discusses installation costs of EHRs to be around $44,000 for full-time providers with yearly costs around $8,000 (339–340). While reduction of clerical staff can be a benefit, the small "fee for service" clinics that Mechanic discusses have it difficult because they are not compensated for checkup fees, be it updates, follow-up problems through e-mail consultations, or educational services, which they still must pay for when investing in the technology and recuperating money spent on it for depreciation and technical difficulty purposes. Many physicians require training and updating, some multiple sessions for extended periods of time, compared to others, so it can range from $2,500 at the low end to almost $45,000 at the high end of the spectrum (p. 340). Looking at a more recent article in 2011, costs for first-year implementation of GE's EMR system were estimated for a five-physician practice to be $233,297, with average per-physician costs of $46,659 and maintenance costs during the first year estimated at $85,500. This was based on a study of 26 primary care practices in a fee for service network called HealthTexas (AHRQ, 2011) using GE's Healthcare's Centricity* EMR system. Also considering other charts from a few years ago, which may be needed to adjusted for inflation, the benefits seem to be in improved coding, prescription refills, chart management, transcription savings, and others. Some examples of the actual costs and benefits estimated are provided in Table 4.1 for two different organizations (example 1 and example 2).

From this originates the idea of a patient payment specifically for EHRs because these electronic systems are benefiting the patient and are for the betterment of society's healthcare network as a whole. Two ways to do this would be either to include the EHR cost as a fee in the patient's bill or

Table 4.1   Example 1: American Medical Software Cost-Benefit Analysis

Cost-Benefit Analysis Matrix (Single Provider Office)	Initial Year	2nd Year	3rd Year	4th Year	5th Year	5-Year Total
COSTS						
Software Licensing	$10,000					
Implementation Computer and Network Setup	$2,000			$1,000		
Hardware: 1 × Tablet PC	$2,500			$2,000		
Hardware: 4 × Workstations	$4,000			$2,000		
Hardware: Network Server	$2,000			$1,000		
Support and Updates: Software	$1,800	$2,400	$2,400	$2,400	$2,400	
e-Scripts, Patient Portal Subscriptions	$1,000	$1,000	$1,000	$1,000	$1,000	
Support and Maintenance: Hardware	$1,000	$1,000	$1,000	$1,000	$1,000	
Productivity Loss during Implementation and Training	$10,000					
Total Annual Costs	**$34,300**	**$4,400**	**$4,400**	**$10,400**	**$4,400**	**$57,900**
BENEFITS						
Improved Coding/Charge Capture	$9,600	$19,200	$24,000	$24,000	$24,000	
Transcription Savings	$2,880	$5,760	$7,200	$7,200	$7,200	
Chart Management	$7,200	$14,400	$36,000	$36,000	$36,000	
Prescription Refills	$5,600	$11,200	$14,000	$14,000	$14,000	
Total Annual Benefit	**$25,280**	**$50,560**	**$81,200**	**$81,200**	**$81,200**	**$319,440**
NET BENEFIT (COST)	**($9,020)**	**$46,160**	**$76,800**	**$70,800**	**$76,800**	**$261,540**

to charge them a tax on top of their normal bill to pay for the EHR system. In the study by Burton, Gerard, and Irvin (2004), the estimate the study provides is only about $5 extra as a fee to complete the EMR, which they estimate will add to the Medicare expenditures by $4 billion dollars (475). However, making patients pay for a system may be unfair since this is a long-term transition and may not go into effect all over the nation for some time. Therefore, patients may opt out of going to clinics with EMR facilities if they are required to pay more. Possibly this kind of a system would be advantageous once the nation is electronic so that it's fair on patients to be assessed a fee

Table 4.1   Example 2: EMR Experts Consulting Cost-Benefit Analysis

Cost-Benefit Analysis Example (Single Provider Office)	*Initial Costs*	*Year 1*	*Year 2*	*Year 3*	*Year 4*	*Year 5*	*5-Year Total*
Cost (Per Provider)							
Software License	$10,000						
Implementation: Software Customization ($100/hr × 10 hrs)	$1,000						
Implementation: Training ($100/hr × 25 hrs)	$2,500						
Implementation: Travel Expenses	$1,500						
Implementation: Computer and Network Setup	$1,000				$1,000		
Hardware: 1 × Tablet PC	$2,500				$2,000		
Hardware: 3 × Workstations	$3,000				$2,500		
Hardware: Network/Server	$2,000				$1,000		
Support and Maintenance: Software		$2,000	$2,000	$2,000	$2,000	$2,000	
Support and Maintenance: Computer		$1,000	$1,000	$1,000	$1,000	$1,000	
Induced Costs: Productivity Loss (40 hrs)	$10,000						
Gross Annual Costs	**$33,500**	**$3,000**	**$3,000**	**$3,000**	**$9,500**	**$3,000**	**$55,000**
Additional Physician Adjustment (10%–30%)							
Net Annual Costs							

(continued)

Table 4.1 Example 2: EMR Experts Consulting Cost-Benefit Analysis (continued)

Cost-Benefit Analysis Example (Single Provider Office)	Initial Costs	Year 1	Year 2	Year 3	Year 4	Year 5	5-Year Total
Benefits (Per Provider)							
Improved Coding		$12,500	$25,000	$25,000	$25,000	$25,000	
Transcription Savings		$3,000	$6,000	$6,000	$6,000	$6,000	
Chart Management		$2,400	$4,800	$4,800	$4,800	$4,800	
Searching for Charts		$1,000	$2,000	$2,000	$2,000	$2,000	
Prescription Refills		$3,250	$6,500	$6,500	$6,500	$6,500	
Capitated Benefits (If applicable)			$29,000	$29,000	$29,000	$29,000	
Total Annual Benefits		22,150	$44,300	$44,300	$44,300	$44,300	$199,350
Net Benefit (cost)	$(33,500)	$19,150	$41,300	$41,300	$34,800	$41,300	$144,350

based on the EMR system. Another question that would develop would be whether the EMR fee would be flat or different for each physician/clinic based on the operating EMR system. The idea would be that clinics with a more expensive EMR may expect to have higher patient fees or taxes on EMRs as a surcharge for usage, whereas those clinics with government subsidies or help may charge less fees as they would anyways be targeting lower-income patients.

Interestingly enough, certain parts of the health system have followed the first suggestions in this chapter in creating a uniform system of HIT that will coordinate care identically, using one system throughout the United States. Such systems are typically government based, such as one created by the Veterans Health Administration (VHA) and Department of Defense, known as the CPRS or Computerized Personal Record System with an associated TRICARE online record system as well. Another system that CMS came out with to encourage small practices to adopt EMRs was VistA software that was provided in 2005, which had free distribution. Yet, licensing fees were present along with hardware fees, data upgrades, customization, and many more costs that deterred many (Mechanic, 2008). So, technically, this was not as good an adoption marketing scheme as it seemed. These periphery costs are the ones that add to the disadvantages of a low basic cost to go electronic. It is typically the laborious and expensive training sessions, repairs, and technical difficulty problems that are typically more in the initial stages which make electronic medical records unaffordable to smaller clinics, rather than just the startup costs of installing the technology.

Looking at the government initiatives so far, there has been about $27 billion kept aside for financial incentives toward helping organizations adopt, providing anywhere from $15,000 to $20,000 in incentives if organizations adopt in a certain year with the amount decreasing as organizations delay adopting by more than one year from now. Table 4.2 specifies some of these incentives from 2011 onwards.

These incentives, as mentioned before, only go toward Medicare- or Medicaid-heavy organizations that may not have the capital to invest in an electronic infrastructure based on their

Table 4.2 Example of Medicaid Incentive Payments

Medicaid Year of Adoption	HITECH Incentive Payout Over Time					
2011	$21,250					
2012	$8,500	$21,250				
2013	$8,500	$8,500	$21,250			
2014	$8,500	$8,500	$8,500	$21,250		
2015	$8,500	$8,500	$8,500	$8,500	$21,250	
2016	$8,500	$8,500	$8,500	$8,500	$8,500	$21,250
2017		$8,500	$8,500	$8,500	$8,500	$8,500
2018			$8,500	$8,500	$8,500	$8,500
2019				$8,500	$8,500	$8,500
2020					$8,500	$8,500
2021						$8,500
TOTAL	$63,750	$63,750	$63,750	$63,750	$63,750	$63,750

low-income patient base. The total estimate looks to be around $10,625/year over 6 years for Medicaid versus $8800/year over 5 years in the Medicare program. States have to voluntarily begin the Medicaid EHR Incentive Program in their region and offer registration, and the healthcare provider must have between 20 to 30% Medicaid patient volume to qualify for these incentive programs. Medicare is based on federal funding without direct state involvement. The problem with such incentive programs, again, are that they lean toward the more liberal populace, and are helpful during a recession, but may increase deficit spending, especially at a time when welfare programs take up quite a portion of the nation's spending. They also come across as further rooting the cycle of poverty by making citizens who are dependent on the government to lead their lives; whereas a fee or tax on all citizens to use EMRs seems more uniform, government spending on underprivileged may be considered unjust. At the same time, with a growing base of low-income population and baby boomers of the senior citizen age group, it may be necessary to provide such aids.

It is much harder to create an integrated model of EHR that will be used throughout the United States, especially when competition is present in a free market. While it is difficult to create regulation and sell only one product, by ensuring that all organizations adopt the same Continuity of Care Record system, this will at least allow for one format with all the up-to-date patient information throughout networks to inform physicians all over the country what is going on with patients both over time and over different hospitals/healthcare organizations. At the same time, it is important that these organizations all meet the HIPAA (Health Insurance Portability and Accountability Act) requirements as they are an important and growing part of HIT standards today. Making sure that EMRs meet the interoperability and privacy clauses will be another source for auditing and regulation for the healthcare industry as the nation moves forward into an electronic system.

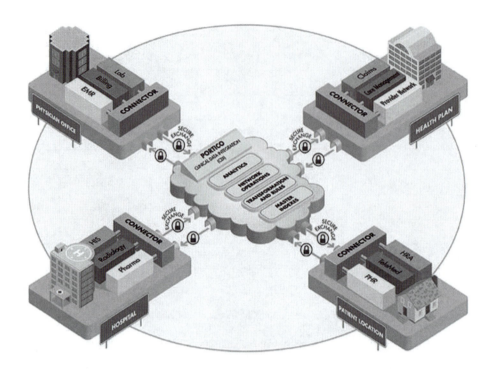

Figure 4.1   Health information exchange diagram.

For this reason, HIEs could greatly benefit the current healthcare model because they allow for an open assessment of the healthcare marketplace and have an invisible hand over demand, supply, and trade of healthcare plans, electronic prescription drugs, EMRs, and other healthcare-related packages. Exchanges would require a uniform electronic interface to operate that will allow the same type of information to be merged and sent across networks about the patient, drugs, medical errors, radiology, and specialized testing procedures that wouldn't need to be rerun, charting costs, drug recalls, and many more. The presence of exchanges may heavily benefit the HIT environment where EMRs are concerned, possibly helping reduce the cost of healthcare overall as suggested by Walker et al. (2005, 10–17). At the same time, another stance on health information exchanges taken by more politically conservative organizations is that it could control and regulate the industry too powerfully by providing only advantages to the disadvantaged organizations and not providing fair standards and impact for all. Only time will tell whether or not exchanges are in society's favor. Through studies done by Walker et al., the amount of redundancy is between 8.6 and 20%, which is quite a lot of avoidable redundancy. Overall, the model also calculated a total avoidable cost of $87.81 a year, per person per year, from avoided tests and avoided administrative costs. An example of a health information exchange is seen in Figure 4.1.

The adoption model procedures, such as the HIMSS EMRAM system, have their pros and cons. While it is an extra fee initially while adopting the technology, it may save a company more money in the long run. To do some may require getting the organization quickly caught up to speed through an oversight and or an audit board that is ensuring that all wings of the organization understand the proper usage of the technology. At the same time, smaller clinics that do not have many departments or have adjusted with more ease to the technology may see no benefit in such an adoption model ranking system; it will be just an extra expense for them. If more adoption

Table 4.3   EMR Adoption Model^{SM}

Stage	*Cumulative Capabilities*
Stage 7	Medical record fully electronic; HCO able to contribute CCD as byproduct of EMR; data warehousing in use
Stage 6	Physician documentation (structured templates), full CDSS (variance and compliance), full R-PACS
Stage 5	Closed-loop medication administration
Stage 4	CPOE, CDSS (clinical protocols)
Stage 3	Clinical documentation (flow sheets), CDSS (error checking), PACS available outside Radiology
Stage 2	Clinical Data Repository, Controlled Medical Vocabulary, Clinical Decision Support System, may have Document Imaging
Stage 1	Ancillaries: Lab, Rad, Pharmacy; all installed
Stage 0	All three ancillaries not installed

Source: Data from HIMSS Analytics^{SM} Database.

model systems are present, the automatic supply and demand for them may balance out as well as lower prices to initiate and be a part of these systems. It only makes sense to have such a system while adopting such a large-scale electronic medical record project if a smooth transition into the technology needs to occur. Example of such a system are shown in Table 4.3.

Conclusion

Looking from a more global perspective, it seems as though developed nations all over the world that represent the beacon of progress for the globe feel the need for electronic medical records. This was documented as 43 to 66% of physicians in Australia, Canada, New Zealand, the United States, and the United Kingdom see the need for EMRs as being effective in improving quality of care (Blendon et al., 2001). Thus, as this trend progresses and makes a uniform change for the better, the United States has important decisions to make. It has to decide whether the healthcare industry, with its move toward a regulated, universal system will benefit from the presence of many possible policy changes: patient fees for usage of EMRs; one integrated government-run EMR system, such as the one being used by the Veterans Administration; more government grants and financial incentives only to welfare-based (Medicare/Medicaid majority) practices; HIEs; and/or adoption model systems. These various possibilities have their flaws and their benefits, but they consist of good choices for the free flow of the healthcare industry with some level of regulation. The least expensive choice is the patient fees for usage of EMRs, and the most expensive would possibly be the government grants toward welfare practices as well as the health information exchanges. The way these different policy initiatives will impact the government is daunting, looking at the financial repercussions. Looking at patient-focused solutions, such as fees for usage for EMRs and adoption model systems, these take a more deregulated GOP approach and may be more ideal if the economy is in good condition and individuals are willing to pay a bit extra for the long-term progress of their practice or healthcare provider. A more liberal leaning is toward health information exchanges, government grants and initiatives, as well as the possibility of an integrated government run EMR network system.

These solutions make the possibility of an EMR more accessible in the near future because they provide financial incentives for smaller startups and fee for service clinics to adopt the technology as well. At the same time, they weigh in on the federal deficit and again may lead to eating up more of the budget in the future. Yet, since these initiatives have already begun and are moving in the direction of an HIT-based infrastructure, it makes sense to spend more in the short run than to have obstacles and a slow transition. A slow transition could become more expensive in the long run for the government as well as for patients because it will only add to the medical errors, coordination problems, unorganized training, and communication barriers with patients and between hospitals/clinics and healthcare providers. If they are able to impact the healthcare industry for the better, there may be greater savings in the long run by putting in short-term investments into the industry.

Chapter 5

Impact of Organizational Behavior Characteristics on Usage of a Healthcare Provider's Health Information Technology (HIT) Services

Overview

While the subject of organizational behavior and competition among nonprofits and for-profits is fairly well researched, how organizational behavior across health providers differs in their ability to integrate technology still has not been fully uncovered. This subject is important because of the amount of technology funding present in the healthcare industry and the inability and disinterest of hospitals in taking advantage of these resources. This chapter presents comparisons across organizational characteristics of different health providers to see which types of HIT are most efficiently used by different health providers and why this phenomenon is such, assuming these differences exist. The more quickly this is understood, the more efficient utility of HIT can be achieved by impacting training and efforts to derive greater technology penetration in specific healthcare industries.

Introduction

What makes not-for-profit and for-profit hospitals interesting is that they provide similar services and are impacting the community through outreach to patients with a presumed interest in quality of care and service. Yet, literature has shown that the two diverge in many aspects of performance, possibly due to differences in ownership, management style, specialty services, physicians present, etc. To add to this literature, it will be important to analyze changes and differences between these management characteristics across various healthcare providers and see how they are using and incorporating health information technology (HIT) into their infrastructure, assuming organizational behavior differences. Incentives to adopt have been on the national agenda, including funds from the American Recovery and Reinvestment Act of 2008, which brought about the HITECH (Health Information Technology for Economic and Clinical Health) Act with funding and subsidies for organizations that want to adopt HIT. Besides the financial motivation to access HIT, the issue has been on the agenda since the late 1990s and the electronics age of the past decade. While it may seem like a heated issue because funds are involved, it is actually considered a bipartisan issue, and one of the few pieces of legislation to be introduced by former President George W. Bush, and now reaffirmed in importance by President Barack Obama. Government sees importance in HIT because it may revitalize as well as standardize healthcare systems such that effectiveness and efficiency to both patients and the communities will be provided, which is a major necessity during a period of healthcare reform and changes to come.

So, the advantages of HIT aside, the purpose of this chapter is to analyze the impact of ownership and management characteristics on a variety of health information technology proxies that indicate how much the organization is making use of its electronic processes. The question this chapter analyzes is: How does the management structure of a healthcare provider (kind of agency/practice (government, private, or not-for-profit) as well as ownership status and physician specialty) affect the likelihood that specific services (with a focus on health information technology and electronic services) are provided and public health needs are being met?

This will help deduce the current state of HIT across specific providers, and analyze which types of organizations and management have the greatest likelihood in adopting. Another important part of the analysis is to see how organizational characteristics impact the improvements in spreading awareness of diseases, double checking errors made, and impacting patients through improvements in quality of care indicators. Some of these indicators include identifying out-of-range errors and lab results, surveillance of information, and dissemination of information. Possible hypotheses to the question include that the ownership status, especially larger organizations with private practice focus and specialists, will make use of technology more efficiently and see use in it compared to smaller community health centers that are being mandated by the law to use technology, but do not meaningfully use or derive benefits from it. Training is another component that may need testing in this chapter, but there is no proxy for training efforts to adapt to the technology. Use of technology to avoid errors is a key component and ownership status may have impacts on the use of technology in improving the error rate. A smaller physician-run practice may see less need to avoid errors or spread public health awareness as a community health center or government clinic that requires large-scale regulation. Government regulation also is analyzed from this chapter, based on the results of which types of organizations are able to have the greatest information dissemination and quality care. Finally, the chapter takes the theory apart that health information technology diffusion is one fluid process across all organizations. Rather, different aspects of health information technology may be more useful to some organizations than others, which is possibly a predictor for the slow penetration of HIT across organizations. It's quite possible that some HIT, such as EMRs or electronic billing, is better suited for certain kinds of organizations over others, whereas governments and policymakers are grouping HIT into one category and trying to see benefits from organizations adopting and using all types of HIT equally. This idea is explored further through some analysis in the data.

Past Literature

Skimming the literature in the past, little analysis has been done of how cross provider variation in ownership characteristics impacts the use and dissemination of health information technology. Lack of adoption of HIT currently divides many organizations, and a possible reasoning for these differences is variations in organizational behavior characteristics that define the organization's infrastructure, work flow, innovation, and progress. Examples of organizational behavior in this context will include (1) ownership, be it a physician-run practice, academic center, HMO, or others; (2) the specialty care services and presence or lack of specialists at an organization; (3) the kind of employment status of the physician, be it owner or employee or contractor; and (4) the type of setting, be it a community health center, nonprofit, for-profit, or healthcare corporation. These differences can have an impact on the kind of electronic services provided at the clinic because infrastructure changes and improvements may be indicative of a provider's mission, decisions to invest profits into the organization, community benefit provisions, and profitability of services from use of technology. Some organizations may see technology as a hindrance, whereas other organizations, with a great number of specialists, may use technology if they see it improving their services or quality of care.

An article by Timothy West (1998) analyzes how organizational components between the Veterans Administration (VA) system, nonprofits, and for-profits act. He does an analysis on VA hospitals and how they may differ across type of hospital as well as across a region. He finds that VA hospitals may place higher importance and focus on quality care, but disregard the relationship between improvements in quality care and performance. Yet, he claims that VA staff are least concerned with cost issues, especially with turnover. Cutting back on staff was not seen as a priority even during periods of rising costs. This is interesting as it notes the characteristics that may have an impact on cost and quality care (by organization) that will be attempted to be tested through the NAMCS (National Ambulatory Medical Care Survey) dataset in this chapter. He also notes the importance hospitals in general place on short-term improvements. This may be key, as many hospitals don't see health information technology as important due to its lagged effect. "Cross functional teams" was an important lacking characteristic, something that can be observed more closely by how well coordinated the staff is within the hospital setting. For this reason, ownership and management characteristics are even more important when analyzing technology implementation across hospitals because, without them, the disconnect may grow wider between teams of staff in various departments.

Next, Sloan and Vraciu (1983) tested a few ownership characteristics. They placed focus on investor-owned hospitals' treatment of welfare patients who are of Medicare, Medicaid, or charity care status; investor-owned hospitals that typically look for profitability of services as a major objective, whether or not not-for-profit hospitals earn no profit at all; and whether investor-owned hospitals tend to have more expensive services. There were no statistically significant indicators to substantiate these claims that investor-owned and not-for-profit hospitals had differences in "scope of services," "treatment of nonpaying patients," and "economic performance" (32). There was not much difference in the areas of radiology, laboratory, and the department of pharmacy. However, differences may be seen once information technology is introduced, especially with electronic prescribing, so this may be a good update. Finally, CT scans, surgery, and cardiac catheterization, which are considered profitable in nature, were provided by not-for-profits, so ownership didn't provide an edge over profitability.

Sloan et al. (1988) discusses the free rider problem of larger hospitals, where less efficiency may persist due to lack of consensus when problems arise across various hierarchies of staff. Most evident in this study is the finding of greater structure in departments with more beds (224). The study states that physician-operated not-for-profits do seem to have significance as compared to other ownership categories. Physicians' presence on a board or committee also seems significant to performance of the hospital as well as chain or nonchain for-profits, specialty physicians in radiology and pathology, and relationship between medical staff and administration (225). This may go in supporting the theory that larger hospitals may have inefficiency when using health information technology, merely due to the sheer numbers and training required to assist all staff. Coordination also may be an issue in ensuring everyone is on the same page in using the technology and communicating with each other across departments and across chains (multiple sets of the same brand hospital in various locations) if the for-profit or not-for-profit is chain in nature.

The dataset used is the NAMCS data of 2009. The data are "a national probability sample survey of visits to office-based physicians conducted by the National Center for Health Statistics." These data were weighted to produce national estimates that describe the utilization of ambulatory medical care services in the United States. The 2009 NAMCS sample included 3,319 physicians: 3,093 medical doctors and 226 doctors of osteopathy. (Specialties not included in the sample had backgrounds in anesthesiology, pathology, and radiology.) Of these, about 1,293 were active participants and filled out the survey, which was an unweighted response rate of 62.1% (62.4 weighted).

Methods

The chapter engages in analyzing behavior of health providers in interacting with technology, looking at survey answers of "yes," "no," or "maybe" that have been better modified for analytical purposes. The unit of analysis is the clinic setting or organization where the provider is involved in caregiving to patients. The best form of analysis for such a study, engaging in survey answers of a binary nature, is a logistic regression model. Regression analysis alone will not explain the variation in the answer choices of the survey or explain the relationship between key organizational characteristics and attitudes and acceptance of technology in the healthcare setting. First, descriptive analysis engages in organizing the key characteristics of meaningfully using technology—the three most important characteristics, which include EMR (electronic medical records) usage, electronic billing, and electronic prescribing, and a few subcategories, such as electronic imaging usage.

Descriptive statistics include a chi^2 test to see if there are significant differences in the observed versus expected frequencies of the various variables being tested across different organizational categories, such as office setting, specialty group, employment status, and ownership. Based on the basic chi^2 tests, there will be reason to test further how these variables impact the organization's ability to use health information technology because the chi^2 test is showing variation across the ownership type, employment status, type of setting, and more, in order to identify how these characteristics are different in their impact on technology penetration. Correlations also were run to predict how many of the instrumental variables interact and ensure there is no multicollinearity between the variables.

Descriptive and Inferential Statistics

Running these few chi^2 tests alone shows that electronic billing and EMR usage varies by multiple organizational characteristics at a statistically significant level, of a .01 level (Table 5.1). This

Table 5.1 Descriptive Statistics

Variation in Presence of EMRs by Physician Specialty: Chi Squared Association

Physician Specialty

Electronic Medical Records	General/f	Internal	Pediatric	Generals	Obstetrics	Orthoped.	Cardiovas.	Dermatol.	Total
Not Present = 0	168	1	105	0	54	68	62	25	628
	26.75	0.16	16.72	0.00	8.60	10.83	9.87	3.98	100.00
Present = 1	1,287	357	451	99	243	140	143	86	3,255
	39.54	10.97	13.86	3.04	7.47	4.30	4.39	2.64	100.00
Total	1,455	358	556	99	297	208	205	111	3,883
	37.47	9.22	14.32	2.55	7.65	5.36	5.28	2.86	100.00

Physician Specialty

Electronic Medical Records	Urology	Psychiatry	Neurology	Ophthalmology	Otolaryngy	Total
Not Present = 0	24	15	10	66	30	628
	3.82	2.39	1.59	10.51	4.78	100.00
Present = 1	91	0	102	64	192	3,255
	2.80	0.00	3.13	1.97	5.90	100.00

(continued)

Table 5.1 Descriptive Statistics (continued)

Variation in Presence of EMRs by Physician Specialty: Chi Squared Association

Physician Specialty

Electronic Medical Records	Urology	Psychiatry	Neurology	Ophthalmology	Otolaryngy	Total
Total	115	15	112	130	222	3,883
	2.96	0.39	2.88	3.35	5.72	100.00

Note: Pearson chi² (12) = 387.6643 Pr = 0.000.

Variation in Presence of EMRs by Type of Office Setting

Type of Office Setting

Electronic Medical Records	Private Sector	Freestand.	Community	Health Maintenance Organization	Total
No EMR = 0	541	15	72	0	628
	86.15	2.39	11.46	0.00	100.00
EMR Present = 1	2,682	230	288	55	3,255
	82.40	7.07	8.85	1.69	100.00
Total	3,223	245	360	55	3,883
	83.00	6.31	9.27	1.42	100.00

Note: Pearson chi²(3) = 33.6470 Pr = 0.000.

Variation in Presence of E-Billing by Type of Office Setting

Type of Office Setting

Electronic Billing	Private Sector	Freestand	Community	Health Maintenance Organization	Total
No E-billing = 0	776	15	150	0	941
	82.47	1.59	15.94	0.00	100.00
E-billing = 1	2,447	230	210	55	2,942
	83.17	7.82	7.14	1.87	100.00
Total	3,223	245	360	55	3,883
	83.00	6.31	9.27	1.42	100.00

Note: Pearson chi^2(3) = 120.9900 Pr = 0.000.

Variation in Presence of EMRs by Ownership

Who Owns the Practice?

Electronic Medical Records	Physician	Health Main.	Community	Medical/a	Other Hosp.	Other Health	Total
Not Present = 0	466	25	72	0	40	25	628
	74.20	3.98	11.46	0.00	6.37	3.98	100.00
Present = 1	2,573	79	288	85	56	174	3,255
	79.05	2.43	8.85	2.61	1.72	5.35	100.00
Total	3,039	104	360	85	96	199	3,883
	78.26	2.68	9.27	2.19	2.47	5.12	100.00

Note: Pearson chi^2(5) = 74.5465 Pr = 0.000.

(continued)

Table 5.1 Descriptive Statistics (continued)

Electronic Medical Records	Does Practice Have Computerized System for Public Health Reporting?		
	Yes	No	Total
Lack of EMR = 0	238	390	628
	37.90	62.10	100.00
EMR Present = 1	1,176	2,079	3,255
	36.13	63.87	100.00
Total	1,414	2,469	3,883
	36.42	63.58	100.00

Note: Pearson chi^2(1) = 0.7115 Pr = 0.399.

means that we can reject the null that there is no difference between these groups and that there may be at least one difference between these groups and the electronics usage. Yet, running the chi^2 test on impacts of electronic medical records and public health reporting, there is not enough evidence to reject the null that the groups are similar. For this reason, it is interesting to continue the analysis with a simple logistic regression analysis of the various binary variables.

Logistic Regression Methods

First, the discussion will be organized around how organizations interact with HIT's meaningful use criteria: EMR usage, electronic billing, and electronic prescriptions. Then, we will be using a newly created interaction term variable that is a combination of specialty and ownership. This way, the analysis can better predict how being both a specialist and the owner of the organization may sway the chances in adopting and meaningfully using technology. Finally, the chapter analyzes how technology is used to generate awareness and how it will impact the community through error and fact checking as well as providing public health support. Using McFadden R^2 models, the regressions are compared for their ability to predict the variation in the relationships, and then a specificity and sensitivity test is run, with the best results displayed. Also, for the sake of space, we display in the following tables *only* those variables that were statistically significant.

Model 1: Outcomes: Differences in HIT Usage across Organizational Providers and Characteristics

Table 5.2 depicts an interesting relationship between EMR usage and the organization. As can be seen, if the physicians are employees, they are 60% less likely to use an EMR compared to if they were the owners of the practice. Household income, rural classification of zip code, and percentage of bachelor's degree in the zip were significant, and had an interesting impact on EMR usage, as increasing household income reduced EMR usage likelihood. This could mean that organizations in areas with higher household incomes are not using EMRs efficiently, a surprising note from the study, which may need to be analyzed further. This could be because there is less regulation for implementation in high-income neighborhoods, and less incentives for high-income hospitals and freestanding clinics compared to low-income clinics that have greater Medicaid and Medicare populations attending. So, looking at the Medicaid populations, the higher the percentage of patients using Medicaid, there was an increase in EMRs, but surprisingly, the higher the Medicare population, the lower the EMR usage rate in that region. Even though federal incentives to use EMRs are present with presence of both types of patients, this could mean that areas with high income, retired, and elderly populations, as well as elderly Medicare populations seek professional help from clinics that currently do not have EMR capacity. If the patient's zip was rurally classified or there was a higher percentage of bachelor's degrees, there was also a higher likelihood of EMR usage, possibly due to new economic funding to promote EMR usage in rural and underserved areas.

Table 5.2   Likelihood of Using an EMR across Various Organizational Traits

Number of observations	3808	
LR	164.44	
Log likelihood	−328.784	
Pseudo R^2	0.2	
Variables	β	*Standard Error*
Employment status of physician: employee	0.41 *	0.1004852
Household income	0.52**	0.1153204
Percent of adults with bachelor's degree or higher in zip code	1.56**	0.2198137
Rural classification of patient's zip code	3.17*	0.5056321
Racial classification: white, black, or other	4.72*	5.970298
Age in days, if under 1 year	1.00**	0.0018663
% of revenue from Medicare	0.80***	0.09993
% of revenue from Medicaid	1.40**	0.1917889
Source of visit was a referral	0.94**	0.0259945

Note: Base category for employment status assumes that the physician is the owner of the practice.

* p <0.00
** p <0.05
***p <0.10

Model 2: Installing a New or Replacing an Old EMR within an Organization

This model (Table 5.3) is a continuation of studying which practices are most likely to adopt a new EMR in the next few years. This is equally as important as knowing which practices currently have EMRs. This proxy is a sign of ability to adapt to new systems, innovation, interest in having new technologies as well as updates to older technologies, and ability to perform organizational change. While the study as a whole is cross sectional, such a predictor that is forward looking can provide insight a few years into the future to see how likely specific organizations are in having new EMRs. Interestingly, other HMOs and healthcare corporations, which are primarily private and for-profit in nature, were less likely to adopt a new EMR system. This may be an interesting finding. It could be that they have the capital and already have an EMR system, or that their capital is not being used toward HIT. This may be leading to the idea that EMRs may be more important for low-income hospitals, as they do not currently have an infrastructure for electronic communication and connectivity, whereas high-capital and high-power hospitals may already be supporting such an infrastructure and not need to make changes to their current system for the

Table 5.3   Installing a New or Replacing an Old EMR within an Organization

Number of observations	3162		
LR chi^2 (39)	980.28		
Prob > chi^2	0		
Log likelihood	−936.141		
Psuedo R^2	0.3436		
Likelihood of Replacing an EMR			
Variables	*Odds*	*Std. Error*	*P > |z|*
Ownership			
HMO: Health Maintenance Organization	0.0477135*	0.022	0.000
Other Hospital	0.2208772*	0.069	0.000
Other healthcare corporation	0.6122035***	0.158	0.058
Specialty Group Practice			
Surgical care	24.16307*	9.058	0.000
Employment Status			
Physician is an employee	26.64*	5.200	0.000
Physician is a contractor	13.38544*	5.150	0.000
Physician Specialty			
Internal medicine	2.98*	0.693	0.000
Pediatrics	11.52*	2.583	0.000
Orthopedic surgery	0.068*	0.026	0.000
Type of Office Setting			
Free standing clinic/urgicenter	0.2558813*	0.082	0.000
Percent in poverty	1.536169*	0.182	0.000
Household income	1.495964*	0.167	0.000
Percent of adults with bachelor's degree or higher in zip code	0.6917478*	0.051	0.000
Rural classification of patient's zip code	0.8463709*	0.050	0.005
Use of Medicare as payment	1.342236***	0.234	0.092
Use of Medicaid as payment	2.765049*	0.663	0.000

(continued)

Table 5.3 Installing a New or Replacing an Old EMR within an Organization (continued)

Likelihood of Replacing an EMR			
Variables	Odds	Std. Error	P > |z|
Use of self pay as payment	0.3793278**	0.168	0.029
Ethnicity: Hispanic or not	0.3581016***	0.218	0.092
% of revenue from Medicare	1.343312**	0.117	0.001
% of revenue from Medicaid	0.5718581*	0.054	0.000
Month of visit	1.282882*	0.028	0.000
Day of week of visit	1.13414**	0.051	0.005
Major reason for visit	0.9343292**	0.026	0.014
Total number of chronic conditions	1.104649*	0.037	0.003
Time it took to get an appointment	1.696318*	0.116	0.000

Note: Ownership has a base category of physician or physician group owned.

Primary care is the base category for specialty group.

For employment status, owner is the base category.

For physician specialty, the base category is general and family practice.

For type of office setting, the base category is private/solo/group practice.

* p <0.00
** p <0.05
***p <0.10

time being. This could have serious implications on government policies that need to focus more on helping low-income hospitals adopt HIT than the high-income hospitals, as well as state government policies that need to provide better Medicaid funding for new EMRs, because Medicaid has a state-based component whereas Medicare is a nationally funded program.

The tables also are turned in this context because when a physician is an employee or contractor he/she is 13 to 20 times more likely to replace an EMR. Internal medicine and pediatrics were the most likely specialties to have a new EMR system. This time, percentage of revenue from Medicare would have a positive impact on adopting a new EMR compared to Medicaid. Similarly, the more the number of chronic conditions, the more likely the practice would have an EMR, which is linked to the specialty physicians who were likely to adopt and the Medicare percentage of revenue variables.

Model 3: Likelihood of E-Billing and Electronic Claims

Electronic billing seems to be most prevalent at hospitals—nearly five times as many as solo or group practices (Table 5.4). On the other hand, community health centers are 67% less likely to use e-billing systems. There are a number of different reasons for this discrepancy. It could be that the complicatedness of the billing process at government centers, where much of the patient

Table 5.4   Electronic Billing Presence Across Providers

Number of observations	3102	
LR chi^2 (36)	1028.1	
Prob >chi^2 (36)	0	
Log likelihood	−1310.3987	
Pseudo R^2	0.2818	

Electronic Billing and Claims		
Variables	*Odds Ratio*	*Standard Error*
Ownership		
Community health center	0.3311657*	0.067
Other hospitals	4.737847*	1.426
Specialty Group Practice		
Surgical care	3.793974*	1.394
Employment Status		
Physician is an employee	0.752536**	0.096
Physician is a contractor	3.284294*	1.038
Physician Specialty		
Internal medicine	8.026811*	1.880
Pediatrics	2.083446*	0.332
Obstetrics/gynecology	4.604915*	1.275
Orthopedic surgery	0.1104287*	0.042
Percent of adults with bachelor's degree or higher in zip code	0.8239474*	0.051
Rural classification of patient's zip code	1.099338**	0.050
Use of private insurance as payment	0.5247249*	0.080
Use of Medicare as payment	0.6071539*	0.088
Use of Medicaid as payment	0.4198214*	0.078
Use of self pay as payment	0.295209*	0.066
% of revenue from Medicare	0.7794452*	0.053
% of revenue from Medicaid	1.786717*	0.128

(continued)

Table 5.4   Electronic Billing Presence Across Providers (continued)

Electronic Billing and Claims		
Variables	Odds Ratio	Standard Error
Month of visit	0.8979217*	0.015
Sex of patient	0.988	0.100
Source of visit was a referral	1.05688*	0.021
Major reason for visit	1.053338**	0.027
Total number of chronic conditions	1.014	0.029

Note: Ownership has a base category of physician or physician group owned.

Primary care is the base category for specialty group.

For employment status, owner is the base category.

For physician specialty, the base category is general and family practice.

For type of office setting, the base category is private/solo/group practice.

* p <0.00
** p <0.05
***p <0.10

mix is either on a government-funded billing program or many of the patients are on free or charity/sliding scale care, could be dissuading community health centers (CHCs) from using e-billing. E-billing also may require quite a bit of training for the CHC and being that there are a larger percentage of volunteer staff at these facilities, including volunteer administration and physicians, they may not perceive e-billing as being in their best interest or ability to participate. Surgical care was four times more likely to adopt e-billing than primary medical care facilities, and, once again, internal medicine and pediatrics seem to be most prevalent in using electronic billing. Gynecology also seems to appear in this list as seeing e-billing as important. Interestingly, specialists may be more likely to use e-billing because they don't normally accept all forms of insurance and may have larger client bases that pay out of pocket. Here, if the physician is a contractor, this seems to be significant in achieving electronic billing standards in the organization.

Model 4: Electronic Prescriptions

The use of e-prescribing was again extremely prevalent, nearly 12 times more likely for someone in internal medicine than someone who was a primary care family practice physician (Table 5.5). CHCs actually seem to be more likely to use e-prescribing, possibly because of the connectivity and benefits to the local pharmacies that now provide pharmacy services, such as Walmart, Target, and more. Usually CHCs are in areas with low-income and rural residents, so this was surprising, but may be the most effective method for rural populations to be getting care because they may live far from the closest hospital, pharmacy, or clinic. This shows some positivity and hope in the healthcare system because it means that CHCs are properly able to

Table 5.5 Electronic Submissions of Prescriptions to Pharmacy

Number of observations	3576	
LR chi^2 (38)	804.87	
Prob >chi^2	0	
Pseudo R^2	0.201	
Log likelihood	−1599.64	

Electronic Submissions of Prescriptions to Pharmacy		
Variables	Odds	Standard Error
Ownership		
Community health center	1.691739**	0.411
Medical/academic health center	0.0970217*	0.028
Other healthcare corporation	0.2369969*	0.060
Specialty Group Practice		
Surgical care	1.826217*	0.234
Physician Specialty		
Internal medicine	12.90191*	5.552
Pediatrics	0.3386529*	0.049
General surgery	2.914046**	1.336
Orthopedic surgery	0.2469418*	0.052
Cardiovascular diseases	0.822	0.200
Urology	2.094929**	0.698
Neurology	4.85324*	2.179
Ophthalmology	0.30476*	0.080
Otolaryngology	0.2065004*	0.043
Rural classification of patient's zip code	1.163004*	0.050
Use of Medicare as payment	0.7815292***	0.106
Use of self pay as payment	0.4484304*	0.100
Ethnicity: Hispanic or not	2.667963**	1.294
Detailed race	1.620079**	0.394
Age in days, if under 1 year	1.001891***	0.001

(continued)

Table 5.5   Electronic Submissions of Prescriptions to Pharmacy (continued)

Electronic Submissions of Prescriptions to Pharmacy		
Variables	*Odds*	*Standard Error*
% of revenue from Medicare	1.124099**	0.066
Month of visit	1.053779*	0.015
Source of visit: Referral	0.9514983*	0.014
Total chronic conditions	1.094146*	0.026
Time for appointment	0.8178622*	0.034

Note: Ownership has a base category of physician or physician group owned.

Primary care is the base category for specialty group.

For employment status, owner is the base category.

For physician specialty, the base category is general and family practice.

For type of office setting, the base category is private/solo/group practice.

* $p < 0.00$
** $p < 0.05$
*** $p < 0.10$

use e-pharmacy mechanisms to their benefit. It also may be that they are advancing quickly in e-pharmacy initiatives and this causes a lag in e-billing, which may involve quite a bit of electronic paperwork and effort to sort out. Because rural classification of the zip code was significant, and Medicare percentages were again significant, it may be that many senior citizens who have retired in rural and suburban areas are getting care using e-prescribing as well because there is easy connectivity.

Interaction Term

Generating an interaction term that combined the effects of both ownership and specialty group of practice created two impacts that were statistically significant: the electronic orders and public health component. Public health awareness was about 10% more likely to occur when the organization was physician-owned as well as part of a specialty group. Electronic orders were nearly 22% more likely to occur using the interaction term variable. Again, only the statistically significant interaction term is shown (Table 5.6). A physician who would be considered part of this "interaction term" variable would have to be a specialist and be the primary owner of the practice. This interaction term takes both of these characteristics into consideration, and has an impact on the dependent variable. For this case, there is a high likelihood that someone who is of both of these categories, in specific specialist categories, would have an electronic order system, which was significant at the .00 level. For example, internal medicine would be nearly 11.5 times more likely to engage in electronic order entry. Gynecology again is impacted similarly. Yet, some specialists were not positively impacted, as pediatrics, general surgery, urology, and the others

Table 5.6   Interaction Term Effects on Electronic Orders

Variables	Odds Ratio	Std. Error
Interaction of ownership and specialty group	1.030886*	0.011745
Ownership		
Medical/academic health center	0.0639704*	0.020862
Other healthcare corporation	0.1533444*	0.045368
Employment status	1.795701*	0.231029
Specialty Group Practice		
Internal medicine	11.27261*	4.883345
Pediatrics	0.2886788*	0.046002
Obstetrics/gynecology	2.472948**	1.154247
General surgery	0.5763266**	0.12716
Orthopedic surgery	0.1875371*	0.043949
Urology	0.5977342***	0.161985

* $p < 0.00$
** $p < 0.05$
***$p < 0.10$

listed do not seem to have much impact by having ownership and a specialist in the field. This was a bit of a conundrum, and the variable may need to be explored further, possibly by looking at other organizational characteristics teamed with specialist categories, to see if they make an impact on electronics usage, and if, by specialists, the utility level varies.

Next, it is important to analyze how technology has repercussions on the greater community, and whether information dissemination and analysis is more quickly reaching the public. To do this analysis, the variable HIT used to report public health issues was analyzed, again by looking at these same organizational dimensions.

From Table 5.7, it was found that CHCs are less likely by about 40% to e-report on public health issues. So, this links to both the use of EMRs and e-billing systems. Only if the CHCs have multiple components of their HIT set up and in use can they be having a measurable impact on public health. CHCs tend to populations of high need, high risk, chronic, and acute conditions, especially with low-income individuals who do not have access to primary care, thus this finding is a problem. But, more worrisome is that the category of "other healthcare corporations" is about 75% less likely than small, solo practices to e-report on public health. This is problematic because many of these organizations have the funds to invest in research, development, and lobbying for various causes. The fact that electronic reporting is still lagging in the community is a major point for concern. From the model, general surgeons were the specialists most likely to report on public health issues in an electronic format. As many famous doctor/reporters, such as Dr. Sanjay Gupta, get a lot of press coverage for their knowledge on the surgical side of medicine, this could be due

Table 5.7   Analyzing Effects on Public Health Reporting

Number of observations	2983.000	
LR chi^2 (25)	941.950	
Prob >chi^2	0.000	
Pseudo R^2	0.2372	
Log likelihood	−1514.973	
Impact on Public Health Reporting		
Variables	*Odds*	*Std. Error*
Community health center	0.5879098*	0.1126521
Other healthcare corporations	0.2584749*	0.0670882
Physician as employee	3.712923*	0.4351244
Internal medicine	0.5393401*	0.0920125
Pediatrics	2.076586*	0.2898335
General surgery	2.665891*	0.7466668
Obstetrics and gynecology	2.010644*	0.3300879
Urology	1.858463**	0.6191557
Otolaryngology	0.5762977**	0.1298228
Use of private insurance as payment	1.753025*	0.2434909
Use of Medicare as payment	1.362623**	0.1839716
Use of self-pay as payment	1.670791**	0.3628497
% of revenue from Medicare	2.860452*	0.2987531
% of revenue from Medicaid	3.071656*	0.2474183
Percent in poverty	1.221661**	0.1060091
Percent of adults with bachelor's degree or higher in zip code	1.619665*	0.0929351
Urban–rural classification of patient's zip code	0.8997568*	0.0358495
Wait until appointment	0.7842393*	0.0292887

* $p < 0.00$
** $p < 0.05$
***$p < 0.10$

Table 5.8 Interaction Term on Public Health Reporting

Category	Odds Ratio	Std. Error
Interaction of ownership and specialty group	1.106843*	0.031
Community health center	0.3931449*	0.085
Other healthcare corporations	0.0420835*	0.024
Surgical care	0.2469606*	0.113
Internal medicine	0.4255031*	0.079
Pediatrics	1.465433*	0.272
General surgery	13.43225*	5.837
Obstetrics and gynecology	1.632391**	0.409
Urology	5.265611*	2.212

* $p < 0.00$
** $p < 0.05$

partially to the amount of influence the media has on what gets into the news and what has been electronically reported and then passed to audiences in an emphasized manner.

Here, compared to owning, when physicians are employees, they are 3.7 times more likely to impact public health reporting. This could be a time issue; administration takes up time and, when physicians run the practice, they may not have as much time to be reporting on issues as if they have help from an overseeing body that does the research and development as well as policy consulting and lobbying for them. Pediatrics, general surgery, and obstetrics are more than two times as likely to report on public health using electronics. Otolaryngology and internal medicine actually are less likely to e-report on public health, and this could just be due to the complexity of the field, or again based on the media and issues that are hot button items, such as surgery or birth, compared to chronic conditions in internal medicine. Finally, a surprising finding is that if the clinic has private patients, they are more likely to report findings, so this could mean that, again, affluence and power has a lot to do with organizational information dissemination. The wealthier the hospital, the more likely it is to provide information on health conditions, and also the more likely it is to engage in needs assessments and other consulting reports that provide analysis of its programs, targeted issues in the community, and its own patients' most prevalent conditions.

This would be interpreted as an 11% higher likelihood of reporting electronically on public health issues to raise awareness if the organization is both a specialist and owns the organization him/herself. Otherwise, general surgery and urology were the only other categories that majorly were impacted on their own if they were not part of the interaction term effects (Table 5.8). So, compared to being a primary care physician, as a specialist who owns the firm, there is a significant impact on the ability to report in an electronic format.

Robust and Reliable Outcomes Check

The McFadden R^2 can be compared across the three models, to see which models were able to depict the best relationships between the independent and dependent variables. As can be seen, the range was in the 20% range, and the second model that discussed organizational behavior effects on electronic billing had the most impactful relationship with the highest McFadden R^2 of 28%. This is still not as high as could be and may mean that the models over all are missing some important variables or this model is not able to do justice to the true relationship present between the variables. There may need to be more manipulation of variables, possibly more interaction terms, for more meaningful results.

Using the predict command, they tested for multicollinearity. Then, specificity and sensitivity, or the probability of predicting negative and positive outcomes, were analyzed, respectively.

The model found for electronic prescribing has correctly classified the data at about 80%. But, the sensitivity is high, about 92%, and the specificity is low at about 50%. This could be fixed by including more relevant variables in the model and checking to see if there are numerous correlated variables in the model and adjusting for this. This also could mean, due to the lower specificity in the model, that there is a high type 1 error rate.

Policy Analysis and Implications

This chapter has some interesting policy implications for physicians, healthcare providers, as well as the community as to how their organizations may be more or less adaptable, utilitarian, and flexible in use of HIT. One of the interesting findings is that the Center for Medicaid and Medicare Services' (CMS) terminology of "meaningful use" may need to differ by specialty group. Rather than classify all healthcare physicians as necessarily needing to use technology in similar ways, some, such as higher specialty doctors (a gynecologist or internal medicine expert), may need to be making greater strides with technology because of the level of work they impact, compared to a physician treating the common cold. Also, the type of office, be it a government clinic or private solo practice or even a healthcare corporation, may be deriving more utility from different kinds of HIT, so there should be some differentiation in the objectives to get these organizations to adopt different kinds of HIT. More analysis, especially field work, may help investigate what differences there are in deriving utility from e-billing versus e-prescribing and so on. This will help in better implementing policies and procedures to speed up adoption in particular areas rather than on HIT as a whole. The same thing may have to do with incentives, as financial incentives may be better spent if there is knowledge of which components are the biggest trouble spots in technology adoption.

Model 1 depicts that a large percentage of Medicaid populations are receiving care at organizations with EMRs, but there is some lacking in the clinics that serve Medicare populations. The difference in technology adoption that should be targeting both Medicare and Medicaid programs could be in the state versus national incentives and interest, and also could be due to the population demographic differences in these two categories. For the elderly, their level of services may be speeded up through usage of HIT at providers' offices, but they may not be using CHCs as frequently as a low-income patient. Therefore, small businesses may be deriving more benefit from Medicare incentives, and CHCs may be deriving more benefit from Medicaid incentives. This also could be causing the differences in the HIT services at solo or group physician practices versus CHCs, as CHCs have major difficulties in electronic billing. Physicians who run the practice also have more control over the usage of EMR systems, but seem to be negligent on public health reporting compared to physicians who are employees. This is an extremely important finding, as public health reporting can be an ethical and invasive issue as the community is very much affected by being aware of major issues that impact their health. More collaboratives and marketing strategies that target the community may be necessary, both between and within the providers, to ensure that there is better outreach and mechanisms to engage the public through electronic reporting. As the mobile health generation has come to fruition, other and, surprisingly, many developing countries have actually been very successful at reporting on public health through the use of electronic devices, including cell phones, which also may need to become a greater focus for the United States.

As is known, the Medicare Electronic Health Record (EHR) Incentive program provides $44,000 over five years to health professionals and hospitals that are willing to use HIT and undergo the compliance standards. There's an even higher incentive for those professionals who provide services in a Health Professional Shortage Area (HSPA), many a time including CHCs and low-income government or charity clinics. On the other hand, Medicaid EHR incentive programs have better incentives, up to $63,750 over the six years, but this is partly a state-based program, which has seen to be impactful on some states more than others depending on how much the state has in its coffers. For this reason, there may have been a bigger discrepancy between Medicare and Medicaid patient-based organizations, as those with higher Medicaid patients will see more incentives from the program, assuming their state has eligible funding. If not, the state politics may play a big role on public health and community health, which will again influence electronic reporting standards as well. Hence, as can be seen, it is an interconnected cycle.

The complications of the hospital billing processes makes it also a problem for community health centers and government hospitals, especially those who do not contract out, to bear the brunt of work on analyzing how to compute their patient mix billing system, with ratios that are less than simple for Medicaid and Medicare patients. Again, Medicaid patients are difficult because it is dependent on state policies for aid as well. Another source of contention with electronic billing is the ability for nonprofit hospitals to carefully identify where there major community benefit percentage is, and how much they are able to document going back to society. With improvised IRS regulations[*] that require community benefit and community needs assessments as supplementary to hospitals' tax returns, nonprofit hospitals have to be especially careful in reporting these numbers and also in analyzing the impact it may have for their tax exempt status. They will have to accordingly reallocate funding toward programs for cultural competence and be more aware of conditions and health concerns for their specific community. Otherwise, they face many financial, ethical and social risks: audit, tax penalties, and other consequences.

Nonprofit hospitals not meeting the requirement must register under a separate section of the tax code, a penalty resulting in the inability to issue tax exempt bonds or receive tax-deductible contributions.

---

[*] Press Release, U.S. Senate Committee on Finance: Grassley Asks Non-Profit Hospitals to Account for Activities Related to their Tax-Exempt Status (2005), available at http://www.ahp.org/Resource/advocacy/us/giftstaxesIRS/taxexemptstatus/Documents/prg052505.pdf; Taking the Pulse of Charitable Care and Community Benefits at Nonprofit Hospitals: Hearing Before the Senate Finance Committee, 109th Cong. (2006), available at http://finance.senate.gov/hearings/hearing/?id=e6a6e518-bc40-78f7-ee63-a9993d182e5c (collecting testimony).

Training for information technology (IT) also will need to differ based on what the organization sees as its strengths versus weaknesses. It is clear that organizations are not utilizing technology for the same purposes nor are they being rational actors in managing technology across divisions, so there will be a need for major focus on research to come. This will help ease the transition into using HIT services.

Limitations of the Study

Major limitations in this study include cost, cross-sectional data that has no adjustment for time, and possibly a lack of a variety of demographic constants and clinic characteristics, such as size and ranking of clinics. These variables, if included in a new survey that is done in waves, may be able to paint a better picture of the analysis and the data, and provide increased external validity for the greater population.

Chapter 6

Quality of Care and the Patient

Overview

The use of electronic medical records (EMRs) is a recent phenomenon that has been introduced into the hospital workplace within the last 15 years. Though they are still in their preliminary stages of adoption and implementation in organizations around the country, there is importance in reviewing their performance to understand the benefits and/or flaws of the system and to see how they have impacted societal needs. For this reason, this chapter includes a series of multinomial logistic regressions to study the impacts of EMR systems on patient quality, coordination, and service. Dependent variables measured are quality of care, communication problems encountered, time spent with patients, and medical errors detected. Discrete effects also are analyzed to measure the impact that technology usage has on each problem in quality of service and care.

Past Literature on Quality of Care

As discussed earlier, EMR technology is still in transition and implementation phases in many organizations. So far there have been some beneficial results, some negative results on patient quality of service, thus, on the whole, mixed reviews. It should be noted that many organizations are at different stages of implementation, thus for some who are still getting used to it, it may be more of a hassle than an aid.

Kaiser Permanente is a cost-effective healthcare system that provides for coverage to nearly 8 million members all over the United States. It used a Clinical Information System (CIS) electronic medical record program that began in October of 2000, and wanted to test out how operability of electronic medical record systems would impact healthcare teams in four departments of the hospital in Oahu, Hawaii. The purpose was to "identify critical events in system implementation," organizational behavior during the transition to complete EMR meaningful use, and measuring the impacts of EMR usage on patient quality and service within and across departments.

Evaluation was based on interviews with 12 clinicians, 5 managers in the 4 teams, and 9 CIS project managers concerning major implementation issues: the major events in CIS implementation, how leadership and culture played a role in the organization, and "CIS-related changes in clinical practice" (Hsu et al., 2005). Within each category (implementation, leadership, culture, and CIS-related changes), recurring themes and issues were found from respondents' perspectives. Approval ratings were quite low, with 18 respondents reporting dissatisfaction and the remainder showing conflicting priorities within the organization's implementation coordinators. Software delays and implementation time were another big point of criticism as nine respondents criticized this and the costs of implantation as being higher than originally planned for (Hsu et al., 2005). Completeness and clarified charting as well as responsibility sharing was greatly improved as a majority opinion by all respondents. Extra burdens from using the CIS and navigation problems caused decreased clinician productivity and less one-on-one time with patients than before. It was also found that organization culture had a big impact on reducing resistance to implementation, but could inhibit constructive criticism.

In 2001, HCI (Healthcare Change Institute) conducted a study on technology adoption for clinics and hospitals in California. Through the program of adoption, quality of care was to be improved and organizational performance was to be improved by a certain percentage as the baseline objective. Medical practices, clinics, and management organizations were given an opportunity to participate in two different activities: a survey and a focus group. Surprisingly, objectives that were less important were improving medical errors and patient safety, whereas improving quality of care and service were among the top of those suggested in the focus group. From survey results, financial factors ranked as causing the greatest barriers to technology by 85% of respondents. Most statistically significant were leadership support, capital, and infrastructure as effective enablers of implementation. Important in acceleration of adoption were "access to funding (70%), support for R&D (57%), training (22%), and access to talent at (8%)" (p. 8). So, there have been comprised results when looking at organizations that were in the trial and testing phase of the technology.

Other organizations have shown primarily positive effects of use of EMR technology. In Des Roches et al. (2008), there was enough statistical evidence to indicate "positive effects of quality care and high levels of satisfaction." This study uses a simple chi^2 test, but from its large sample size, it only analyzes those physicians who have completely installed and have fully functioning EHRs in their organizations. This actually brings down the original sample size from 3,000 to near 120 physicians, or about 4% of the original sample size. Therefore, its results were primarily positive. Delivery of preventive care, chronic illnesses, and quality of clinical decisions, as well as communication with patients and decision making, were impacted while avoiding medical errors and timely access to patients were not statistically significantly impacted in the study. Multinomial or ordinal logistic regressions were not used, which could better the study.

Quality of care delivered to minorities was specifically evaluated in Reschvosky and Boukas (2009). This study uses simple chi^2 tests and regression analysis to indicate correlations between communication barriers and use of interpreter services for minorities in healthcare. While it provides evidence that minorities are benefiting from using EMR in the healthcare workplace, its results are somewhat skewed because the presence of a detailed nonlinear logistic analysis is lacking. It also mainly represents the numbers of providers with the tools, with no evidence of use of the services or how the IT (information technology) plays a role in physician decision making in the study. These are problem areas to build on and better the studies conducted previously.

There have been studies that show that through the use of EMR/EHR (electronic health record)/IT services, the quality of service and treatments to healthcare have been improved, but some drawbacks of use that include change to organizational culture and style of work ethic must be changed for there to be progress. Specifically, research is not consistent as to whether there are distinct improvements and/or differences in use of an EMR-based system compared to a paper-based system in different categories, such as medical errors, communication with minority patients, and quantity of time spent with patients.

Improvements and better assistance to minorities that are presumed may be due to a number of reasons, such as language translators being present in the technology, easier access to medical records and insurance paperwork, and even better education and training sessions held for assistant and healthcare professionals doing the treatment. The system has been known to capture more errors and provide better time and employment utilization, so these are important effects of the EMR services, which should be tested as well. Being a recent study (just two years old), it is difficult to say whether there are advantages or disadvantages to introducing EMR to the healthcare arena. Also, due to how recent the data are, which was collected in 2008, many of these effects may be more long term, and there is the possibility that until transition into the technology is complete, there will be volatility and unsatisfactory results as individuals are not trained properly on the correct use.

Data Source

The data are derived from the Interuniversity Consortium for Political and Social Research (ICPSR) Web site (www.icpsr.umich.edu/) and consists of a Health Tracking Physician Survey of 2008. It is ICPSR 27202. As a nationally representative sample of U.S. physicians providing direct patient care, the data do not include changes among communities as do previous data collected similarly, such as the CTS (Community Tracking Study). The respondents were selected using stratified random sampling and answered a mail questionnaire. Divided into 20 strata (10 regions cross-classified by primary care/not primary physician type), the sample frame was derived from a list of physicians provided by the American Medical Association.

Methodology

By conducting different kinds of logistic analyses—basic logistic and use of multinomial logistic model on each of the important dependent variables—results on each of the categories and factors influencing the dependent variables can be found. Depending on which nonlinear functional form generates more reasonable and robust results, this will be conducted and analyzed for the study's purpose. Each dependent variable has multiple categories; for example, a difficulty communicating with patients has categories 1, 2, 3, and -9, which have been converted for easier ranking procedure as binary. This chapter also may test more variables than necessary to ensure no omitted variable bias is present.

Variables

The independent variables that were analyzed were EMR technology usage as a whole, As well as more specific IT variables such as "IT for emails" and "IT for decision making" that specifically impacted the major areas of problems faced by patients. The reason for separating the EMR usage and IT variables is that each IT variable seemed to have a different purpose, thus by breaking each one down separately, like IT for decision making versus IT for email usage, it could be seen which IT variables benefited the patient service and which ones were actually hindrances.

Descriptive and Inferential Statistics

First, it is important to look at correlations, especially among the various individual IT variables that together combine to form the EMR use variable. These IT variables are tested separately to see how a variable like "IT used in email" defers from "IT used for decision making" on the quality of care, time spent with patient, medical errors, and communication problems dealt with. Spearman correlations are used for this purpose.

I: Quality of Care

First measured is the impact of overall EMR use or lack of use by organizations on quality of care. Use of EMR as a whole wasn't statistically significant on the quality of care in the multinomial logistic model. This could have to do with it being relatively new and that, though organizations have the technology, it is not being implemented and used after adoption. Possibly also, quality of care of patients isn't dictated by the EMR technology itself, but some specific IT variable that involves how the patient isn't cared for. For this reason, Table 6.1 presented is each IT variable's impact on the quality of patient care.

Using the odds ratios listed in Table 6.2, the statistically significant variables on quality of care were on certain levels of agreement. For example, for measuring how quality of care increases based on IT use on prescriptions, the odds of physicians disagreeing somewhat to strongly agreeing that there was increasing quality of care is about 28% more likely. This means IT used for prescriptions was not as helpful, or possibly not well implemented and didn't generate satisfaction or ease of use. IT for guidelines actually had a positive effect, though those who agreed somewhat on the use of IT versus agreed strongly were 37% higher. For decision making, the odds of a physician disagreeing strongly to disagreeing somewhat was 40% less. Therefore, though the overall EMR use didn't affect quality of care, specific IT variables were in fact important to the quality of care with which physicians felt they could impact patients.

On the other hand, when the IT variables "Financial Incentives," "IT for Drugs," and "IT for Email Use" were tested on quality of care, these were not statistically significant and no conclusions can be drawn to say that they impact quality of care.

II: Quality of Service Based on Medical Errors, Time Issues, and Arising Communication Problems

For the next group of Patient Quality of Service, again EMR use is tested in general by itself. Then, specific IT variables are tested.

When measuring minor versus major problems in technology use compared to a base category of no problems, minor problems were statistically significant on all the issues. On the other hand, major problems were not statistically significant. This could mean that, as a whole, EMR use has produced minor problems due to start-up issues and transitional problems from adoption and implementation of EMR systems (Table 6.3 and Table 6.4).

Table 6.1 IT Variable on Quality of Care

Variables	Disagree Somewhat	Neither Disagree Nor Agree	Agree Somewhat	Agree Strongly
IT for Prescriptions	–0.0331	–0.118	–0.157	–0.282*
	(0.172)	(0.483)	(0.156)	(0.158)
IT for Guidelines	0.421	1.867	0.489*	0.173
	(0.301)	(1.145)	(0.279)	(0.279)
IT for Decisions	–0.512**	–0.552	–0.383	–0.452*
	(0.253)	(0.612)	(0.236)	(0.237)
Black Percentage	–0.00143	0.0117	–0.00448	–0.00753
	(0.00539)	(0.0142)	(0.00492)	(0.00499)
Hispanic Percentage	–0.00754	–0.000692	–0.0130***	–0.0139***
	(0.00536)	(0.0155)	(0.00486)	(0.00492)
Asian Percentage	0.00281	–0.0262	0.00499	0.00783
	(0.0136)	(0.0447)	(0.0124)	(0.0125)
Constant	1.238***	–3.587***	2.382***	2.614***
	(0.241)	(1.092)	(0.220)	(0.220)
Observations	4,134	4,134	4,134	4,134

Note: Standard errors are in parentheses.

* $p < 0.1$
** $p < 0.05$
*** $p < 0.01$

Here, for these issues, the odds suggest no statistically significant major problems with medical errors, time issues, or communication problems. Rather, the minor problems to no problems were statistically significant. For medical errors, this meant that the odds of having minor problems were 12% higher than no problems at all using the technology. With time, the odds of having minor problems was 15% lower than having no problems at all, which is a positive aspect of EMR on these issues. For communication problems, the minor problems were 18% more likely to occur when EMR is used compared to no problems at all.

Next, each IT variable is looked at more closely to identify how they impact each issue.

Patient Quality of Service Based on Specific IT Variables

Many of the IT variables didn't cause any major problems. The exception was except IT used in decision making in medical errors. This was statistically significant and the odds ratio was a 50% chance of having major problems to no problems at all when IT was used in decision making.

Table 6.2 Odds of Comparing the Various Alternatives

IT for Prescriptions		
Category	**Probability**	**Odds**
Disagree Somewhat to Agree Strongly	0.015	1.2829
IT for Guidelines		
Category	**Probability**	**Odds**
Agree Somewhat to Agree Strongly	0.007	1.3721
IT for Decisions		
Category	**Probability**	**Odds**
Disagree Strongly to Disagree Somewhat	0.043	0.5991

This is quite the opposite of what was expected and should be analyzed further to see whether IT itself had technical difficulties and caused errors in decision making as well as medical errors. The minor problems on medical errors mainly resulted from IT used for decision making, which again was around a 30% chance of having minor problems than no problems at all. This is a trend that shows that IT used in decision making may be causing more medical errors than necessary and should be reevaluated to ensure better results or more training should be present so that IT is generating correct results.

With time issues, specifically IT on decision making did seem to decrease time issues once again, which is a growing trend and one of the benefits of IT in the healthcare field. Here, the chances of there being minor time problems is actually 30% less than no problems at all if IT is used for decision making. On the other hand, with communication problems, when IT is used for prescriptions, there is 16% higher chances of there being minor problems to no problems at all.

Next, the last three IT variables are analyzed. The chances of there being minor problems when using IT for drug labeling was actually about 20% higher than having no problems in medical errors. There were no significant major problems due to IT variables.

These also were analyzed under logistic regression conditions where answer choices were coded as only three categories, such as agree, not sure, and disagree. But when this was conducted, the robustness actually decreased because less answer choices are being coded and the model loses data. Accuracy decreases as well because answer choices have to be assumed in one direction or another and biasedly may increase one value in the "agree" category versus that of the "disagree" or vice versa.

III: Computing Discrete Change Based on Technology Use

As marginal effects are not useful when binary variables are computed, such as technology usage which is either used or not used, it is preferred to use a discrete change method rather than computing marginal effect. Below are illustrations of how an increase in technology usage by 1 unit impacts each quality of service and care problem (Figure 6.1).

Table 6.3   Patient Quality of Service Based on EMR Usage

Variables	Medical Errors	Time Issues	Communication Problems
Minor Problem Indication			
Black Percentage	0.000504	–0.0133***	0.0121***
	(0.00214)	(0.00301)	(0.00210)
Hispanic Percentage	0.000204	–0.0119***	0.0216***
	(0.00222)	(0.00312)	(0.00223)
Asian Percentage	0.00461	0.00944	0.0352***
	(0.00526)	(0.00748)	(0.00526)
Technology Usage	0.117**	–0.156**	0.168***
	(0.0457)	(0.0758)	(0.0484)
Constant	0.317***	1.463***	–0.841***
	(0.0597)	(0.0909)	(0.0611)
Major Problem Indication			
Black Percentage	0.0113***	–0.00254	0.0251***
	(0.00416)	(0.00292)	(0.00487)
Hispanic Percentage	0.00564	–0.00299	0.0367***
	(0.00439)	(0.00303)	(0.00471)
Asian Percentage	0.0249**	–0.00210	0.0610***
	(0.00978)	(0.00752)	(0.0106)
Technology Usage	0.0254	–0.135*	0.0324
	(0.0851)	(0.0756)	(0.0955)
Constant	–2.186***	1.256***	–3.803***
	(0.128)	(0.0914)	(0.170)
Observations	4,590	4,649	4,656

Note: Standard errors are in parentheses.

* $p < 0.1$
** $p < 0.05$
*** $p < 0.01$

Table 6.4   Odds Ratios

Medical Errors		
Category	**Probability**	**Odds**
Minor Problem to No Problem	0.01	1.1241
Time Issues		
Category	**Probability**	**Odds**
Minor Problem to No Problem	0.039	0.8553
Communication Problems		
Category	**Probability**	**Odds**
Minor Problem to No Problem	0.001	1.1827

Looking at this, the discrete change for increasing the use of technology one more time causes nearly a 7% decrease in having no problems with communication, but also an increase in having minor problems by almost 6%. With errors, there is a decrease in the chance of there being no problems in medical errors, whereas the chances of having minor problems increases by 4.71%. Yet, the chances of there being major problems actually decrease 0.13%. With time constraints as proved before when conducting the multinomial logistic model, there is a decrease in minor and major problems of time efficiency by 1%, whereas with no problems there is an increase of 2.25%.

Next, the discrete change in quality of care, which is based on five rather than three outcome measures, is computed (Figure 6.2).

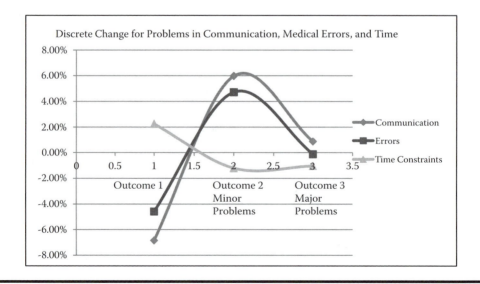

Figure 6.1   Discrete change of technology use on problems.

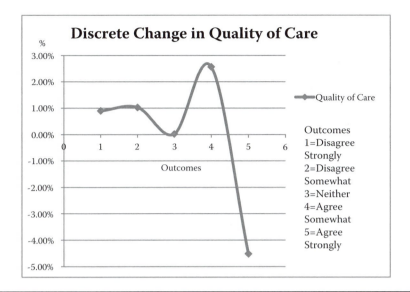

Figure 6.2   Discrete change of technology use on quality of care.

Here, with an increase of technology usage by 1 unit, the chances of agreeing strongly that quality of care improves decrease almost 4.5%, but will increase 2.57% for agreeing somewhat, and increases 1% for disagreeing somewhat. Disagreeing strongly that the quality of care improves increase almost 1% as well. Thus, the respondents are split between the benefits of technology on quality of care, though they are suggesting that quality of care most likely does not improve with an increase in technology usage.

Limitations

The study is based on one survey and, while it has a number of variables, there may be correlates to the variables that are still not accounted for. This may be undermining or weakening the significance and/or changing the positive/negative impact on the dependent variable. Financial issues, such as capital investment, are not addressed and may be included in future literature.

Conclusion

The use of technology has been proved to significantly and positively impact primarily time management issues. Besides this issue, the other quality of care indicators seems to be worsened by EMR technology usage. This could have a variety of reasons. While medical record technology was not statistically significant in the majority of major problems of patient quality and care, it was significant in the majority of *minor problems* that occurred. This means transitions are difficult for employees and staff that are getting used to the technology. Possibly by reanalyzing the survey results in a longitudinal data source in the future, a better research design can be created that will take time into consideration and enough time would have passed to see true patterns and impacts on patients and staff. From this point forward, we want to see healthcare IT solve problems, i.e., reduce medical errors, increase quality of care, and help promote better communication and time management, which can only be done if organizations have stronger tactics to analyze progress and flaws of the system and smoothen the transition (some of which was discussed in past chapters). Time management is already one factor that has benefited from EMR usage, and it is definitely a critical factor as a matter of life and death can be changed by a split second difference. At the same time, a factor as critical as medical errors was not statistically impacted by major problems in IT, while minor problems were impacting medical errors, which need to be taken care of as soon as possible. Communication problems were not reduced by providing IT with interpreter services, nor by IT used for email and prescription selection. This could be because the technology is relatively new and many clinics prefer a verbal approach until they get the hang of using the interpreter services.

In conclusion, there is much hesitancy and insecurity related to the adoption of electronic medical/health records, leading to the initial obstacles and problems faced for first time users. However, as studies have shown, over the long term, the EMR and EHR systems may actually derive greater benefit than the current, though obsolete, paper-based records. Problems present in the current paper-based system include rising costs in healthcare and inefficiency as well as poor quality of patient care and services. Examples of these include billing- and order-based problems, errors and misuse of prescription medication, inefficiency of prescribing medicines, communication barriers with ESL (English as a second language) families, patient safety and confidentiality issues, and occupational efficiency of staff. Mortality rates also are still high and need to be and can be lowered by a better system that synthesizes data and reduces the time necessary to find cures and medical assistance for patients, especially those who are immobile and need care from home.

Long-term usage of EMR should have some seriously positive outcomes for society. This will include an increase in efficiency through the process of completely switching over for the majority of hospitals to an electronic record-keeping system. Improved patient safety and, to a lesser extent, reducing healthcare costs should result. Through a possible link between electronic record keeping and reduced mortality, there is research being done on lower patient death rates under certain conditions, most likely because the electronic medical records systems helped cut down on a combination of major medication errors while reducing the time necessary to make patient assessment decisions. Adverse drug and prescription coding errors are a leading cause of mortality in hospitals and should be followed over time as well, so that EMR benefits and obstacles may be seen with the possibility of EMR systems flagging errors that aren't caught by the human eye in prescriptions, drugs, billing, scanning, and coding.

In the short term, it's not as easy to see the benefits as this study has shown. EMRAMs (EMR adoption models), such as those developed by HIMSS Analytics, allow "scoring to help electronic documentation, funding and budgeting suggested that may speed up management related problems and cut down costs." Implementing electronic medical records, hospital stays can be shortened by "reducing delays in the ordering process for services, streamlining discharge planning, and minimizing complications from preventable errors." Likewise, "automating manual tasks, streamlining documentation, and enhancing communication among caregivers through computerized records" was expected to improve nurse efficiency and result in reduced staffing requirements (Furukwa, Raghu, and Shao, 2010). Hopefully, the short-term benefits will be sped up using such adoption models that can identify the stages where hospitals are at, and quicken the process through benchmarking and reporting.

Technology is the beacon of the future and unless hospitals keep up with the changes that are being made, they will be losing ground on important progress that can be made in saving human lives. For this reason, there must be better ways to transition into it and smooth the process of adoption and implementation of EMR rather than seeing it as a hindrance. There is much that can be done to buffer the process, especially involving staff training sessions, hosting webinars within hospitals, and using benchmarking systems like the ones created by HIMSS Analytics and other healthcare technology organizations in order to effectively measure how the hospital is utilizing its technology. This study shows that technology so far has achieved the status quo and to a lesser extent a negative undertone, so looking toward the future, the effectiveness and efficiency of technology usage must be improved to positively benefit society and improve quality of life as we know it.

Chapter 7

Physicians and Perceptions on HIT Medical Malpractice Lawsuits: Can Physicians Reduce Their Chances by Using Health Information Technology?

Overview

There has been discussion of revamping the current medical malpractice infrastructure. However, one component that should be in the limelight is health information technology (HIT) because it will soon be having effects on quality of care, insurance premiums, and potential reduction in lawsuits for the physician. For this reason, it is important to understand what is holding back physicians from using health information technology to possibly reduce their chances of medical malpractice, and then analyzing the actual effects of HIT on medical malpractice lawsuits, claims, and mediation amounts. For this reason, this chapter does two analyses. First, it analyzes perceptions of physicians and interest in reducing medical malpractice, and, second, it derives a theoretical model of what major factors can be modeled to see effects on the medical malpractice system in the new technological age.

Introduction

Medical malpractice is an interesting domain during this age of health information technology. This is because there are indirect and direct effects of technology on healthcare practices. The use of technology by physicians may impact medical malpractice directly, through improved communication, collaboration and coordination networks across practices and within departments of one practice, and reducing electronic billing, electronic prescriptions, and other errors that occur. Also, there can be indirect effects of technology, such as not needing unnecessary tests that would have previously been needed during paper records standards, just to ensure that there is no lawsuit filed against the company for not having additional tests as backup in case the paper records are lost. What makes the concept intriguing is that many physicians have not yet picked up the use of technology in their practices, as it is still held questionable whether technology may be reducing or increasing the presence of medical malpractice. What is evident, though, is the differences between physicians, as conducted in the model in this chapter, to analyze what these features are, and how to incorporate these features such that there can be some direct effect seen from use of technology at various healthcare providers and the filing of medical malpractice lawsuits on these providers who use technology.

This chapter first analyzes a recent survey, the Health Tracking Physician Survey of 2008, to visualize perceptions of physicians on the use of health information technology (IT), and to categorize those most likely to use IT to prevent medical malpractice, based on their opinions of IT's usefulness. Then, the chapter constructs a theoretical model of how HIT can be incorporated into the current infrastructure in reducing medical malpractice, analyzing older papers that could now be obsolete.

Writings on the subject of malpractice, ethics, and reform provide some background on the subject being discussed. Miller and Tucker (2009) discuss the ethics of the usage of electronic medical records in court, sort of like a paper trail, but instead an electronic one, on medical malpractice, and sees that some states may be greatly impacted by litigation when there are cases allowing electronic medical records (EMRs) to be taken to court. They do an excellent job of analyzing the important features to physicians of small practices and how their chances of being taken to court may change, by state and EMR rules, in the future. For this reason, Miller and Tucker's study will be a good platform for usage for the construction of the chapter being written. This chapter discusses in greater detail the type of physicians most likely to be taken to court for HIT usage violations, and how physicians may use HIT to their benefit to prevent malpractice litigation. Other papers, discussed next, provide information on medical malpractice that has been analyzed in the past, but many leave out the importance of health information technology today, possibly due to their datedness and/or lack of data on the matter. Health information technology actually does impact many economic components of this issue by impacting insurance premiums and the risk predicted to be accepted by an organization that goes electronic; HIT can impact state tort reforms, based on what that state's tort policies are for physicians in the state and total lawsuit damages amounts; and HIT impacts the physician's ability to possibly save himself from medical malpractice at large. Physicians may save time, money, and effort and improve quality of care for patients, in having HIT backup their records and documentation while also having a system to verify their transactions if taken to court. These ideas are first discussed by other works, and then put into perspective through the methods section of this chapter.

Studies on Malpractice Concerns

Many malpractice studies today discuss how high malpractice premiums are jeopardizing the career and interest of doctors in pursuing medicine. The long-standing debate remains on whether the insurance premiums remain high relative to the economy, insurance companies' "price gouging" techniques, and may have nothing to do with the actual injury of the patient or negligence in the case. Tabarrak and Agan (2006) break down the discussion by analyzing the "co-integration" that is present between premiums and awards. This means that the statistical relationship shows a trend of awards and premiums typically moving together, though not necessarily consistent in every point in time. The relationship between premiums and awards is as follows: "the theoretical error-correction mechanism is easy to see: if premiums in the insurance industry long exceed awards (plus expenses), competition will drive premiums down; and if premiums long fall below awards (plus expenses), bankruptcy, exit, and survival behavior will drive premiums up." Yet, the opposite, of awards being impacted by premiums, is not true. Premiums are determined by a prediction or expected value of future awards, and without a fixed mean, this means past awards do not provide an indicator of future awards. The task of predicting a point in the future with few data points is a challenge, to say the least, in setting premiums. "The variation in the average award per doctor is surprisingly large. Mean awards range from a low of $1,688 in Wisconsin to a high of $10,025 in Pennsylvania." The authors point out that it is unlikely for Pennsylvania to have a system that is fraught with errors such that its tort awards should be so much higher. However, what they have not included in their discussion is the possibility that inclusion of health information technologies may be driving the predicted value of tort awards up as well as the price of premiums. The short-term costs of health information technology, which have questionable long-terms results, may be a driver of high costs and higher premiums in the future, due to prediction of higher tort awards from settlements that will be due to expensive law suits filed on technology breakdown and inefficiencies that could be fatal. At the same time, because malpractice premiums are higher in certain specialties, such as obstetrics, there may be marginal changes in the difference in premiums over time, between obstetrics and primary care physicians, because in the long run, health information technology may help to drive down the predicted and actual value of tort awards in these specialties. This will be further analyzed in the methods section of this chapter as well, to see whether certain features impact the premiums and predictions of physicians on their likelihood of having medical malpractice suits filed against them.

A study by Singh et al. (2007) generated the conclusion that graduate and medical school trainees were more likely to make errors, including judgment and teamwork errors. This could be costly to both the school and to the trainee, as malpractice does not condone mistakes. Diagnostic decision making was the most common agenda on which trainees were likely to make errors. This could mean that including years of practicing medicine as a proxy for experience and knowledge of HIT is important, yet at the same time, older generations may be ignorant of technological uses and developments due to the newness of the technological generation. For that reason, there must be a careful balance between weighing the years of practice and those who are of a past generation who have not used technology before for a large part of their practice.

Roberts and Hoch (2008) discuss how medical malpractice litigation has had an impact on the U.S. costs and financing of healthcare. They discuss a Weighted Least Squares (WLS) regression model that incorporates various variables, from time variables across 1999 through 2002, as well as various demographic constants, and, finally, regional specifications and differences in state law policies that impact the cap on malpractice lawsuits filed and claimed. Their model found a positive relationship between malpractice litigation and increasing costs. It is possible that certain regions, metropolitan or that have errors in billing or other issues may be generating the highest costs in the system. The fixed-effect model was a thorough one, but the study may have been more useful had it been taken one step farther to analyze what major types of medical malpractice behavior are driving up costs, be it errors in coding, billing, technological change, or prescribing. This is possibly a more important issue today than ever before.

Another study by Garber and Adams (2007) looks directly at physician histories and how medical malpractice payments may be less depending on the variation in physician background and decision making. The easy access to malpractice litigation history, developed in this study through the indemnity payments made by physicians, has led to an information asymmetry problem found in choosing physicians, especially when patients have resources to analyze their physicians' backgrounds and decide who has or hasn't been taken to court over negligence. The study showed some relationship, though a weak one, in the number of indemnity payments that patients found their physicians having made, and choice of physician. This proxy was not a strong one for the actual medical malpractice history of the physician, as payment made did not have a high correlation or possible causation with having a malpractice lawsuit filed against the physician. For this reason, this study failed to really provide a strong economic analysis or external validity in its impacts on consumer information knowledge and use of knowledge to choose a physician. This study could be extended by understanding what physicians see as important in preventing malpractice and whether certain practices, based on number of physicians present, years worked as a physician, and other components, are more likely to have issues with malpractice when using technology than others.

A white paper by Ozeran and Anderson (2011) analyzes how EMRs could increase liability in the initial stages of health information technology use, but later reduce liability once clinicians and staff are accustomed to the technology. This is an interesting debate. They state that so far, the initial stages have been very expensive to physicians who have seen actual increases in insurance premiums due to the rising errors and initial lack of understanding about how to use EMRs and other technology in the hospital or clinical practice. Harvard researchers who published a study in 2008 found that only about 6% of physicians with electronic records were affected with malpractice settlements, compared to nearly 11% who had no electronic records, which the researchers interpreted as the physicians having an EMR or HIT system as being the reducer in the malpractice litigation as well as possibility for insurance premiums to go down since less risk is involve (Virapongse et al, 2008). Some of the reasons noted as possibilities for technology to reduce malpractice claims and insurance premiums are control and accessibility to patients' histories that is secure, confidential, and easily available; possibly fewer errors in documentation and other steps; and better documentation and electronically available paperwork with a history and electronic filing system in the event a lawsuit was to come about.

Zuger (2004) noticed that physicians of 44 of the 50 states are having major issues with paying the rising insurance premiums and receiving malpractice insurance that is cost effective and affordable. For this reason, it may be interesting to work this into a model that accounts for technology and weighs how health information technology may reduce the cost of malpractice insurance and reduce the overall number of lawsuits filed as well.

Also, Hiller et al. (2011) analyze the impact of states with varying ethics and regulations of which may impact and actually notice rises in litigation compared to the European Union (EU) standards of privacy and confidentiality as well as uniformity across the nations in their EMR adoption.

Focus of the Chapter

This chapter will analyze the impact of characteristics of the healthcare provider/practice and fondness with using technology to see the impact on medical malpractice trials that are either dropped, settled, or taken to trial, and the amount of the mediation award. There are two components to this research question: (1) to see how perceptions of physicians impact their gravity to using technology in prevention of medical malpractice, and, then, (2) seeing if incorporating such characteristics will actually impact mediation amounts and lawsuits filed in court for medical malpractice.

The unit of analysis is the practice, looking at what characteristics of the practice impact the perception to rely on technology to reduce malpractice. Here are two hypotheses that are being evaluated:

Hypothesis 1: The survey will demonstrate that physicians who are highly specialized and using technology will be less likely to worry about malpractice over time, and less likely to be a part of malpractice suits in 10 years.

Hypothesis 2: If extended outward, the data will show that the same number of lawsuits, analyzed by organizational dimensions and adaptiveness to technology, will have differing numbers of medical malpractice suits. This means that organizations using technology will be sued less.

The second component is theoretical in nature— taking a look at data presenting the number of lawsuits filed, either taken to trial, settled out of court, or dropped. A theoretical framework is developed, using organizational characteristics learned from the previous survey findings, to analyze how changes have occurred in technology, simultaneously with the malpractice lawsuits filed.

Analysis

The first part of the research is done using a logistic regression, to analyze the perceptions of physicians in the year 2009. Based on the results, these perceptions will be incorporated into the theoretical model that will predict how lawsuits will be impacted, both in terms of mediation amount and the chances of being taken to trial, by physician perceptions of technology. The theoretical model will use data from 1977 through 1989 and then devise a predicted model for the year 2009 based on assumptions drawn from the first logistic regression that analyzes physicians' attitudes toward malpractice and what contributes to them.

1. Perceptions of Physicians and How Ownership Impacts Chances of Medical Malpractice

    a. $\mathrm{Ln}\left(\dfrac{\text{Probability of being involved in medical malpractice in 10 years}}{\text{Probability of not being involved in medical malpractice in 10 years}}\right)$

    $= \alpha + \beta$ ownership $+ \beta$ competitiveness $+ \beta$ HIT (health information technology) usage$+ \beta$ use of EMR $+ \beta$ year began practicing $+ \beta$% Medicaid patients $+$ more control and demographic variables

    b. $\mathrm{Ln}\left(\dfrac{\text{Probability of level of pressure form malpractice litigation}}{\text{Probability of no level of pressure from malpractice litigation}}\right)$

    $= \alpha + \beta$ ownership $+ \beta$ competitiveness $+ \beta$ IT usage $+ \beta$ use of EMR $+ \beta$ year began practicing $+$ more control and demographic variables

    c. $\mathrm{Ln}\left(\dfrac{\text{Probability of using technology to prevent malpractice}}{\text{Probability of not using technology to prevent malpractice}}\right)$

    $= \alpha + \beta$ ownership $+ \beta$ competitiveness $+ \beta$ use of EMR $+ \beta$ year began practicing $+$ more control and demographic variables

This test would not have IT usage variables as independent variables because the IT variables may then be correlated with the outcome, which involves usage of IT. Instead, the practice's characteristics are used to analyze what features of the physician and practice are impacting usage of IT in preventing malpractice.

Hypothesis 1: Ownership characteristics, such as usage of health information technology will reduce the chances of a physician predicting his/her own malpractice in 10 years. A physician using HIT will be more confident that he/she will not get medical malpractice, showing that he/she believes that technology will prevent medical malpractice lawsuits.

Hypothesis 2: Pressure from medical litigation will be reduced by usage of health information technology.

Hypothesis 3: Using technology to prevent medical malpractice will be impacted by using an EMR and a practice that has many employees, which is specialty care and is extremely competitive in nature.

Outcomes of Medical Malpractice Perceptions

Table 7.1 outlines the most relevant independent variables and their descriptive statistics used in the study.

The results from the logistic regression showed that the statistically significant features of the first model, being involved by medical malpractice in 10 years, was most affected by the traits shown in Table 7.2.

Looking at this, those characteristics that prevented physicians from being involved in medical malpractice include using IT for decision support, the years the physician had been practicing, competitiveness of the firm, number of hours visiting outpatient or clinic, wanting to spend enough time with patients, and percent of patients who are on Medicaid.

There are some interesting reasons for these characteristics being significant. This shows that physicians were less likely to feel that they would be involved in medical malpractice if IT is used; the earlier the year that the physician was practicing, there was a 52% higher likelihood of medical malpractice in 10 years; the more competitive the firm, there was a 70% less chance of medical malpractice; the time spent with patients increases the chances of involvement; and the higher the percent of patients on Medicaid, they were less likely to be involved in medical malpractice by 4%. Competitiveness of the firm, as has been established in other papers and works, can be a proxy for nonprofit or for-profit firms, as typically for-profits are more competitive and goal-oriented in nature. Experience of a physician seems to be an important feature, because the number of years they have practiced may bias them to not want to use a new form of decision making, or may jeopardize their intuition in the field. On the other hand, newer, younger physicians who have been trained since schooling to use EMRs and other technology may be more adaptive and better at using IT in preventing errors as well as malpractice. This could mean that for-profits have a lower likelihood of perceiving malpractice litigation through use of technology. Medicaid percentage indicates that understanding patient mix at a healthcare organization is extremely important.

Similarly, the model run for pressure of litigation is shown in Table 7.3.

This model shows that those using health information technology actually feel the most pressure from medical malpractice, nearly 48 times more than those who feel little pressure. This could be a good indicator of prevention of medical malpractice, especially for those firms of a competitive nature who want to prevent chances of getting into malpractice lawsuits. These results can be justified by Table 7.1 where perceptions of having medical malpractice in 10 years were decreased

Table 7.1   Example Variables Chosen

Variable	Number of Observations	Mean	Std. Dev.	Min.	Max.
Use of technology to prevent malpractice	140	0.8285714	0.3782363	0	1
Use IT for decision support	392	0.3214286	0.4676217	0	1
Use IT for prescription support	140	0.8357143	0.3718651	0	1
Use of an EMR	140	0.9071429	0.2912743	0	1
Year began practicing	140	4.75	1.91595	1	8
Primary care physician	140	0.45	0.4992801	0	1
Specialty of physician	140	3.614286	1.852805	1	7
Number of physicians in practice	140	53.65	44.29186	2	101
Competitiveness	140	2.092857	0.6448069	1	3
Weeks working in year	140	47.36429	2.746379	40	52
Hours providing charity care	140	3.628571	5.934102	0	40
Provide high quality care	140	0.8642857	0.3437147	0	1
Medical errors found	140	0.3642857	0.4829572	0	1
Percent of patients on Medicaid	140	14.02143	15.77014	0	90

by the use of HIT. Time spent on the phone with other physicians and the number of physicians in the practice also were important variables in predicting malpractice pressure. Finally, the use of formal written guidelines, if present, was 45% more likely to be a predictor of high pressure of medical malpractice. So, summing this up, those who had formal guidelines and used technology were the most likely to worry that they would be involved in medical malpractice and feel the pressure from it now. All indicators used in the model are in the figures. Finally, predicting usage of HIT to prevent medical malpractice is given. Again, the entire table of indicators is presented in Table 7.4.

Here, the most important predictors were the years that physicians had been practicing, which increased the presence of technology usage for prevention of medical malpractice almost 80%. Next, the weeks practicing medicine, the number of hours visiting a clinic, and hours providing charity care also were important. Finally, the quality of care that the physician strives to provide decreased usage of technology by 55%, showing that the higher the quality of care, the less likely

Table 7.2 Physician's Concern of Being Involved in Medical Malpractice in Another 10 Years

Variables	Odds or β	Interpretation–Likelihood of Med. Malpractice	Std. Error
How often IT is used for decision support	0.1004085***	Those who used IT were **90%** **less** likely	0.131623
Year physician began practicing	1.524829*	The later the year practicing, **52%** **more** likely	0.27159
Competitiveness	0.3013706*	The more competitive the firm, **70% less** likely	0.141536
Number of hours visiting outpatient or clinic	1.018022***	The greater the number of hours spent working, **2% more** likely	0.009581
Adequate time spent with patients	0.5674514**	The more time spent with patients, **44% less** likely	0.144799
Percent of patients who use Medicaid	0.9650552***	The greater the Medicaid patients, **5% less** likely	0.019093

* p < .01
** p <.05
***p <.10

the physician is to use technology to prevent malpractice. The higher the charity care hours, the less likely, by 10%, the practice was to use technology, possibly because charity care is more expensive to the firm (because it usually is on a sliding scale or out of pocket ratio rather than the full cost of the visit) and it may not require as advanced technology, if it is a basic preventive care need.

Using these findings of physician perceptions in 2009, the study will now create a theoretical predictive model of data that utilizes the physician perceptions and statistically significant characteristics that may impact medical malpractice in the future. This also will have an economic

Table 7.3 Level of Pressure from Malpractice Litigation

Variables	Odds	Interpretation–Pressure from Malpractice Suits	Std. Error
Use technology to prevent medical malpractice	48.08343*	**48 times more likely** to have pressure	42.68953
Career satisfaction	0.1638352***	**84% less likely**	0.179896
Number of physicians in practice	0.98304***	**2% less likely**	0.0089742
Time spent on phone with other physicians	2.621727**	Almost **three times more** likely	1.120052
Formal written guidelines	1.459128***	**45% more likely**	0.3204204

* p < .01
** p <.05
***p <.10

Table 7.4 Characteristics that Impact a Practice's Ability to Use Technology in Preventing Malpractice

Variables	Odds Ratio	Likelihood that Usage of Technology Prevents Malpractice	Std. Error
Year physician began practicing	1.808496*	**80% more likely**	0.3694335
Weeks practicing medicine in 2006	0.793355***	**20% less likely**	0.1082786
Number of hours visiting outpatient or clinic	1.027242*	**3% more likely**	0.0113992
Hours providing charity care	0.9115294*	**9% less likely**	0.0438949
High quality of care	0.5502155***	**45% less likely**	−0.63

* $p < .01$
** $p < .05$
*** $p < .10$

component because the mediation amount of a lawsuit is impacted by some interesting and important economic variables, such as insurance premiums, presence of tort reform by a particular state, the amount of charity care at the organization, and the amount of incentive given to the organization to adopt technology based on the state's charity care incentive policies.

2. Theoretical Model: How Physicians Using Technology Will Impact Medical Malpractice Lawsuits

In 2009, 1,076 of the total 260,000 cases filed in the U.S. District Court were civil cases on medical malpractice. In 2010, this number was 1,120 cases. If a survey were to be done in 2011, it would be useful to take into consideration many of the prior physician characteristics, such as age and experience as well as number of physicians practicing and competitiveness, before including the technology variable, as these are important controls. The technology variable, as well as insurance premium changes and presence of tort reform, may be useful additions as well, because through healthcare reform, many states have identified caps to the amount of damages that an organization can be slapped with. For this reason, the model will be shaped as follows.

Analyzing the two equations below, there should be some understanding of mediation amount under the presence of time, and the likelihood of a lawsuit at a given point in time. For this reason, there is a need for cross-sectional survey data for a likelihood estimate and identification of mediation amount in that time period, to see the impacts on the mediation amount based on the different features.

a. $\text{Ln} \left(\dfrac{\text{Probability of going to trial for a lawsuit}}{\text{Probability of not going to trial for a lawsuit}} \right)$

$= \alpha + \beta$ ownership $+ \beta$ competitiveness $+ \beta$ use of HIT $+ \beta$ year began practicing + ins. premium % change $_t+$ more control and demographic variables

b. Mediation Amount $= \alpha + \beta$ ownership $+ \beta$ competitiveness $+ \beta$ use of EMR $+ \beta$ year began practicing + ins. premium % change $_t+$ presence of tort reform + state tort reform cap on damages * use of technology + quality of care + amount of charity care + more control and demographic variables

Hypothesis for This Theoretical Model

Hypothesis 1: The chances of being taken to trial, compared to the chances of the lawsuit being settled out of court or through mediation is going to be lower than previously, due to technological change and ease of information finding, communication, and better quality care in hospitals.

Hypothesis 2: Mediation amount of lawsuit, on average, will decrease based on the technological changes and increase in usage of EMRs, because EMRs are supposed to cut costs and prevent errors. For technology-related lawsuits, mediation amount may increase. Also some states that have established tort reforms such that there are caps on noneconomic damages may have a greater effect on reducing the mediation amount, especially with an interaction term that includes the state's tort reform and use of technology of the provider.

Interestingly, in the first equation, there is a new addition, which is the insurance premium % change. This is because this number, as literature has suggested, is extremely important in dictating whether physicians have the ability to protect themselves against malpractice. What it also can determine is its correlation to usage of technology, as data should find that over time, technology usage will decrease the insurance premium costs for physicians, as technology should bring down the cost on premiums.

Overall Outcomes for the Models

The outcomes can be looked at from a short run and long run perspective. In the short run, the amount of pressure from medical malpractice suits and use of technology in countering medical malpractice were analyzed. Looking at the results, those using technology have more pressure from medical malpractice claims to begin with and, therefore, are trying to counter the number of lawsuits filed by using technology. Thus, for this reason, a practice's years of experience, reputation, and ranking may all need to be observed and incorporated if the study were to be done again with new survey questions. Next, career satisfaction was an interesting measure for whether or not malpractice pressure was faced by physicians, and predictably, the more satisfied the physician, the higher the likelihood he would not face pressure of malpractice. The greater the number of physicians and presence of formal guidelines also increased malpractice as these are standards set, typically when starting the organization, and would be transaction costs of doing business. Of course, if there is more of a paper trail and guidelines present, patients have an option to sue based on what the physician does or does not do for them during their clinical outcome. These results should have interesting projected outcomes on the number of medical malpractice lawsuits filed. The use of these variables, once incorporated, should reduce the number of lawsuits filed overall, if more physicians are satisfied with technology usage and can demonstrate better techniques in their patient interaction. At the same time, the short term has higher uncertainty of physicians being able to adapt and implement the technology successfully and with higher errors, so there may be periods of higher levels of medical malpractice lawsuits. Premiums on malpractice are also risk-driven, so, in the short run, medical malpractice premiums may increase, purely on the basis of uncertainty of technology driven clinical outcomes, and this will have an impact on physician mediation amounts. More physicians using technology in the short run may have high mediation amounts settled at court because of the costs of using technology and the possibility of injuring a patient being more likely in the short run due to unsureness and lack of knowledge. In the short run, it is difficult to know how the hypothesis for number of medical malpractice lawsuits will behave, especially depending on the type of physician, organization, and many of the uncertain characteristics that were provided in this analysis.

The long run results of technology on medical malpractice may have some interesting, though perplexing outcomes. Analyzing physician perceptions, there is hope that specific kinds of physicians who have already been early adopters and see technology as a green light to doing business will benefit more so from technology in countering medical malpractice. Going back to the original hypothesis, it was correct when the model implies that ownership characteristics, such as usage of HIT, will reduce the chances of a physician predicting his/her own malpractice in 10 years. Specific ownership characteristics that were particularly impactful were how often IT was used in decision support, competitiveness of the firm, how much time was to be willingly spent with patients, and the higher patient mix that were Medicaid recipients. One interesting reason for this is that a physician who has IT and sees IT as a good competitive edge may use this also to generate less repercussions in the long run with medical malpractice suits. Because they have the purchasing power to invest in the technology, especially because the majority of such firms that are competitive are wealthy for-profit hospitals or well-to-do nonprofits, they will definitely invest heavily in technology and use that as a tool for countering malpractice. It could be presumed as well that these organizations perceive technology as a big reducer of risk in such expensive businesses, because their transaction costs for doing business is already high. Organizations with a high percentage of patients on Medicaid were actually reducing malpractice, which is kind of an anomaly because the more likely reasoning was that profitable organizations that have low or no Medicaid patients typically use HIT. While it could be that Medicaid has a more complicated billing system, many nonprofit organizations are adopting HIT, which will more easily translate the billing rates using electronic billing and electronic records. For this reason, nonprofits should realize that they may benefit quite generously by having lower medical malpractice suits. Time spent with patients is an interesting predictor of reduction in malpractice because the more time spent with patients, the lower the medical malpractice lawsuits. This also could be interacted with technology to gain efficiency because more can be achieved by taking notes electronically or deducing a patient's condition by spending enough time, while also having an electronic mechanism to facilitate the process. This may need to be tested in further studies.

These analyses should translate into the outcomes for the theoretical model, which demonstrates that using these statistically significant variables, technology will have a reduction in malpractice lawsuits that reach trial, but, on the other hand, mediation amounts may go up, just by the sheer amount for which patients may be able to sue the physicians because of how expensive technological errors may be. Technology may not only leave an electronic and permanent record, it also may provide patients with an option to engage in game theory and try to blame the physician for every technological error that comes their way and, therefore, reap much higher mediation amounts in trial. For this reason, the state tort reform policies may have influence as well on the mediation amounts won by the patient.

Finally, this model should help interpret the impact of HIT on medical malpractice mediation amounts from lawsuits, and the likelihood of a lawsuit filed going to trial. While currently data are not present to predict these factors, this model may be a good predictor of what is necessary to gauge the mediation amounts in the future as well as the presence of lawsuits, based on a number of past studied factors, such as state tort reform policies and insurance premiums as well as new factors like technology.

The prediction for this model is that presence of technology will lower mediation amounts in trial and lower the number of cases taken to trial.

Policy Implications and Conclusion

This chapter should be useful in identifying how the prediction of medical malpractice has evolved over the years, how it may impact medical malpractice in the short run, between three to five years from now, and, finally, in the long run, around 10 years from now. It will be very necessary to include new organizational characteristics and state-wide tort reform policies that are interacted with technological change, using an interaction term, in new models, because there are multiple underlying factors that influence technology penetration at an organization. Technology usage is cutting edge and may impact efficiency and effectiveness of medical malpractice, while hopefully reducing, in the long run, the number of medical malpractice lawsuits filed. It is suggested that in the short run, though, there may be some mistakes to be learned from by the incorrect usage of technology and mishandling of inefficiencies in the adopted system. It is possible also that there may be an initial rise in lawsuits when technology is not well understood and contributes to some unexpected errors in patient diagnosis and treatment; however, in the long run, there should be some presence of change and progress.

The importance of this subject is derived from the likelihood of the healthcare reform law to take effect and a larger percentage of patients being covered under Medicaid. The reason to study such a topic is because, as more providers see a rise in Medicaid patients, they may automatically see some reduction in malpractice as well, as the earlier survey results in the chapter suggest. Healthcare reform laws have brought about great pushes toward increasing funds in HIT that will indirectly and directly impact medical malpractice claims and mediations. It is highly likely that other characteristics, such as the number of physicians practicing in a clinic and ethics, play a role in how carefully technology is used in the practice, such that medical malpractice may be predicted by the ethical nature of the practice. Age of a physician also may play a role in how technologically savvy the physician is and how adaptive he/she is in picking up new technologies, as well as impacting medical malpractice or keeping the number of lawsuits filed the same. For this reason, the first survey results are fairly important before analyzing a full throttle model of what major characteristics impact medical malpractice claims, lawsuits, and mediations.

A very interesting variable that should be tested in the future is the reputation and ranking of an organization, which is a better version of the competitiveness variable in this study, because it will be a predictor of whether those organizations with better rankings are upholding a higher standard of medical errors and reducing their medical malpractice suits. It would be interesting also to see if they are more efficiently using technology through better training of staff, personnel, better cultural competence, and higher levels of graduate education. They may have the funds as well to incorporate into their organization and higher profits to be gained, so their goals and strategy to adopt technology and reduce malpractice may be much different than nonprofits and low-capital organizations that don't do these things. Government regulation will be interesting to watch to see whether it impacts progress of technology and whether technology lawsuits can be brought to court for medical malpractice. It will be partially in the government's hands to say how far a patient can go in blaming the physician for an error that the technology has solely caused, and where the gray area lies in which the physician has made mistakes himself in using the technology incorrectly or interpreting the wrong diagnosis.

Next up, policy implications may be felt globally as well as domestically. Interconnectivity and expansion of HIT across the United States may be extremely important in producing better collaboration networks and reducing internal errors, almost a way of ensuring better standards for all. Otherwise, the initial players in technology usage may not see any repercussions for wrongful usage until more organizations have caught up with the new technology. Thus, the more organizations using HIT may increase the overall number of medical malpractice lawsuits files, just in sheer numbers, but may reduce the mediation amounts settled at court and the insurance premiums that physicians carry, if there is less risk involved because most physicians would be using the same system. This uniformity could be greatly beneficial to medical malpractice premiums and may reduce physician shortages and provide more physicians flexibility to practice. Globally, the use of HIT will have repercussions on research and development, and many other industries, and if the United States begins to uphold a higher standard of medical malpractice lawsuits, the rest of the world may want to follow in this country's footsteps. While corruption and other issues may have their impact on developing countries, countries like China and India that want to grow and show their global footprint may need to conform to medical malpractice standards set by the United Kingdom and the United States as well as other HIT innovative nations that are using technology to reduce medical malpractice claims. Again, it may have an interesting policy implication on the ethical nature of medicine and how doctors are perceived for nations using technology and those who choose not to use HIT in their practices. HIT may give nations that really invest in HIT a competitive edge that they have since been lacking, especially a country like the United States that has been known for very high costs in healthcare and high malpractice insurance and premiums. Using HIT may help the United States gain back its place as a driver of strong medical services, whereas, right now, it has lost some of its potential to "medical tourism" and offshoring medical services to countries where there is cheaper, low-quality services.

On the whole, this chapter takes a look at the incentives driving physicians to adopt technology as well as how technology is perceived to be impacting the medical malpractice litigation world. While there is currently a limit of data on the subject, the interesting part would be to analyze if healthcare reform and its laws between 2008 and 2012, two years before and after the passing of the law that provided incentives to invest in HIT, have shown great impact on medical malpractice or if it seems unaffected. A possible limitation of the research is that medical malpractice is classified as one category rather than identifying genres, such as the kind of errors made, be it regarding prescribing, diagnosis, symptoms, treatments, or issues in other parts of the process. With a more extended data set and better survey questionnaire, this limitation may be ironed out as well. This research makes a good case for further research on the subject that takes into consideration the physician and his/her beliefs on HIT, state tort reform policies, insurance premium changes, organizational characteristics, and, most importantly, the factor that many papers thus far have been lacking in identifying—the amount of impact HIT has on malpractice lawsuits.

Chapter 8

Community Impacts from the Detection of Bioterrorism Using EMRs

Overview

This chapter emphasizes the importance of electronic medical records (EMRs) in the detection of bioterrorism in the past, and what it may hold for the future as well. It analyzes past cost-benefit studies regarding EMRs in the tracking of bioterrorism and the financial implications of EMRs to society.

Introduction

In considering the issue of bioterrorism surveillance, one must more clearly specify the bounds of the definition of bioterrorism. Bioterrorism has been defined by the Center for Disease Control and Prevention (CDC) as terrorism using biological agents with an intentional purpose. While a majority of "select agents" including viruses, bacteria, fungi, and/or biological toxins are grouped by the CDC into a list of Category A, B, and C biological agents, bioterrorism is not limited to this list, and additions are possible. Because many of these natural occurrences, such as viruses and bacteria, can be found in nature, it doesn't seem right to classify accidental occurrences as terrorism. Rather, it is the unlawful and intentional use of these agents on people, property, or a government to frighten or intimidate the civilian population for an objective, be it politically or socially motivated. Examples of past presence of such agents include *Bacillus anthracis,* which caused anthrax; *Yersinia pestis,* which caused the plague; salmonella outbreak, which caused food poisoning; and the influenza virus that caused influenza.

Since the late 1990s, studies have been done to test the importance of EMR and electronic health record (EHR) systems in detecting and rapidly reporting such outbreaks of agents and their harm on large groups of people in different geographic regions. For the purpose of this chapter and the minute details that differentiate EHR and EMR systems, the two terms will be used interchangeably from this point forward. Evidence from research suggests the importance in switching over to an electronic system from the paper record system as there is great ease of use, efficiency, and effectiveness gains in these surveillance methods along with possible cost savings in the long run and a healthier overall community. This chapter is a detailed analysis of past case studies and research on the subject, as well as a policy analysis and policy implications of how switching over to such a system may cause changes to the American society's infrastructure. While it mentions the current systems in place including BioWatch, ESSENCE, and other automated reporting systems, there is still room for improvement, and analysis of what can be used to provide progress for the future of bioterrorism EHR and automated reporting systems.

President George W. Bush issued the Directive 21 or HSPD-21 in 2007 to promote a state of health preparedness and protection through the use of biosurveillance mechanisms, including EMR and EHR systems (or also known as *automated reporting systems*). After this, President Obama's administration has pushed for many initiatives, including the ARRA (American Recovery and Reinvestment Act) and the HITECH (Health Information Technology for Economic and Clinical Health) Act, which is under the PPACA bill (Patient Protection and Affordable Care Act) that has taken strides to create a fundamental united national healthcare system. As the directives toward greater HIT initiatives came around the same time as bioterror initiatives, this means the two are closely linked in the national agenda and need to be worked on simultaneously. Government initiatives so far have included tremendous focus on grants, incentives, and help to organizations, especially impoverished- and Medicare/Medicaid-based clinics to be granted support for adopting EHR and EMR systems with proper implementation and meaningful use standards. At the same time, a push for biodefense spending has been granted within the past decade as well, which makes their goals quite intertwined. There should be further focus on developing both goals together as they are related and influence society as a whole, as will be discussed in the Policy Implications section of this chapter.

Literature Review

Examples of past studies of EMR/EHR identification of bioterrorism, also known as bioterror surveillance systems, are slowly becoming a more closely scrutinized topic. A few studies have taken place directly by the CDC and date back to the late 1990s when this subject was first being broached. In the first study of Massachusetts anthrax cases in a hospital, the hospital had a well-known brand of EMR, Epicare. The way it worked was that within 24 hours, "ambulatory and telephone encounters recording patients with diagnoses of interest are identified and merged into major syndrome groups. Counts of new episodes of illness, rates calculated from health insurance records, and estimates of the probability of observing at least this number of new episodes are reported for syndrome surveillance" (Lazarus et al., 2001). Using a linear mixed model, the quantitative research shows that the EMR system had the ability to better cluster illnesses that were beyond the norm of day-to-day problems found by groups of people and better identified their symptoms and causes. In cases such as influenza where diagnostic tests are not performed, EMRs were especially helpful as normally nothing would have been detected.

Another set of authors did a slightly different study that had interesting findings. Rather than evaluate the work that EMRs did at a specific hospital, Bravata et al. (2004) compiled 17,510 article citations and 8,088 government and nongovernmental Web sites and reviewed these to see trends on how prepared EMRs are for preventiveness of bioterror. Looking at the results, very few surveillance systems, 29 of the 115 surveillance systems at the time, were designed for surveillance of illnesses and syndromes associated with bioterrorism-relevant pathogens. This may be a valuable focus in the future because bioterror has become a well-known epidemic and could be the new trend for terrorists in the twenty-first century. This means that the building of more EMRs that specifically counter terror threats of biological pathogens are developing in importance to the same extent as EMRs in a normal hospital setting.

The next study is by BMC Public Health, which had a longitudinal focus of studying 250,000 enrolled health plan members in the Boston area over a three-year period. A paper-based record system had shown weak results in four areas: bioterrorism, pandemic influenza, antimicrobial resistance, and growing infections when it was under review by the U.S. Department of Health and Human Services (HHS). The electronic reporting of such problems would expedite reporting in real-time records of current data and patients infected as well as facilitate access to symptoms, causes, consequences, and past historical cases for patients with each of these issues.

After analysis, a Level 1 national standards need for an automated system was reported because this would provide not only rapid real-time reporting that is valuable for trend analysis and efficient data mining and storage, but efficiency in providing accurate medical care to patients. Harvard Vanguard Medical Associates', a multispecialty group practice, main electronic record system is the Epicare system, which is commercially recognized. It uses unique identifiers for coding observations before analysis is conducted to meet privacy standards. Cases that typically go unreported can be assigned a grouping through an electronic system as an extra consideration that could not be done through a paper-based record-keeping system. Even more important, data are not only available immediately, but fewer biases may be perceived in reporting. The study in Boston specifically looks into a narrow field of care, the lower respiratory infection area, to identify the impact electronic medical records have. By conducting the study, it was indicated that having an electronic recording system helped ascertain about 2% of the cases as being due to influenza caused by respiratory manifestations, an important point that needs in-depth research. The LRI (lower respiratory infection) episode incidence rates are easily projected and provide an idea of how soon after the first instance the second bout of the influenza or condition occurred again to the same individual as well as to other individuals. This will be of use when comparing lab reports that identify frequency of a condition typically weeks after the first round of the condition has occurred (BMC Public Health).

The United States remains low on the list in terms of the world's health systems, at 37th place, ranked by a study conducted from the World Health Organization (WHO). Other countries, such as New Zealand, Great Britain, and Australia, have already set the wheels in motion and have developed strong EMR and EHR systems in their countries, making their healthcare framework strong. Looking at these nations, Australia has had the quickest results; by May 2000, nearly 70% of practices were using an electronic format for consulting purposes (Bates et al., 2003). This is due to the wide base of financial incentives that the government provided to assist small and large practices, hospitals, and organizations with electronic equipment. While the United States has started down this path, it has been a very slow and an abrupt transition in comparison to other countries. On the other hand, Great Britain has had a very successful system, though at a slower pace. In 2002, nearly 98% of practitioners had access to electronic record-keeping systems and 30% claimed that all components of the practice (e-billing, prescriptions, etc.) were paperless. Looking at these results from a bioterror perspective, the two are closely related. These nations, especially England, have shown greater interest in bioterror research, especially Great Britain's INTERPOL network (Bates et al., 2003).

Yet, as can be seen from most industrialized nations (excluding the United States), due to government involvement and large investment of citizen's taxes toward buildup of the health infrastructure, it is easier for these nations to subsidize the processes and possibly develop a universal automated reporting system. On the other hand, in the United States, the healthcare networks are run at every level—the local, state, and federal levels—with typically state autonomy, making for multiple types of automated reporting systems (government run, private reporting systems, etc.) in existence. This makes a greater challenge for the United States in linking its state-run and government-run health information networks and coordinating them so they all have similar interfaces.

Financial Issues for the Nation Regarding Bioterrorism

While many research issues regarding bioterrorism speak of ways to prevent it through better surveillance systems and a healthier nation, it is more difficult to analyze how costly these changes are to a nation. Looking from the scope of bioterror prevention mechanisms, proposed solutions have been in the form of bioterror vaccines that have been granted high amounts of funding. Project Bioshield was a 2004 Act passed by Congress utilizing $5 billion worth of vaccines over a 10-year span, yet since the distribution and compilation were not to undergo FDA regulation, there was some tension involved in the Act. While debate has ensued between a prevention and postattack solution, funding for prevention activities more than doubled in 2007, with distribution to 11 federal agencies. Within this funding has been resources for electronic surveillance systems and for this reason, Project Bioshield must be noted when discussing measures to increase automated reporting systems for bioterrorism research. Before discussing different methods, programs, and research that have taken place so far, it is wise to first look into the overall spending for biodefense purposes that has occurred in the past decade, especially in recent years, and then look at such comparisons.

First it's important to consider the current biodefense budget projected for the 2011 year and then work backwards looking at past years' estimations. An analysis by the Center for Biosecurity suggests a 4% increase in the presidential budget, a total of around $271.3 million above the previous year's estimates. This means a 2011 budget of $6.48 billion, specifically for the purpose of civilian biodefense (Franco and Sell, 2010). The diagram in Figure 8.1 provides an overview of the different agencies that will take part in the spending of the biodefense estimates.

The importance of what agency gets the most funding may be based on electronic health records and which organizations are focusing in on developing new automated rapid reporting systems for bioterrorism detection. HHS, which most heavily uses biodefense allocations, should be spending a good proportion of these allocations toward developing its electronic systems, but it splits the brunt of its funds between the CDC and the NIH (National Institute of Health). While some of its projects are subcontracted to other agencies, such as the Department of Defense (DOD) and Department of Homeland Security (DHS) as well as nongovernment agencies, not enough focus has been placed on developing the electronic portions of biodefense security. A reason for this is that HHS has goals that are both biodefense and nonbiodefense related to which it caters. Therefore, even though it has been granted the largest sum toward biodefense, it may have indirect biodefense programs and goals that it will take care of under the umbrella of this money. An example of this is "HHS's Hospital Preparedness Program (HPP), which helps to improve healthcare surge capacity around the country for multiple hazards" (Franco and Sell, 2010). This includes bioterrorism, but is not limited to bioterrorism needs and may include such programs as the National Institute of Allergy and Infectious Diseases (NIAID).

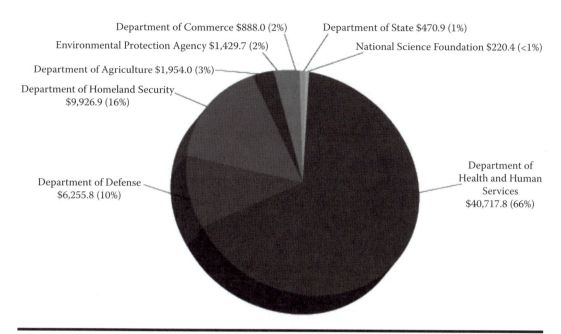

Figure 8.1 Cumulative biodefense spending by agency, FY 2011–2012.

There are also two ways to look at the federal budget. From a long-term perspective, analyzing how the money for the next 11 years will be spent, and a short-term analysis of this year's spending. From a long-range view, only about $11.28 billion will go toward strictly biodefense goals, out of a total of $61.86 billion devoted to the cause in the next 11 fiscal years. This is about 18.23% of the total budget for the next 11 years. Looking at just the 2011 estimated budget, about 9% ($577.9 million) of the FY 2011 biodefense budget is going to be spent strictly on biodefense-related issues for the year, with around 91% spent on a range of issues directly and indirectly touched: healthcare, international and national security, and more. Looking more closely at the Project Bioshield funding trends also is important because it is a long-term allocation of funds, so investment towards it gets used for new projects and grants over extended periods of time. The diagram in Figure 8.2 is again proposed by the Center for Biosecurity (Franco and Sell, 2010).

Next, instead of looking at bioterror as an overarching concept, it will be separated into a range of specific bioterror encounter studies and analyzed based on each cost-benefit situation. Some examples taken into consideration so far have been the cost-benefit analysis of countering the nation postdisease. For example, in an article on the cost effectiveness of defending the nation once the anthrax virus occurred, postattack strategies were created. They included "no prophylaxis, vaccination alone, antibiotic prophylaxis alone, or vaccination and antibiotic prophylaxis, as well as preattack vaccination versus no vaccination." These strategies were then analyzed in a regression model to test for what works best, adjusting for the cost, quality-adjusted life-years, life-years, and cost-effectiveness incrementally. The conclusion derived from such a study suggested that a specific vaccination—"postattack prophylactic vaccination"—as well as antibiotic therapy were both the most effective and cost-efficient strategy (Fowler et al., 2005).

Literature that analyzes both the prevention and postattack costs produced a wealth of data and provided more insight into analyzing bioterror. Schmitt et al. (2007) did an analysis of both prevention and postattack programs for bioterror on anthrax, analyzed a reattach vaccination

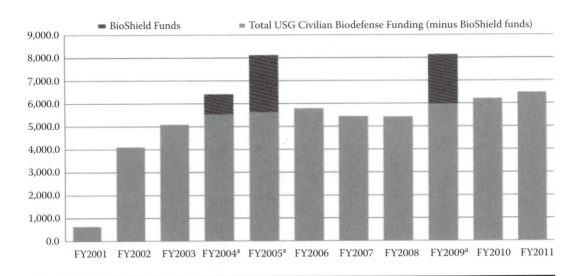

Figure 8.2 Civilian funding by fiscal year, FY 2001–2011 (in $millions).

for U.S. postal workers, and then a postattack antibiotic therapy afterward. The results showed that by an incremental cost-effectiveness method, there was about $60,000 per quality-adjusted life-year using postattack antibiotic therapy *and* vaccination compared with postattack antibiotic therapy alone. Preattack strategies did not prove cost effective. Yet, these studies don't take into consideration the possibility of using an HIT system that may have vital and beneficial results on cost. HITs may prevent redundant tests, better connected networks all over, and lower costs to bioterrorism prevention in the long run. This was a study done in 2007, nearly 10 years after the introduction of electronic surveillance systems, so a vital link is missing in the study, which may be inclusion of HIT costs and benefits from use. On the contrary, other studies have shown that by increasing prevention and detection methods of such diseases, there can be very robust results in cost effectiveness and cost savings. One such study was constructed using a model of three biologic warfare agents—*Bacillus anthracis*, *Brucella melitensis*, and *Francisella tularensis*—and deduced how they impacted the suburb of a major city. The economic impact of the model showed that such a bioterrorist attack ranges from the brucellosis scenario, with estimated $478 million per 100,000 persons exposed, to the anthrax scenario, with about $26 billion per 100,000 persons exposed. The ability to rapidly identify persons at risk also would have significant impact on costs. Because the ratio of unexposed to exposed individuals is around 15:1, it becomes vital to rapidly detect and create preparedness programs that lower the overall "threshold costs" compared to the intervention costs (Kaufmann, Meltzer, and Schmid, 1997).

Another set of articles explore the actual cost of bioterrorism surveillance in reference to defense spending and if the price is justified or if there is some level of price gauging occurring. One article explores a cost-benefit model of actually having a specific bioterrorism surveillance equipment, known as BioWatch, in place, and sees economic gains of anywhere from $1 billion to $50 billion depending on how the statistical life is calculated. In this model, the costs of using the BioWatch program are justified when there is a probability of 1.26% bioterror threat crossed. The BioWatch program also is one to be analyzed further. Deployed by DHS in 2003, the BioWatch program serves "as an early warning system for aerosolized pathogen releases by monitoring high threat urban environments for the presence of airborne pathogens." Yet, again, one of the flaws of this program is that it can't serve as a prevention or early detection system. Due to the high cost, and relatively slow rate of detection, some counter arguments and comparative operating programs include government programs such as BioSense by the CDC and ESSENCE by the DOD.

Policy Implications/Analysis

After the passing of the PPACA and the HITECH Act that mandates EMRs and EHRs to be present throughout all hospitals and primary care practices, the healthcare system is changing and is moving toward a well-connected and coordinated network of professionals who will able to access highly secure data through electronic machines, even if they are separated by large distances of space and time. This would involve EHR and EMR systems that have a high level of accuracy and prediction while also documenting and clustering data relevantly. Through the clustering and sampling, there will be patterns detected in the data that can demonstrate any public health risks, especially those of a bioterror nature.

In this regard, GIS (geographic information systems) and mapping systems become crucial in the mix. The 2001 postal letters anthrax outbreak was one of the periods when GIS served a vital part of spatial modeling and imaging of the areas "of potential exposure" (Rotz and Hughes, 2004). GIS, mapping, and programming are skills that are progressing and will have high impact in the next few decades as the merger of industry, government, and business intelligence occurs. Yet, going back to the original statement, political concerns always raise issues with the level of regulation that should be allowed by governments and/or private institutions in accessing patient records and citizens' information.

Other problems with technology, such as complexity and reliability, opacity, providing good backup systems, design errors, and maintenance, all very much apply in the realm of biosurveillance design techniques (Dumas, 2010). An example like this relates back many years to an occurrence in a Soviet military facility. In 1979, due to an accidental release of anthrax, nearly 60 civilians of the Sverdlovsk community were killed. Also, at the Children's Hospital Oakland Research Institute, a report suggested that there was an accidental exposure of anthrax to researchers when the Southern Research Institute of Maryland sent what they considered to be live germs, but accidentally turned out to be anthrax (Goodman, 2004).

More concerns are lurking relating to the enormous transitions of the healthcare system that will need to be made in rural parts of the United States. As mentioned before, these zones may have the most access and face time with plants, animals, and airborne as well as seaborne diseases (not to mention many other kinds), and lack the critical access to quality healthcare that must be present. Some external healthcare networks are working to change this. As a part of the HITECH Act, HIEs (health information exchanges) will play a fundamental role in unifying the different sectors of healthcare, but progress has been slow and danger may originate from these obstacles. An interesting way to link both bioterrorism and HIT goals together in the United States can be seen through Hawaii's example. Hawaii's QHA (Quality Healthcare Alliance) is a connected system of networks that includes the entire state's HIT network through the stated-funded Medicaid program, while at the same time working with the Department of Health's bioterrorism systems. This way its goals are united to bridge both opportunities together and define a stronger HIT network altogether (Rosenfeld et al., 2006). This also may link with some of Hawaii's proposed budgeting toward a state HIT some day, more HIT conferences, and a strong push for HIT legislation. If proposed in more states, this could be a good plan of action that serves a means to many ends. Also, with the kind of clout that the HHS has and the amount of money it allocates toward biodefense spending, it must take some important steps in bridging the gaps between HIT across regions, both local and state boundaries (Nuzzo, 2009).

Conclusion

Defense spending and healthcare have traditionally been thought of as separate budgets for spending as well as large chunks of the U.S. federal budget in specific election years. Yet, as the fusion of technology and healthcare has become a new goal, the development of the biodefense area of research has blurred the lines between spending specifically toward automated reporting systems for national defense and specifically in prevention of health risks and hazards. This means that more departments have to work together and see eye-to-eye on issues, such as better surveillance and prevention mechanisms as well as pre- and postattack preparations, monitoring, and recording systems.

Many papers have noted past and present examples of electronic and rapid reporting systems that have presented quick solutions and detection of widespread viruses and pathogens, such as SARS (severe acute respiratory syndrome) and anthrax. There is more work to be done in stringing together better networks and coordination of the health information network and providing financial incentives to make these changes possible for citizens. While financial concerns may mount, there is plenty being done through legislation and government funding to provide hope for the United States in supporting a stronger healthcare system. Besides this, individuals also will have to take on some level of the risk, through taxes or healthcare coverage, in order to sustain better healthcare for the nation. More clinics and hospitals will need to switch over to an electronic record-keeping system and link themselves with other clinics and bioterrorism prevention networks as well. This way, the advantages of the HIT network can be reaped early on rather than waiting until the last possible moment to transition and having difficulties in the process. Hopefully, this will benefit the United States in the long run, as European nations and some parts of the world with a universal healthcare system have shown.

Also, it remains important to remember that America is a beacon for other nations in many aspects, and the way it handles the current HIT framework will speak volumes of its abilities to implement a strong infrastructure where it was previously lacking. What cannot be forgotten is that international concerns also persist and remain important to global security. Measures must be taken to get developing countries up to speed on bioterror prevention, security with biodevelopment as the roots so that these countries with persisting bioterror problems are not left behind. In essence, such problems, especially bioterrorism-related, do not remain in the host country, but are transferred to the United States and other nations through changing migration, globalization, and travel patterns.

Chapter 9

Health Informatics and the New Direction of Healthcare: Mobile Health, PHRs, Mobile Health Apps, and More

Overview

Electronic medical records (EMRs) are not the only component of the health industry that has been steered by technological advancements. There also has been rapid expansion in the usage of (1) mobile health, or healthcare applications on mobile devices (laptops, cell phones) that cater to a patient's health in the form of patient-controlled health records, as well as (2) patient–physician interactive health technology (like EMRs), which includes telemedicine and telehealth. The focus of this final chapter is the patient, as patient-controlled health records (PHRs) are an extremely important part of the dynamic electronic health industry. The patient also may be the root of the e-health industry, especially if outcomes are to be patient-focused going forward in the future.

Introduction

The electronic health (e-health) industry is not limited to the presence of the electronic health records (EHRs) and EMRs found in small and large health provider settings. Rather, there are record-keeping mechanisms that are marketed to the consumer who also is typically the patient. The patient looks for easy access to stored records, ways to monitor his/her own care, and possibly a way to connect his/her own records to the hospital's records. This is all possible through a PHR, which has grown in presence and prevalence in the health industry today. Patients of all ages, from the technology savvy younger generations to the eldest senior citizens, are seeing value in PHRs due to how easy it is for patients to have control over their own records and take charge of their condition. PHRs allow for control and record keeping of co-morbidities, public health issues and bioterrorism scares, provide quicker surveillance of disease in a region through instant mapping, monitoring of health conditions, and, finally, prevention of both diseases and illnesses.

Patient-controlled health records, also known as PHRs, are designed to assist individuals in managing their own conditions, health records, and healthcare services. Just how well they will anticipate the needs of patients and improve health outcomes remains to be seen. However, there is some correlation between the growth and use of electronic medical record systems and the spread of PHRs in the households of chronic disease patients themselves.

There are a number of products—ranging from mobile phone applications to software programs to online sites—that provide patients easy access to their own health records. While the early beginnings of PHRs were actually paper-based, the current market contains a combination of computer-based products that store patient data on a flash drive or CD, and Internet-based programs that allow for password-protected organization and input of health information. There are also hybrid-style services that are available both on CD, flash drive, and other devices as well as online.

In addition, smart phones with Internet capabilities that can be used to support health management support tools, also known as mobile health, are a growing trend in PHR usage. "M-health" (also known as mobile health or Mhealth) varies greatly in PHRs. While some mobile applications spread awareness or give research capabilities to individual patients, others are used to support particular healthcare needs, conditions, and concerns. More specifically, Mexico has Vidanet, India has the Freedom HIV/AIDs application, and New Zealand has VensaHealth. Each application utilizes things like interactive games and texts to raise awareness of patients regarding disease surveillance, remote data collection, and epidemic outbreak tracking.

Another large field for Mhealth is chronic disease management. In 2009, the U.S. Army started giving the mCare application to wounded soldiers so they could have easy access to wellness tips, appointments, and other assistance tools for a healthy lifestyle. Moreover, Kenya's "Weltel" application helps HIV-positive patients, while Mexico's "Diabediario" application supports people with diabetes. Other Mhealth applications target everything from cardiovascular disease to heart arrhythmia.

Free mobile apps are provided by drugstores like CVS and Walgreens, as well as the Department of Veterans Affairs and large insurance giants like Anthem Blue Cross/Blue Shield, Wellpoint Inc. and United Health Group, and Kaiser Permanente. However, not all insurance companies provide online programs and applications for free.

The cost of PHRs depends on the provider and the brand of the product, and could be subject to certain changes over time. Because it is just the beginning, there is still limited government-based aid for purchasing PHRs, and healthcare providers and/or employers who are willing to provide free or marked-down PHRs to their employees. Some of the most famous companies providing aid and who believe PHRs promote healthier living for employees include Dossia, Dell, and IBM.

As mentioned regarding the mobile health applications, insurance providers differ in cost and availability of mobile health applications and PHRs for patients. A few examples, such as Blue Cross/Blue Shield and Kaiser Permanente, actually provide PHRs free of cost in some provider plans. The Department of Veterans Affairs provides free PHRs as well.

To reduce disparities and provide these resources to low-income individuals, new pilot programs are providing PHRs free of cost or at a sliding scale to individuals of low income to gauge trends and benefits in usage. In South Carolina, Medicaid launched its first pilot programs to provide fee for service (FFS) recipients with federally funded PHRs in 2008, whereas Medicare launched its own programs in 2009 in Utah and Arizona. While conclusions are still being drawn as to the feasibility of federally funded PHRs, there is work going on between CMS and some of the major health providers so Medicare and Medicaid recipients can gain access to PHRs.

There are over 200 PHR products on the market today. Many vary across format, features, functionality, and how they can be utilized in accordance with PHRs from other provider networks (information often needs to be transferred if an individual leaves one healthcare and/or insurance provider for another). Microsoft Vault, Google Health, RevolutionHealth, and Apple are some of the more famous independent PHR sellers in the market. These PHRs each have high levels of interoperability with multiple providers and are low, if not free, of cost. Of course, it would require that the consumer/patient have frequent access to the Web and/or a computer. Apple has mobile health applications as well with "Drchrono" being used on Ipads. Some of the cutting edge services that PHRs can provide include blood glucose and blood pressure monitoring, BMI checks, immunizations, allergy data entry, lab results, and access to a patient's history of medications. PHRs can even offer guidance and medical advice based on the latest health trends and facts. Table 9.1 is a list of examples of PHR and mobile health technologies in the market today.

Companies involved in the production of the interface, online tools, and databases for PHRs are (but are not limited to) Markle, AHIMA, AHIC, and HL7, among others. Each seems to have developed interfaces that have comparable yet distinct characteristics. Some differences between interfaces include the ability to hold information for a lifetime versus shorter periods, whether it provides prepopulated medication histories and its access, and interoperability.

The Robert Wood Johnson Foundation also has developed projects in the direction of healthcare technology. In 2008, the Foundation established a $5 million program for nine research teams to design competing "tailor-made" applications that would allow individuals to personalize their health record at their own convenience. The applications were for various purposes—chronic illness care and self-help applications to name a few—and the groups included various not-for-profit organizations and universities including Vanderbilt University, Stanford, RIT (Rochester Institute of Technology), and University of Massachusetts, among others.

Today, the e-health industry is moving in the direction of a patient-centered outcomes focus and a telemedicine focus used by healthcare professionals, but the impacts of e-health are felt by the community as a whole. E-health will impact job creation and innovation domestically, but also collaboration and communication globally. It is deriving benefits as well as generating uncertainties in its quest for a better state of health for the world's populations, from bettering mortality rates to improving quality of care indices and medical errors. Yet, with great power comes great responsibility and it will be left to be seen whether the e-health industry causes more help than harm to the world at large.

Table 9.1   Mobile Health Application Examples

Mhealth List of Examples				
Intervention	*Patient Condition*	*Purpose*	*Outcome Types*	*Sources*
Vidanet–Mexico	HIV/AIDS	Patients have the ability to register to receive messages to help improve their adherence to their specific treatment.	Generate changes in attitude toward a self-health care, health risk prevention, and adherence to specific prescribed treatments assigned to people living with HIV.	Vital Wave Consulting (February 2009). *MHealth for Development: The Opportunity of Mobile Technology for Healthcare in the Developing World.* United Nations Foundation, Vodafone Foundation. p. 9.
Freedom HIV/AIDS–India	HIV/AIDs	Awareness; four mobile games spreading education on HIV/AIDS targeting different mindsets and psychology of mobile users.	Not been studied	Vital Wave Consulting (February 2009). *mHealth for Development: The Opportunity of Mobile Technology for Healthcare in the Developing World.* United Nations Foundation, Vodafone Foundation. p. 9.
Vensa Health–New Zealand	Primary care access for patients; no condition necessary	Improve access to primary care services and hospital appointment attendance in accordance to Ministry of Health targets. Daily text messages sent to patients to improve appointment attendance, immunization rates of children, cervical smear screenings, breast screening, flu vaccinations and more.... .	On average, GP surgeries and hospitals achieve 50% reduction in missed appointment rates and achieve six times greater response in recall/precall activities with patients.	Vital Wave Consulting (February 2009). *mHealth for Development: The Opportunity of Mobile Technology for Healthcare in the Developing World.* United Nations Foundation, Vodafone Foundation. p. 9.

(continued)

Table 9.1   Mobile Health Application Examples (continued)

	Mhealth List of Examples			
Intervention	*Patient Condition*	*Purpose*	*Outcome Types*	*Sources*
Text to Change– Uganda	HIV/AIDS	HIV/AIDS awareness via an SMS-based multiple choice quiz in exchange for free airtime; correct answers provided; participants encouraged to come in for testing (fee waived for participants)	40% increase in the number of patients who came in for HIV/ AIDS testing.	Vital Wave Consulting (February 2009). *mHealth for Development: The Opportunity of Mobile Technology for Healthcare in the Developing World.* United Nations Foundation, Vodafone Foundation. p. 9.
mCare–U.S.	Wounded soldiers	Disease management, wellness tips, appointments, and other assistance tools	Helps with changing and maintaining a healthier lifestyle	Vital Wave Consulting (February 2009). *mHealth for Development: The Opportunity of Mobile Technology for Healthcare in the Developing World.* United Nations Foundation, Vodafone Foundation. p. 9.
Pilot Programs– South Carolina, Utah, Arizona	Medicaid recipients specifically; some pilot programs on chronic care patients use of informatics	Testing out low-income groups on Medicaid and effectiveness of Mhealth on them	No findings as yet	http://healthsciences. utah.edu/phc/grants/ pilotgrants.html
Drchrono– Apple app	No condition necessary, useful to monitor any patient conditions, electronic prescribing and appointments	Blood glucose and blood pressure monitoring, BMI checks, immunizations, allergy data entry, lab results, and access to a patient's history of medications	No findings as yet	http://thenextweb.com/ apple/2011/07/28/ doctors-using- drchronos-ipad-app- can-now-receive-44k- from-the-government/

(continued)

Table 9.1   Mobile Health Application Examples (continued)

Mhealth List of Examples				
Intervention	*Patient Condition*	*Purpose*	*Outcome Types*	*Sources*
Nike's Fuelband Mhealth product	No condition necessary	Tracks fitness regimens; it converts real-time data and acts as an app to compete with friends, train for marathons, or use for daily tracking of physical activity.	No findings as yet	http://bigthink.com/ideas/42250
Philips' Telestation	No condition necessary	Self-managing chronic diseases and heart failure	No findings as yet	http://www.healthcare.philips.com/phpwc/main/shared/assets/documents/homehealthcare/telehealth/rpm_452296227751.pdf
Honeywell's HomMed system: LifeStream View	No condition necessary	Ability to instantly and easily see both symptom status and critical biometric information, such as weight and blood pressure; encourages patients to take an active role in their health.	No findings as yet	http://www.hommed.com/News/LifeStream_View_and_LifeStream_Connect.asp
Point of Care (PoC)– separate from mHealth, but still considered e-health	Abbott's iStat blood gas meter, diabetes meters like Lifescan by JNJ, or portable products like Sonosite's ultrasound or cardiac impedance devices	Used within a defined space and are "diagnostics"	No findings as yet	http://thenextweb.com/apple/2011/07/28/doctors-using-drchronos-ipad-app-can-now-receive-44k-from-the-government/

(continued)

Table 9.1   Mobile Health Application Examples (continued)

		Mhealth List of Examples		
Intervention	*Patient Condition*	*Purpose*	*Outcome Types*	*Sources*
Blue Angel	Asthma patients	Asthma	1. Therapeutic and monitoring adherence among children with asthma 2. Saw significant effect on adherence and decreased nighttime and daytime symptoms	Gibbons et al. *Impact of Consumer Health Informatics Applications.* Evidence Report/Technology Assessment No. 188. (Prepared by Johns Hopkins University Evidence-Based Practice Center under contract No. HHSA 290-2007-10061-I). AHRQ Publication No. 09(10)-E019. Rockville, MD. Agency for Healthcare Research and Quality. October 2009.
Health Buddy app	Elderly in rehab centers	Provides instant assistance and alert calls to monitor emergencies for elderly	Health Buddy-impacted having no limitation of activity; significantly less likely to report peak flow readings in the yellow or red zone or to make urgent calls to the hospital	Gibbons et al. *Impact of Consumer Health Informatics Applications.* Evidence Report/Technology Assessment No. 188. (Prepared by Johns Hopkins University Evidence-Based Practice Center under contract No. HHSA 290-2007-10061-I). AHRQ Publication No. 09(10)-E019. Rockville, MD. Agency for Healthcare Research and Quality. October 2009.

(continued)

Table 9.1   Mobile Health Application Examples (continued)

Mhealth List of Examples				
Intervention	*Patient Condition*	*Purpose*	*Outcome Types*	*Sources*
Web-based CBT	Mental health study: Proudfoot et al.	inventory (BDI), Beck Anxiety Inventory (BAI) and Work and Social Adjustment Scale	Improved depression/mental health conditions	Gibbons et al. *Impact of Consumer Health Informatics Applications.* Evidence Report/Technology Assessment No. 188. (Prepared by Johns Hopkins University Evidence-based Practice Center under contract No. HHSA 290-2007-10061-I). AHRQ Publication No. 09(10)-E019. Rockville, MD. Agency for Healthcare Research and Quality. October 2009.
Fearfighter	Phobia, panic disorders	Product on the market	Online CHI app that reduced symptoms of phobia and panic disorders	Gibbons et al. *Impact of Consumer Health Informatics Applications.* Evidence Report/Technology Assessment No. 188. (Prepared by Johns Hopkins University Evidence-Based Practice Center under contract No. HHSA 290-2007-10061-I). AHRQ Publication No. 09(10)-E019. Rockville, MD. Agency for Healthcare Research and Quality. October 2009.

(continued)

Table 9.1   Mobile Health Application Examples (continued)

	Mhealth List of Examples			
Intervention	*Patient Condition*	*Purpose*	*Outcome Types*	*Sources*
CHESS	Breast cancer patients	Support product	Level of info competence, social support	Gibbons et al. *Impact of Consumer Health Informatics Applications.* Evidence Report/Technology Assessment No. 188. (Prepared by Johns Hopkins University Evidence-based Practice Center under contract No. HHSA 290-2007-10061-I). AHRQ Publication No. 09(10)-E019. Rockville, MD. Agency for Healthcare Research and Quality. October 2009.
BtB or Beating the Blues interactive multimedia CBT program	–	Product on the market	On anxiety and depression, had no significance	Gibbons et al. *Impact of Consumer Health Informatics Applications.* Evidence Report/Technology Assessment No. 188. (Prepared by Johns Hopkins University Evidence-Based Practice Center under contract No. HHSA 290-2007-10061-I). AHRQ Publication No. 09(10)-E019. Rockville, MD. Agency for Healthcare Research and Quality. October 2009.
MoodGym	Depression	Consists of five modules, an interactive game, anxiety and depression assessments, downloadable relaxation audio, a workbook, and feedback assessment.	Teaches the principles of cognitive behavior therapy—a proven treatment for depression	http://moodgym.anu.edu.au/welcome/faq

(continued)

Table 9.1 Mobile Health Application Examples (continued)

	Mhealth List of Examples			
Intervention	*Patient Condition*	*Purpose*	*Outcome Types*	*Sources*
Run Zombie Run	No condition necessary	Product on the market	Increase targeting of health/fitness	
Lumosity	No condition necessary	Product on the market	Brain health and performance	http://www.lumosity.com/about/press
HopeLab	Young people with chronic illnesses	Product on the market	Positive outcomes reported	http://www.hopelab.org/our-research/re-mission-outcomes-study/
Zamzee	Childhood obesity	Tracks physical movement	Alleged 30% increase in movement by participants within first month	http://www.hopelab.org/innovative-solutions/zamzee/
Bejeweled	Anxiety and clinically depressed conditions	Video games for youth depression	Research indicated games had both short-term (after 30 minutes of game play) and long-term (after one month) effects; offer convincing evidence casual video games should be widely available to those who suffer depression	http://blog.ecu.edu/sites/poeight/blog/2011/02/01/1252/
Peggle	Anxiety and clinically depressed conditions	Video games for youth depression	Research indicated games had both short-term (after 30 minutes of game play) and long-term (after one month) effects; offer convincing evidence casual video games should be widely available to those who suffer depression	http://blog.ecu.edu/sites/poeight/blog/2011/02/01/1252/

(continued)

Table 9.1 Mobile Health Application Examples (continued)

Mhealth List of Examples				
Intervention	*Patient Condition*	*Purpose*	*Outcome Types*	*Sources*
Bookworm	Anxiety and clinically depressed conditions	Video games for youth depression	Research indicated games had both short-term (after 30 minutes of game play) and long-term (after one month) effects; offer convincing evidence casual video games should be widely available to those who suffer depression.	http://blog.ecu.edu/sites/poeight/blog/2011/02/01/1252/
Re-Mission	375 young adults and teens with cancer	Impacting positive behavior of patients with chronic illnesses, such as cancer, playing video games	Improved key behavioral and psychological factors associated with successful cancer treatment; higher levels of chemotherapy in their blood and took their antibiotics more consistently; self efficacy	Tate, Haritatos, & Cole. HopeLab's Approach to Re-Mission. (2009). *International Journal of Learning and Media*, 1(1): 29–35
IBREAST-CHECK	Breast cancer patients	Shows and videos to demonstrate how to perform breast self-exams, lets you set up regular reminders, and helps you assess your risk	No findings as yet	http://ibreastcheck.com/

(continued)

Table 9.1 Mobile Health Application Examples (continued)

Mhealth List of Examples				
Intervention	*Patient Condition*	*Purpose*	*Outcome Types*	*Sources*
POCKET FIRST AID and CPR	For emergency purposes	Text and video app walks you through what to do when someone's bleeding, bruised, bitten, burned, or no longer breathing.	No findings as yet	http://jive.me/apps/firstaid/
MelApp	For those who want to check for melanoma; no condition necessary	Snap a photo of a mole using MelApp and get a near-instant evaluation of potential melanoma risk.	No findings as yet	htt://www.melapp.net/how_it_works.php

Bibliography

Introduction

The History of Health Informatics. Health Informatics, Nursing Informatics and Health Information Management Degrees. University of Illinois at Chicago.

November, J. A. (2012). Biomedical Computing: Digitizing Life in the United States (1st ed.). The Johns Hopkins University Press.

Collen, M. F.(2006a). A History of Medical Informatics in the United States, 1950 to 1990. Bethesda, MD: American Medical Informatics Association.

Collen, M. F. (2006b). Fifty years in medical informatics. Yearbook of Medical Informatics, 174–179.

Chapter 1

Annas, G. J. (2003). HIPAA Regulations—A New Era of Medical-Record Privacy? New England Journal of Medicine, 348(15), 1486–1490. doi:10.1056/NEJMlim035027

Armstrong D, K.-R. E. (2005). Potential impact of the HIPAA privacy rule on data collection in a registry of patients with acute coronary syndrome. *Archives of Internal Medicine, 165*(10), 1125–1129. doi:10.1001/archinte.165.10.1125

Attar, E., Gokdemirel, S., Serdaroglu, H., and Coskun, A. (2002). Natural contraception using the Billings ovulation method. *The European Journal of Contraception and Reproductive Health Care: The Official Journal of the European Society of Contraception, 7*(2), 96–99.

Collen, M. F. (2006). Fifty years in medical informatics. *Yearbook of Medical Informatics*, 174–179.

Christephero, T. 2005. Information privacy as required by the Health Insurance Portability and Accountability Act of 1966 (HIPAA): Awareness and barriers to compliance as experienced by small health care practitioners in rural West Virginia. Nova Southeastern University, 126.

DHHS. OCR Privacy Brief. (2003). Policy Brief, Department of Health and Human Services, 1–23.

English, A., and Ford, C. A. (2004a). The HIPAA Privacy Rule and Adolescents: Legal Questions and Clinical Challenges. *Perspectives on Sexual and Reproductive Health, 36*(2), 80–86. doi:10.1363/3608004

English, A., and Ford, C. A. (2004b). The HIPAA Privacy Rule and Adolescents: Legal Questions and Clinical Challenges. *Perspectives on Sexual and Reproductive Health, 36*(2), 80–86. doi:10.1363/3608004

Galt, K. A., Paschal, K. A., Abbott, A., Drincic, A., Siracuse, M. V., Bramble, J. D., and Rule, A. M. (2008). Privacy, security and the national health information network: A mixed methods case study of state-level stakeholder awareness. *Advances in Health Care Management, 7*, 165–189. doi:10.1016/S1474-8231(08)07008-0

Goldsmith, C.W. (September–October 2001). HIPAA and Higher Education. *Education Review*, 60-61.

Kilbridge, P. (April 2003). The Cost of HIPAA Compliance. *The New England Journal of Medicine*, 348, 1423–1424.

Kingdon, J. W. (1995). *Agendas, Alternatives, and Public Policies*, 2nd ed. New York: HarperCollins.

Kulynych, J., and Korn, D. (2003). The new HIPAA (Health Insurance Portability and Accountability Act of 1996) Medical Privacy Rule: Help or hindrance for clinical research? *Circulation, 108*(8), 912–914. doi:10.1161/01.CIR.0000080642.35380.50

Mercuri, R. T. (2004). The HIPAA-potamus in health care data security. *Commun. ACM, 47*(7), 25–28. doi:10.1145/1005817.1005840

Ness, R. B. (2007). Influence of the HIPAA Privacy Rule on health research. *JAMA: The Journal of the American Medical Association, 298*(18), 2164–70. doi:10.1001/jama.298.18.2164

O'Herrin, J. K., Fost, N., and Kudsk, K. A. (2004). Health Insurance Portability Accountability Act (HIPAA) Regulations. *Annals of Surgery, 239*(6), 772–778. doi:10.1097/01.sla.0000128307.98274.dc

Privacilla.org.(2003). The HIPAA Privacy Regulation: Troubled Process, Troubling Results. HIPAA Privacy One Year Later: Prognosis . . . Negative! http://www.privacilla.org/releases/HIPAA_Report.html

Schneider, A. L., and Ingram, H. M. (1997). *Policy Design for Democracy*. Lawrence, KS: University Press of Kansas.

Slutsman, J., Kass, N., McGready, J., and Wynia, M. (2005). Health Information, The HIPAA Privacy Rule, And Health Care: What Do Physicians Think? *Health Affairs, 24*(3), 832–842. doi:10.1377/hlthaff.24.3.832

Chapter 2

Beal, G. M., Rogers, E. M., and Bohlen, J. M. (1957). Validity of the concept of stages in the adoption process. *Rural Sociology, 22*(2), 166–168.

Betancourt, J. R., Green, A. R., Carrillo, J. E., Fund, C., and Fund, Q. of C. for U. P. (Program: C. (2002). *Cultural competence in health care: Emerging frameworks and practical approaches*. Commonwealth Fund.

Billings, E.L. (2001). Teaching the Billings Ovulation Method, DCH (London).

Billings, E. L. (1991). The simplicity of the Ovulation Method and its application in various circumstances. *Acta Europaea fertilitatis, 22*(1), 33–36.

Chatman, J. A., and Jehn, K. A. (1994). Assessing the Relationship Between Industry Characteristics and Organizational Culture: How Different Can You Be? *Academy of Management Journal, 37*(3), 522–553. doi:10.2307/256699

Cutler, D. M., Feldman, N. E., and Horwitz, J. R. (n.d.). U.S. Adoption of Computerized Physician Order Entry Systems. *SSRN eLibrary*. Retrieved from http://papers.ssrn.com/sol3/papers.cfm?abstract_id=1002694

Davis, F. D., Bagozzi, R. P., and Warshaw, P. R. (1989). User Acceptance of Computer Technology: A Comparison of Two Theoretical Models. *Management Science, 35*(8), 982–1003. doi:10.1287/mnsc.35.8.982

Deal, T., Kennedy, A., Kennedy, A. A., and Deal, T. E. (2000). *Corporate Cultures: The Rites and Rituals of Corporate Life* (1st ed.). Basic Books.

Desmidt, S., and Heene, A. (2007). Mission statement perception: Are we all on the same wavelength? A case study in a Flemish hospital. *Health Care Management Review, 32*(1), 77–87.

Firbank, O. E. (n.d.). Exploring the fit between organizational culture and quality improvement in a home-care environment. *Health care management review, 35*(2), 147–60. doi:10.1097/HMR.0b013e3181cd1780

Ford, E. W., Menachemi, N., Huerta, T. R., and Yu, F. (2010). Hospital IT adoption strategies associated with implementation success: implications for achieving meaningful use. *Journal of Healthcare Management/ American College of Healthcare Executives, 55*(3), 175–188; discussion 188–189.

Foundation, Delmarva.(2003). Healthcare Quality Improvement and Organizational Culture. Executive Summary, Delmarva Foundation.

Harper, M., Hernandez, M., Nesman, T., Mowery, D., Worthington, J., and Isaacs, M. (2006): Organizational cultural competence: A review of assessment protocols (Making children's mental health services more successful). FMHI (University of South Florida), 1-25.

HIMSS Analytics. (February 2012). Hospitals Continue to Move toward Meeting Stage 1 of Meaningful Use. Business Wire.

Horwitz, J. R., and Nichols, A. (2009). Hospital ownership and medical services: Market mix, spillover effects, and nonprofit objectives. *Journal of Health Economics, 28*(5), 924–937.

Liao-Troth, M. A. (2001). Attitude Differences Between Paid Workers and Volunteers. *Nonprofit Management and Leadership, 11*(4), 423–442. doi:10.1002/nml.11403

Office of Minority Health, U.S. Department of Health and Human Services. (2002). Teaching Cultural Competence in Health Care: A review of Current Concepts, Policies and Practices. Washington, DC: American Institute of Research.

Prince, T. R. (1998). A medical technology index for community hospitals. *Health Care Management Review, 23*(1), 52–63.

Puffer, S. M., and Meindl, J. R. (1995). Volunteers from corporations: Work cultures reflect values similar to the voluntary organization's. *Nonprofit Management and Leadership, 5*(4), 359–375. doi:10.1002/nml.4130050404

Reiter, K. L., Sandoval, G. A., Brown, A. D., and Pink, G. H. (2009). CEO Compensation and Hospital Financial Performance. *Medical Care Research and Review, 66*(6), 725–738. doi:10.1177/1077558709338479

Rogers, E. M. (1962). *Diffusion of innovations.* New York: Free Press of Glencoe.

Roomkin, M. J., and Weisbrod, B. A. (1999). Managerial compensation and incentives in for-profit and nonprofit hospitals. *Journal of Law, Economics, and Organization, 15*(3), 750–781. doi:10.1093/jleo/15.3.750

Scott, T., Mannion, R., Davies, H., and Marshall, M. (2003). The Quantitative Measurement of Organizational Culture in Health Care: A Review of the Available Instruments. *Health Services Research, 38*(3), 923–945. doi:10.1111/1475-6773.00154

Seren, S., and Baykal, U. (2007). Relationships between change and organizational culture in hospitals. *Journal of nursing scholarship: an official publication of Sigma Theta Tau International Honor Society of Nursing/Sigma Theta Tau, 39*(2), 191–197. doi:10.1111/j.1547-5069.2007.00166.x

Stronks, A.-W., and Galvez, E. (2007). Hospital, Language and Culture: A Snapshot of the Nation. The Joint Commission.

The Lewin Group.(2002). Indicators of Cultural Competence in Health Care Delivery Organizations: An Organizational Cultural Competence Assessment Profile. U.S. Health Resources and Services Administration, U.S. Department of Health and Human Services, 1-19. Retrieved, January 2012, from http://www.hrsa.gov/culturalcompetence/healthdlvr.pdf

Vandenberghe, C. (1999). Organizational culture, person–culture fit, and turnover: a replication in the health care industry. *Journal of Organizational Behavior, 20*(2), 175–184. doi:10.1002/(SICI)1099-1379(199903)20:2<175::AID-JOB882>3.0.CO;2-E

Wolff, N., Weisbrod, B. A., and Bird, E. J. (1993). The supply of volunteer labor: The case of hospitals. *Nonprofit Management and Leadership, 4*(1), 23–45. doi:10.1002/nml.4130040104

Wurster, C. J., Lichtenstein, B. B., and Hogeboom, T. (2009). Strategic, political, and cultural aspects of IT implementation: improving the efficacy of an IT system in a large hospital. *Journal of healthcare management/American College of Healthcare Executives, 54*(3), 191–206; discussion 206–207.

Chapter 3

Bernet, P. M., Carpenter, C. E., and Saunders, W. (2011). The impact of competition among health care financing authorities on market yields and issuer interest expenses. *Journal of Health Care Finance, 38*(1), 55–70.

Congressional Budget Office. (2006). A CBO Paper: Nonprofit Hospitals and the Provision of Community Benefits. Retrieved, October 2011, from http://www.cbo.gov/sites/default/files/cbofiles/ftpdocs/76xx/doc7695/12-06-nonprofit.pdf

Currie, J., and Fahr, J. (2001). *Hospitals, Managed Care, and the Charity Caseload in California* (Working Paper No. 8621). National Bureau of Economic Research. Retrieved from http://www.nber.org/papers/w8621

Danzon, P. M. (1982). Hospital "profits": The effects of reimbursement policies. *Journal of Health Economics, 1*(1), 29–52.

Dranove, D. (1988). Pricing by non-profit institutions: The case of hospital cost-shifting. *Journal of Health Economics, 7*(1), 47–57.

Ellis, R. P., and McGuire, T. G. (1996). Hospital response to prospective payment: Moral hazard, selection, and practice-style effects. *Journal of Health Economics, 15*(3), 257–277.

Gentry, W. M. (2002). Debt, investment and endowment accumulation: The case of not-for-profit hospitals. *Journal of Health Economics, 21*(5), 845–872. doi:10.1016/S0167-6296(02)00056-5

Getzen, T. (n.d.). Health Care is an Individual Necessity and a National Luxury: Applying Multilevel Decision Models to the Analysis of Health Care Expenditures. *SSRN eLibrary*. Retrieved from http://papers.ssrn.com/sol3/papers.cfm?abstract_id=1112905

Goldman, F., Grossman, M., Nesbitt, S. W., and Mobilia, P. (1994). *Determinants of Interest Rates on Tax-Exempt Hospital Bonds* (Working Paper No. 4139). National Bureau of Economic Research. Retrieved from http://www.nber.org/papers/w4139

Herring, B. (2005). The effect of the availability of charity care to the uninsured on the demand for private health insurance. *Journal of Health Economics*, 24(2), 225–252. doi:10.1016/j.jhealeco.2004.08.003

Hoerger, T. J. (1991). "Profit" variability in for-profit and not-for-profit hospitals. *Journal of Health Economics, 10*(3), 259–289.

Horwitz, J. R., and Nichols, A. (2009). Hospital ownership and medical services: Market mix, spillover effects, and nonprofit objectives. *Journal of Health Economics, 28*(5), 924–937.

Keeler, E. B., Melnick, G., and Zwanziger, J. (1999). The changing effects of competition on non-profit and for-profit hospital pricing behavior. *Journal of Health Economics, 18*(1), 69–86. doi:10.1016/S0167-6296(98)00036-8

McCullough, J. S., and Snir, E. M. (2010). Monitoring technology and firm boundaries: Physician-hospital integration and technology utilization. *Journal of Health Economics, 29*(3), 457–467.

Preyra, C., and Pink, G. (2001). Balancing incentives in the compensation contracts of nonprofit hospital CEOs. *Journal of Health Economics, 20*(4), 509–525.

Sloan, F. A., Valvona, J., Hassan, M., and Morrisey, M. A. (1988). Cost of capital to the hospital sector. *Journal of Health Economics, 7*(1), 25–45.

Weisbrod, B. A., and Lindrooth, R. C. (2007). Do Religious Nonprofit and For-Profit Organizations Respond Differently to Financial Incentives? The Hospice Industry. *SSRN eLibrary*. Retrieved from http://papers.ssrn.com/sol3/papers.cfm?abstract_id=1826143

Whelan, D. (Nov. 2011). America's Most Profitable Hospitals. Prod. Forbes.com. Retrieved from http://www.forbes.com/2010/08/30/profitable-hospitals-hca-healthcare-business-mayo-clinic.html

Wilkerson, G.(2005). The Future of Health Care Finance and its Implications for Athletic Trainers. Chattanooga, TN: University of Tennessee at Chattanooga.

Yaesoubi, R., and Roberts, S. D. (2011). Payment contracts in a preventive health care system: A perspective from Operations Management. *Journal of Health Economics, 30*(6), 1188–1196.

Chapter 4

Audet, A.-M., Doty, M. M., Peugh, J., Shamasdin, J., Zapert, K., and Schoenbaum, S. (2004). Information Technologies: When Will They Make It Into Physicians' Black Bags? *Medscape General Medicine, 6*(4). Retrieved from http://www.ncbi.nlm.nih.gov/pmc/articles/PMC1480565/

Blendon, R. J., Schoen, C., Donelan, K., Osborn, R., DesRoches, C. M., Scoles, K., Davis, K., et al. (2001). Physicians' Views On Quality Of Care: A Five-Country Comparison. *Health Affairs, 20*(3), 233–243. doi:10.1377/hlthaff.20.3.233

Burton, L. C., Anderson, G. F., and Kues, I. W. (2004). Using Electronic Health Records to Help Coordinate Care. *Milbank Quarterly, 82*(3), 457–481. doi:10.1111/j.0887-378X.2004.00318.x

DesRoches, C. M., Campbell, E. G., Rao, S. R., Donelan, K., Ferris, T. G., Jha, A., Kaushal, R., et al. (2008). Electronic Health Records in Ambulatory Care—A National Survey of Physicians. *New England Journal of Medicine, 359*(1), 50–60. doi:10.1056/NEJMsa0802005

Felt-Lisk, S., Johnson, L., Fleming, C., Shapiro, R., and Natzke, B. (2010). Toward understanding EHR use in small physician practices. *Health care Financing Review, 31*(1), 11–22.

Fleming, N. S., Becker, E. R., Culler, S., Cheng, D., McCorkle, R., and Ballard, D. J. (2009). Financial performance of primary care physician practices prior to electronic health record implementation. *Proceedings (Baylor University. Medical Center), 22*(2), 112–118.

Gans, D., Kralewski, J., Hammons, T., and Dowd, B. (2005). Medical groups' adoption of electronic health records and information systems. *Health Affairs (Project Hope), 24*(5), 1323–1333. doi:10.1377/hlthaff.24.5.1323

Grieger, D. L., Cohen, S. H., and Krusch, D. A. (2007). A pilot study to document the return on investment for implementing an ambulatory electronic health record at an academic medical center. *Journal of the American College of Surgeons, 205*(1), 89–96. doi:10.1016/j.jamcollsurg.2007.02.074

HIMSS Analytics. (September 10, 2010). Impact of Electronic Health Records on the Financial Performance of Medical Group Practices—Track 1: EHR Implementation and Adoption. Retrieved from http://www.himssanalytics.org/hc_providers/emr_adoption.asp

Health Affairs: Study puts a price tag on EMR implementation in small practices. (n.d.).*Clinical Innovation + Technology*. Retrieved December 4, 2012, from http://www.clinical-innovation.com/topics/ehr-emr/health-affairs-study-puts-price-tag-emr-implementation-small-practices

Lohr, S. (2008, June 19). Most Doctors Aren't Using Electronic Health Records. *The New York Times*. Retrieved from http://www.nytimes.com/2008/06/19/technology/19patient.html

Loomis, G. A., Ries, J. S., Saywell, R. M., Jr., and Thakker, N. R. (2002). If electronic medical records are so great, why aren't family physicians using them? *The Journal of Family Practice, 51*(7), 636–641.

Ludwick, D. A., and Doucette, J. (2009). Primary Care Physicians' Experience with Electronic Medical Records: Barriers to Implementation in a Fee-for-Service Environment. *International Journal of Telemedicine and Applications, 2009*. doi:10.1155/2009/853524

Maxson, E. R., Buntin, M. J. B., and Mostashari, F. (2010). Using electronic prescribing transaction data to estimate electronic health record adoption. *The American Journal of Managed Care, 16*(12 Suppl HIT), e320–326.

McDonald, C. J. (1997). The Barriers to Electronic Medical Record Systems and How to Overcome Them. *Journal of the American Medical Informatics Association, 4*(3), 213–221.

Mechanic, D. (2008). Rethinking medical professionalism: the role of information technology and practice innovations. *The Milbank Quarterly, 86*(2), 327–358. doi:10.1111/j.1468-0009.2008.00523.x

Miller, R. H., West, C., Brown, T. M., Sim, I., and Ganchoff, C. (2005). The Value Of Electronic Health Records In Solo Or Small Group Practices. *Health Affairs, 24*(5), 1127–1137. doi:10.1377/hlthaff.24.5.1127

Porter, M. E. (2009). A Strategy for Health Care Reform—Toward a Value-Based System. *New England Journal of Medicine, 361*(2), 109–112. doi:10.1056/NEJMp0904131

Walker, J. (2005). The Value Of Health Care Information Exchange And Interoperability. *Health Affairs*. doi:10.1377/hlthaff.w5.10

Wang, S. J., Middleton, B., Prosser, L. A., Bardon, C. G., Spurr, C. D., Carchidi, P. J., Kittler, A. F., et al. (2003). A cost-benefit analysis of electronic medical records in primary care. *The American Journal of Medicine, 114*(5), 397–403. doi:10.1016/S0002-9343(03)00057-3

Winkelman, W. J., and Leonard, K. J. (2004). Overcoming Structural Constraints to Patient Utilization of Electronic Medical Records: A Critical Review and Proposal for an Evaluation Framework. *Journal of the American Medical Informatics Association: JAMIA, 11*(2), 151–161. doi:10.1197/jamia.M1274

Chapter 5

Finance, U. S. C. S. C. on. (2006). *Taking the pulse of charitable care and community benefits at nonprofit hospitals: hearing before the Committee on Finance, United States Senate, One Hundred Ninth Congress, second session, September 13, 2006.* U.S. G.P.O.

Frank A. Sloan, J. V. (n.d.). Cost of capital to the hospital sector. *Journal of Health Economics*, (1), 25–45. doi:10.1016/0167-6296(88)90003-3

Grassley Asks Non-profit Hospitals to Account for Activities Related to Their Tax-exempt Status. (n.d.). Retrieved December 5, 2012, from http://www.grassley.senate.gov/news/Article.cfm?customel_dataPageID_1502=12892

Sloan, F. A., and Vraciu, R. A. (1983). Investor-Owned And Not-For-Profit Hospitals: Addressing Some Issues. *Health Affairs, 2*(1), 25–37. doi:10.1377/hlthaff.2.1.25

Study of Technology Adoption in California Medical Groups, IPAs, and Community Clinics - CHCF.org. (n.d.). Retrieved December 5, 2012, from http://www.chcf.org/publications/2002/05/study-of-technology-adoption-in-california-medical-groups-ipas-and-community-clinics

West, T. D. (1998). Comparing change readiness, quality improvement, and cost management among Veterans Administration, for-profit, and nonprofit hospitals. *Journal of health care finance, 25*(1), 46–58.

Zaleski, P., and Esposto, A. (2007). The Response to Market Power: Non-Profit Hospitals versus For-Profit Hospitals. *Atlantic Economic Journal, 35*(3), 315–325.

Chapter 6

Anderson, J. G., and Goodman, K. (2002). *Ethics and Information Technology: A Case-Based Approach to a Health Care System in Transition.* Springer.

Burke, L., and Weill, B. (2005). Information technology for the health professions. Upper Saddle River, NJ: Prentice-Hall. 10–206.

California Healthcare Foundation. (2008). Study of Technology Adoption in California. 1–82.

Center for Studying Health System Change. (2008). Health Tracking Physician Survey.[United States] [Computer file]. ICPSR27202-v1. Ann Arbor, MI: Inter-university Consortium for Political and Social Research [distributor], 2010-02-16.

DesRoches, C. M., Campbell, E. G., Rao, S. R., Donelan, K., Ferris, T. G., Jha, A., Kaushal, R., et al. (2008). Electronic Health Records in Ambulatory Care—A National Survey of Physicians. *New England Journal of Medicine, 359*(1), 50–60. doi:10.1056/NEJMsa0802005

Furukawa, M. F., Raghu, T. S., and Shao, B. B. M. (2010). Electronic Medical Records, Nurse Staffing, and Nurse-Sensitive Patient Outcomes: Evidence from California Hospitals, 1998–2007. *Health Services Research, 45*(4), 941–962. doi:10.1111/j.1475-6773.2010.01110.x

Goodman, K. W. (1997). *Ethics, Computing, and Medicine: Informatics and the Transformation of Health Care.* Cambridge University Press.

Healthcare Change Institute. (May 2002). Retrieved from http://www.kathykim.com/sitebuildercontent/sitebuilderfiles/StudyofTechnologyAdoptionMedGroups.pdf

Modest and Uneven. (n.d.).*RWJF.* Retrieved December 5, 2012, from http://www.rwjf.org/en/research-publications/find-rwjf-research/2010/02/modest-and-uneven.html

Scott, J. T. (2005). Kaiser Permanente's experience of implementing an electronic medical record: a qualitative study. *BMJ, 331*(7528), 1313–1316. doi:10.1136/bmj.38638.497477.68

United States Department of Health and Human Services,Centers for Disease Control and Prevention, National Center for Health Statistics. (2009). National Ambulatory Medical Care Survey. ICPSR31482-v3. Ann Arbor, MI: Inter-university Consortium for Political and Social Research [distributor], 2011-11-17. doi:10.3886/ICPSR31482.v3

Chapter 7

Adams, J. L., and Garber, S. (2007). Reducing Medical Malpractice by Targeting Physicians Making Medical Malpractice Payments. *Journal of Empirical Legal Studies, 4*(1), 185–222. doi:10.1111/j.1740-1461.2007.00087.x

Chumney, W. M., Hiller, J., McMullen, M. S., and Baumer, D. L. (2010). Privacy and Security in the Implementation of Health Information Technology (Electronic Health Records): U.S. and EU Compared. Retrieved from http://works.bepress.com/wade_chumney/1

Do Policies That Target Physicians Who Make Medical Malpractice Payments Reduce Negligent Injuries? | RAND. (n.d.). Retrieved December 5, 2012, from http://www.rand.org/pubs/research_briefs/RB9280/index1.html

Miller, A. R., and Tucker, C. (2011). Electronic Discovery and the Adoption of Information Technology. *SSRN eLibrary*. Retrieved from http://papers.ssrn.com/sol3/papers.cfm?abstract_id=1421244

Ozeran, L., and Anderson, M. (n.d). Do EHRs Increase Insurance Liability : A White Paper.

Plans, The Association of Washington Healthcare. (2004). Rising Health Care Costs: What Factors are Driving Increases?

Roberts, B., and Hoch, I. (2007). Malpractice litigation and medical costs in Mississippi. *Health Economics, 16*(8), 841–859. doi:10.1002/hec.1195

Roberts, B., and Hoch, I. (2009). Malpractice litigation and medical costs in the United States. *Health Economics, 18*(12), 1394–1419. doi:10.1002/hec.1436

Singh, H., Thomas, E. J., Petersen, L. A., and Studdert, D. M. (2007). Medical errors involving trainees: A study of closed malpractice claims from 5 insurers. *Archives of Internal Medicine, 167*(19), 2030–2036. doi:10.1001/archinte.167.19.2030

Study: Electronic medical records reduce malpractice claims. (2008).*Computerworld*. Retrieved December 5, 2012, from http://www.computerworld.com/s/article/9122063/Study_Electronic_medical_records_reduce_malpractice_claims

Taborrak, A., and Agan, A.. (2006). Medical Malpractice Awards, Insurance, and Negligence: Which Are Related?: *Civil Justice Report*. Center for Legal Policy at the Manhattan Institute.

Virapongse, A., Bates, D. W., Shi, P., Jenter, C. A., Volk, L. A., Kleinman, K., Sato, L., et al. (2008). Electronic health records and malpractice claims in office practice. *Archives of Internal Medicine, 168*(21), 2362–2367. doi:10.1001/archinte.168.21.2362

Zuger, A. (2004). Dissatisfaction with medical practice. *The New England Journal of Medicine, 350*(1), 69–75. doi:10.1056/NEJMsr031703

Chapter 8

Bates, D. W., Ebell, M., Gotlieb, E., Zapp, J., and Mullins, H. C. (2003). A Proposal for Electronic Medical Records in U.S. Primary Care. *Journal of the American Medical Informatics Association: JAMIA, 10*(1), 1–10. doi:10.1197/jamia.M1097

Bellazzini, M. A., and Svenson, J. (2008). Discrete Data from Electronic Medical Records—Next Generation Data Sets for Syndromic Surveillance. Advances in Disease Surveillance 5.

Bravata, D. M., McDonald, K. M., Smith, W. M., Rydzak, C., Szeto, H., Buckeridge, D. L., Haberland, C., et al. (2004). Systematic review: surveillance systems for early detection of bioterrorism-related diseases. *Annals of Internal Medicine, 140*(11), 910–922.

Buckeridge, D. L., Graham, J., O'Connor, M. J., Choy, M. K., Tu, S. W., and Musen, M. A. (2002). Knowledge-based bioterrorism surveillance. Proceedings/AMIA ... Annual Symposium. AMIA Symposium, 76–80.

Dumas, L. J. (2010). The Technology Trap: Where Human Error and Malevolence Meet Powerful Technologies. Praeger.

Enhancing regional anti-bioterrorism efforts focus of New Zealand INTERPOL training session. (Feb 23, 2010.) Retrieved from http://www.interpol.int/public/ICPO/PressReleases/PR2010/News20100223.asp

Fowler, R. A., Sanders, G. D., Bravata, D. M., Nouri, B., Gastwirth, J. M., Peterson, D., Broker, A. G., et al. (2005). Cost-effectiveness of defending against bioterrorism: a comparison of vaccination and antibiotic prophylaxis against anthrax. *Annals of Internal Medicine, 142*(8), 601–610.

Goodman, L. (2004). Biodefense cost and consequence. *Journal of Clinical Investigation, 114*(1), 2–3. doi:10.1172/JCI22418

Hammond, W. E. (2004). Electronic Medical Records: Getting it Right and Going to Scale. Commonwealth Fund.

Haynay, J. (2007).Missouri Hospitals Launch Syndromic Surveillance System to Track Early Signs of Bioterrorism or Disease Outbreaks. Robert Wood Johnson Foundation.

Hripcsak, G., Soulakis, N. D., Li, L., Morrison, F. P., Lai, A. M., Friedman, C., Calman, N. S., et al. (2009). Syndromic surveillance using ambulatory electronic health records. *Journal of the American Medical Informatics Association: JAMIA, 16*(3), 354–361. doi:10.1197/jamia.M2922

Hutwagner, L., Thompson, W., Seeman, G. M., and Treadwell, T. (2003). The bioterrorism preparedness and response Early Aberration Reporting System (EARS). *Journal of Urban Health: bulletin of the New York Academy of Medicine, 80*(2 Suppl 1), i89–96.

Kaufmann, A. F., Meltzer, M. I., and Schmid, G. P. (1997). The economic impact of a bioterrorist attack: are prevention and postattack intervention programs justifiable? *Emerging infectious diseases, 3*(2), 83–94. doi:10.3201/eid0302.970201

Kleinman, K., Lazarus, R., and Platt, R. (2004). A generalized linear mixed models approach for detecting incident clusters of disease in small areas, with an application to biological terrorism. *American Journal of Epidemiology, 159*(3), 217–224.

Klompas, M., et al. (2008). Automated Detection and Reporting of Notifiable Diseases Using Electronic Medical Records Versus Passive Surveillance. Massachusetts. June 2006-July 2007. Center for Disease Control and Prevention, *Morbidity and Mortality Weekly Report*, 373–376.

Kohane, I. S. (2002). The Contributions of Biomedical Informatics to the Fight Against Bioterrorism. *Journal of the American Medical Informatics Association: JAMIA, 9*(2), 116–119. doi:10.1197/jamia.M1054

Lazarus, R, Kleinman, K. P., Dashevsky, I., DeMaria, A., and Platt, R. (2001). Using automated medical records for rapid identification of illness syndromes (syndromic surveillance): the example of lower respiratory infection. *BMC Public Health*, 1, 9.

Lazarus, R., Kleinman, K., Dashevsky, I., Adams, C., Kludt, P., DeMaria, A., and Platt, R. (2002). Use of Automated Ambulatory-Care Encounter Records for Detection of Acute Illness Clusters, Including Potential Bioterrorism Events. *Emerging Infectious Diseases, 8*(8), 753–760. doi:10.3201/eid0808.020239

Martin, S. (n.d.). The Federal Goal of Making All Healthcare Records Electronic By 2014: Differing Viewpoints. Retrieved December 5, 2012, from http://www.libsearch.com/view/595279

Nuzzo, J. B. (2009). Developing a National Biosurveillance Program. *Biosecurity and Bioterrorism: Biodefense Strategy, Practice, and Science, 7*(1), 37–38. doi:10.1089/bsp.2009.1006

Nuzzo, J. (2005). The Global Outbreak Alert and Response Network (GOARN). *International Conference on Biosafety and Biorisks*,1.

Rosenfield, S., Koss, S., Caruth, K., and Fuller, G. (2006). Evolution of State Health Information Exchange/A Study of a Vision, Strategy, and Progress. 1-77.

Rotz, L. D., and Hughes, J. M. (2004). Advances in detecting and responding to threats from bioterrorism and emerging infectious disease. *Nature Medicine, 10*(12 Suppl), S130–136. doi:10.1038/nm1152

Schmitt B. et al. (2007). Responding to a small-scale bioterrorist anthrax attack: Cost-effectiveness analysis comparing preattack vaccination with postattack antibiotic treatment and vaccination. *Archives of Internal Medicine, 167*(7), 655–662. doi:10.1001/archinte.167.7.655

Tice, A. D., Kishimoto, M., Dinh, C. H., Lam, G. T.-K., and Marineau, M. (2006). Knowledge of severe acute respiratory syndrome among community physicians, nurses, and emergency medical responders. *Prehospital and Disaster Medicine, 21*(3), 183–189.

Uscher-Pines, L., Babin, S. M., Farrell, C. L., Hsieh, Y.-H., Moskal, M. D., Gaydos, C. A., and Rothman, R. E. (2010). Research priorities for syndromic surveillance systems response: consensus development using nominal group technique. *Journal of Public Health Management and Practice: JPHMP, 16*(6), 529–534. doi:10.1097/PHH.0b013e3181c7c9bd

Chapter 9

Cassil, Alwyn. (2009). Insurer Personal Health Records (PHRs): Can They Bridge the Information Gap? *Health Affairs*. March 10.

Center for Medicaid and Medicare Services. (2011). CMS Personal Health Record Pilots in South Carolina, Arizona, Utah. September 8.

Council, AHIMA Personal Health Record Practice. (n.d.).Helping Consumers Select PHRs: Questions and Considerations for Navigating an Emerging Market.

Cox, T. HIPAA in Kentucky's Local Health Departments. (2004).Retrieved from http://www.mc.uky.edu/kphli/documents/masterprojects/HIPAA_final_2002.pdf

Hart, B. (n.d.). Health care cell phone apps gain popularity—Dayton Business Journal. Retrieved December 5, 2012, from http://www.bizjournals.com/dayton/news/2011/02/18/health-care-smartphone-apps-gain.html?page=all

Horowitz, B. T. (n.d.). Apple iPad Health Care Check-in App Cuts Duplicate Data Entry. Retrieved December 5, 2012, from http://www.eweek.com/c/a/Health-Care-IT/Apple-iPad-Health-Care-Checkin-App-Cuts-Duplicate-Data-Entry-143913/

Keckley, P. H., and Chung, B. (2011). The Mobile Personal Health Record: Technology-Enabled Self-Care. Deloitte Center for Health Solutions. June. Retrieved from http://www.deloitte.com/assets/Dcom-Mexico/Local%20Assets/Documents/mx(es-mx)Mobile%20Personal%20Health%20Record_2010.pdf.

Misra, S. (n.d.). M'obiSante mobile ultrasound live demonstration at the mHealth Summit, update on Android support #mHS11. *iMedicalApps*. Retrieved December 5, 2012, from http://www.imedicalapps.com/2011/12/mobisante-ultrasound-live-demonstration-mhealth-summit-update-android-support-mhs11/

Index

A

Accounting costs, 40–41
Agan, A., 99
Agency for Health Research and Quality (AHRQ), 11,
    52
AHIC, 121
AHIMA, 121
American Hospital Association (AHA), 8
American Recovery and Reinvestment Act (ARRA), 16,
    29, 51, 64, 112
Amish, 37
Anderson, G. F., 56
Anderson, M., 100
Anthrax, 111, 112, 115–116, 117, 118
Apple mobile health applications, 121
Arbitrage Pricing Theory, 41
Ardent Health Services, 43
Australia, 113

B

Bacillus anthracis, 111, 116, *See also* Anthrax
Beating the Blues (BtB), 127*t*
Bejeweled, 128*t*
Bernet, P. M., 44–45
Betancourt, J. R., 25
Billings Ovulation Method, 24
Bioterrorism surveillance, 111–118
    literature review, 112–113
    policy implications/analysis, 117–118
    programs and financial issues, 114–117
BioWatch, 112, 116
Bird, E. J., 21
Blue Angel, 125*t*
Blue Cross/Blue Shield, 120
Bluefield Regional Medical Center, 43
BMC Public Health, 113
Bond ratings, 28–29
Bonds, tax-exempt, 44
Bonuses, 21

Bookworm, 129*t*
Bounded rationality for technology introduction, 48
Bravata, D. M., 112
Brucella melitensis, 116
Burton, L. C., 56

C

Capital Asset Pricing Model, 41
Carpenter, C. E., 44–45
Carrillo, J. E., 25
Center for Biosecurity, 114
Center for Medicaid and Medicare Services (CMS), 18
    aid for adopting EMR systems, 53
    HIPAA coverage and compliance and, 3
    reimbursement potential for technology adoption, 46
Centers for Disease Control (CDC), 18, 111
CEO compensation issues, 45–46
Charity care patients, 41
Cherry-picking, 40, 41, 48
CHESS, 127*t*
Chi² test, 66, 71, 86
Children's medical records, parental access, 9
Christerepho, Tracy, 11
Chronic disease management, 120
Citizens Memorial Hospital (CMH), Missouri, 29
Clark Regional Medical Center, 43
Clinical Information System (CIS), 85
Cohen, S. H., 53
Collaboration, 30–31
College student medical records, 9
Communication problems, EMR system use and,
    88–90, 94
Community health centers, *See also* Government
        hospitals
    culturally diverse patient mix, 24
    e-billing systems, 74–76
    economic issues of technology adoption, 42
    e-prescribing, 76–78
    health information technology funding, 47
    HIPAA and privacy considerations, 5

Medicaid incentive benefits, 82
organizational culture and information technology
adoption, 16
state funding differences, 29–30
switch from private to charity care, 39
Community health needs assessments, 31
Community Health Systems, 43
Community impacts of health information technology
use, 79
IRS guidelines, 19, 83
public health reporting, 79–81, 83
Community Tracking Study (CTS), 87
Compensation issues, 20–23, 45–46
Competition, 40
bond markets and, 44
health information exchanges and, 55
rural hospitals and, 23, 29
Competitiveness, malpractice litigation risk perceptions
and, 102, 107, 108
Computerized Personal Record System (CPR), 58
Computerized physician order entry (CPOE) system,
24, 30
Confidential information, malpractice considerations, 8
Congress, HIPAA and, 6–7
Continuity of Care Record, 54, 59
Corporate culture, *See* Organizational culture
differences, HIT adoption and
Cost-benefit analysis, electronic medical record system
adoption, 52, 55–61
Cross-functional teams, 65
Cultural competence, 25–28
Cultural diversity issues, *See also* Minorities
cultural competence of hospitals, 25–28
quality of care for minorities, 86–87
training, 23–24
translation, 23–24

D

Danzon, P. M., 40
Deal, T., 17–18, 20
Delmarva Foundation, 25
Demand side of healthcare, 39
Deregulation, 3
Desmidt, S., 18
DesRoches, C. M., 53, 86
Developed nations, EMR systems and, 61
Diabediario application, 120
Diagnostic-related group (DRG), 49
Diversity, *See* Cultural diversity issues; Minorities
Drchrono, 121, 123*t*

E

Economies of scale, 43
Elderly patients or senior citizens, 71, 78, 82
Electronic billing (e-billing) systems, 23, 74–76, 82, 83

Electronic health (e-health) industry, 119
patient-controlled health records, 119–121
Electronic health record (EHR) system, *See also*
Electronic medical record (EMR) systems
bioterrorism surveillance, 111–118, *See also*
Bioterrorism surveillance
government incentives and funding, 58–59
health information exchanges and, 55, *See also*
Health information exchanges
HIMSS Stage 7 award, 30
installation costs, 55
integrated model, 59
Medicaid EHR Incentive program, 59, 83
patient fees, 55–58, 61
Electronic medical record (EMR) systems, *See also*
Electronic health record (EHR) system;
Health information technology
bioterrorism surveillance and, 111–118, *See also*
Bioterrorism surveillance
developed nations and, 61
financial barriers, 52
government funding, 52
health care reform and requirements, 54
health information exchanges and, 60, *See also*
Health information exchanges
HIPAA and privacy requirements, 59, *See also* Health
Information Privacy and Accountability Act
HITECH Act, 16, 52, *See also* HITECH Act
malpractice litigation risk, 98, *See also* Medical
malpractice
Medicaid/Medicare patient mix and usage, 71, 82
need for, 52
new or replacement system installation, 72–74
new physician culture, 53
patient-controlled health records, 120
physician employment status and usage, 71
potential benefits of, 51
quality of care impacts, 85–95, *See also* Quality of
care, impacts of EMR systems
return on investment and, 53
shortening length of stays, 94
smaller hospitals and, 53
standardization, 54
translation, 23–24
user and nonuser characteristics, 53
Electronic medical records, financing and adopting,
51–52
background factors, 52–54
cost-benefit evaluation, 52, 55–61
government incentives and funding, 52, 58–59
patient base and, 53–54
patient fees, 55–58
penalties and incentives, 52–53
policy analysis, 54–55
Electronic prescriptions (e-prescribing), 76–78, 82
Ellis, R. P., 38
EMR, *See* Electronic medical record (EMR) systems

EMR adoption models (EMRAMs), 55, 60–61, 94, *See also* HIMSS (Healthcare Information and Management Systems Society) Adoption Model
English as a second language (ESL) patients, 25
Epicare, 112, 113
E-reporting on public health issues, 79–81, 83
Ethical considerations, health care research, 10–11
Executive incentives and compensation structure, 20–23, 45–46

F

Family Education Rights and Privacy Act (FERPA), 9
Family physicians, use of EMRs, 53
Family planning services, 9, 24
Fearfighter, 126*t*
Food and Drug Administration (FDA), 3
For-profit hospitals, 39
    bounded rationality for technology introduction, 48
    cherry-picking, 40, 41, 48
    competitiveness metric, 102
    financing structure, 35, 38, *See also* Hospital financing
    management characteristics and HIT usage, *See* Organizational behavior characteristics, impact on HIT usage
    mergers and acquisitions of nonprofit hospitals, 42, *See also* Mergers and acquisitions
    mission of, 38
    organizational culture and HIT adoption, 15, *See also* Organizational culture differences, HIT adoption and
        achievement differences, 29
        cultural competence and, 25, 28
        incentives and compensation structure, 20–21
        missions and values, 18
    patient type selection behavior, 48
    profitable services, 41–42
    stages of technology adoption and implementation, 16
Forum Health, 43
Francisella tularensis, 116
Free clinics, 24
Freedom HIV/AIDS application, 120, 122*t*
Free markets and healthcare, 4
Free rider problem, 5, 38, 65

G

Getzen, T., 36
Goal-oriented hospital behavior, 28–31
Google Health, 121
Government funding, 29
    differences across states, 29–30
    incentives for EMR system adoption, 52, 58–59
    physician incentives and, 47

Government hospitals, 39
    causes of failures, 30
    e-billing systems, 74–76
    economic issues of technology adoption, 42
    financial differences across, 29–30
    health information technology funding, 47
    mission of, 38
    organizational culture and HIT adoption, 15, *See also* Organizational culture differences, HIT adoption and
        cultural competence and, 25, 27
        missions and values, 18
        theoretical models, 17–18
    stages of technology adoption and implementation, 16
Graduate school trainees, 99
Great Britain, 113
Green, A. R., 25
Grieger, D. L., 53
Gupta, Sanjay, 79
Gynecology services, 37, 76, 78, 82

H

Harvard Vanguard Medical Associates, 113
Hawaii, Quality Healthcare Alliance, 117
Health Buddy app, 125*t*
Healthcare Change Institute (HCI), 86
Healthcare costs, 3
    malpractice litigation and, 99–100
Healthcare economics, 35–37, *See also* Hospital financing
    absolute versus relative costs, 39
    demand side, 38
    differences in insurance needs, 36–37
    history of, 49
    management performance and, 45–46
    policy analysis and implications, 48–49
    supply side, 37–38
    switch from private to charity care, 39
Healthcare personnel diversity, 25
Health care reform law, *See* Patient Protection and Affordable Care Act
Healthcare reform politics, 53
Health care research, privacy and ethical considerations, 10–11
Healthcare's Centricity EMR system, 55
Healthcare spending, 49
Healthcare workers, HIPAA stakeholders, 7–8
Health information exchanges (HIEs), 41, 55, 60, 117
Health Information Privacy and Accountability Act (HIPAA), 1–3
    compliance costs, 8
    EMR requirements, 59
    enforcement and interpretation, 2
    entities required to comply with, 3
    Health Plan Identifier, 2–3

making the policy window, 3–4
policy analysis and implications, 11–12
public choice theory, 4–6
stakeholder analysis, 4
    Congress, 6–7
    healthcare provider staff, 7–8
    insurance companies/third-party providers, 10
    patients and healthcare consumers, 9–10
    researchers, 10–11
transparency issues, 11
Health information technology (HIT), *See also*
        Electronic medical record (EMR) systems
    bond ratings and, 28–29
    community impacts, 79
    horizontal and vertical integration, 46–47
    medical malpractice and, 20, 97–109, *See also*
        Medical malpractice
    organizational behavior characteristics and usage,
        See Organizational behavior characteristics,
        impact on HIT usage
    potential benefits of, 1
    stages of technology use, 16, 100
        measurement issues, 47
    standardization, 54, 109
    technology adoption as sunk cost, 38, 41
Health Information Technology for Economic and
        Clinical Health, *See* HITECH Act
Health insurance
    differences in individual need for, 36–37
    low-income and uninsured patients, 39
    mandate for required insurance, 39
Health insurance providers, *See* Insurance providers
Health literacy initiatives, 25
Health maintenance organizations (HMOs), 40, 41, 72
Health outcomes research, impact of privacy regulations,
        11
Health Plan Identifier (HPID), 2–3
Health Professional Shortage Area, 83
Health records privacy, *See* Health Information Privacy
        and Accountability Act
HealthTexas, 55
Heene, A., 18
Herring, B., 39
Hiller, J., 100
HIMSS (Healthcare Information and Management
        Systems Society) Adoption Model, 16, 20, 28,
        38, 55, 60–61, 94
    Stage 7 award, 30
HIPAA, *See* Health Information Privacy and
        Accountability Act
HIT, *See* Health information technology
HITECH Act (Health Information Technology for
        Economic and Clinical Health Act), 15–16,
        38, 51, 64, 112
    bioterrorism surveillance and, 117
    cultural competence and, 26
    electronic medical records and, 52

return on investment and, 44
HIV/AIDS application, 120, 122*t*
HL7, 121
Hoch, I., 99
Hofstede's cultural dimensions theory, 17
HomMed system, 124*t*
HopeLab, 128*t*
Horizontal and vertical integration, 46–47
Horwitz, J. R., 40
Hospital cultural competence, 25–28
Hospital financing, 35–37, *See also* Healthcare
        economics
    accounting costs, 40–41
    bond ratings and, 28–29
    bounded rationality for technology introduction, 48
    differences across states, 29–30
    differences in services and, 40, 41–42
    free rider issues, 38
    government funding, 29
    HIPAA compliance costs, 8
    hospital structures and financing mechanisms,
        39–42
    impact of competitive environment, 40
    incentives and compensation structure, 21
    length of stay effects, 38, 41
    management performance and, 45–46
    mismanagement of funds, 40
    policy analysis and implications, 48–49
    return on investment, 44–45
    sunk costs, 38, 41
    supply side of healthcare, 37–38
    tax status, 44
    technology adoption implications, 46–48
Hospital mergers and acquisitions, 22, 42–44
Hospital missions and values, 18–19, 27, 37–38
Hospital Preparedness Program (HPP), 114
Hospitals, for-profit (private), *See* For-profit hospitals
Hospitals, government-owned, *See* Community health
        centers; Government hospitals
Hospitals, nonprofit, *See* Not-for-profit hospitals
Hospitals, organizational culture differences, *See*
        Organizational culture differences, HIT
        adoption and
Hospital size
    EMR use and impacts, 53
    free rider issues, 65
    inefficiencies in technology use, 66
    new technology adoption and, 29
    quality of care impacts, 43
Hospital staff, HIPAA stakeholders, 7–8

I

IBREAST-CHECK, 129*t*
Identification numbers, 3
India, 120
Ingram, H. M., 4–5, 11

Insurance premiums, medical malpractice risk and, 98–99, 100, 106
Insurance providers, *See also* Health insurance
    HIPAA stakeholders, 10
    mobile health applications and, 120
Integrated model, electronic health records, 59
Integration, horizontal and vertical, 46–47
Internal Revenue Service (IRS) guidelines, 19, 83
INTERPOL, 113
Interuniversity Consortium for Political and Social Research (ICPSR), 87

K

Kaiser Permanente, 43, 85, 120
Keeler, E. B., 43
Kennedy, A., 17–18, 20
Kenya, 120
Krusch, D. A., 53
Kues, I. W., 56

L

Laffont, J.-J., 46
Lagged effects, 47, 65
Language translation, 23–24, 87
Length of stay (LOS), 41
    EMR use and shortening, 94
    trends affecting hospital economics, 38
Liao-Troth, M. A., 22
LifePoint Hospitals, 43
Lifestream View, 124*t*
Logistic regression, 66, 71, 85, 87, 100–101
Loomis, G. A., 53
Lumosity, 128*t*

M

Malpractice issues, *See* Medical malpractice
Managed care organizations, 41
Management, top-down and bottom-up, 43
Management compensation, 20–23, 45–46
Management performance, impact on HIT usage, 63–64, *See also* Organizational behavior characteristics, impact on HIT usage
Marion Regional Healthcare System, 43
Markle, 121
Martimont, D., 46
mCare, 120, 123*t*
McCullough, J. S., 46, 47
McFadden R^2 models, 71, 82
McGuire, T. G., 38
Meaningful use of technology, 16, 24
    HIMSS Stage 7 award, 30
    specialty groups and, 82
Mechanic, David, 53, 55

Medicaid, *See also* Center for Medicaid and Medicare Services
    EHR Incentive program, 59, 83
    incentive benefits for community health centers, 82
    patient-controlled health records program, 121
    Quality Healthcare Alliance (QHA), 117
Medicaid patient mix
    billing issues, 83
    EMR systems and, 53–54, 71, 82
    hospital health information technology investment reimbursement and, 38
    new or replacement EMR system installation, 74
    physician malpractice litigation perceptions and, 107, 108
Medical errors
    EMR system use and, 88–90
    trainees and, 99
Medical malpractice
    confidentiality violations, 8
    healthcare costs and, 99–100
    physician litigation history, 100
    policy, 20
    risk-based technology adoption, 20
    studies, 98–100
Medical malpractice, HIT and physician liability perceptions, 97–109
    analysis, 101–102
    competitiveness metric, 102, 107, 108
    global considerations, 109
    information technology expansion and, 109
    outcomes of perceptions, 102–105
    overall model outcomes, 106–108
    policy implications, 108–109
    premiums and awards, 98–99, 106
    pressure of litigation risk, 102–104
    previous studies, 98–100
    quality of provided care, 103–104
    research hypotheses, 101
    stages of technology use, 100
    theoretical predictive model, 104–106
Medical school trainees, 99
Medical tourism, 11, 109
Medicare, *See also* Center for Medicaid and Medicare Services
    incentive benefits for small businesses, 82
    patient-controlled health records program, 121
Medicare patient mix
    billing issues, 83
    EMR systems and, 53–54, 71, 82
    hospital health information technology investment reimbursement and, 38
    new or replacement EMR system installation, 74
    physician malpractice litigation perceptions and, 107
Meindl, J. R., 22
MelApp, 130*t*
Mental health services, 26
Mergers and acquisitions, 22, 30, 42–44

diseconomies of scale, 43
  examples, 43
  pricing effects, 43
Meta-analysis, 11
Mexican Health Project, 25
Mexico, 120
Mhealth, 120
Microsoft Vault, 121
Miller, A. R., 98
Minorities, *See also* Cultural diversity issues
  quality of care of health services, 86–87
  staff diversity, 25
Missions and values, 18–19
  cultural competence and, 27
  supply side of healthcare, 37–38
Mission statements, 18–19
Mobile health applications, 119, 120
  examples, 120, 122–130*t*
Mobile health services, 83
Moodgym, 127*t*
Moral hazard, 39
Municipal bonds, 44

N

National Ambulatory Medical Care Survey (NAMCS),
      65, 66
National Institute of Allergy and Infectious Diseases
      (NIAID), 114
Native Americans, 37
New Zealand, 120
Nichols, A., 40
Nike's Fuelband, 124*t*
Not-for-profit hospitals, 39
  benefits from physician integration, 47
  bounded rationality for technology introduction, 48
  causes of failures, 30
  competitiveness metric, 102
  financing structure, 35, 38, *See also* Hospital
        financing
    impact of competitive environment, 40
    mismanagement of funds, 40
    tax-exempt status, 44
  IRS guidelines for community outreach, 19, 83
  less-profitable services, 41–42
  management characteristics and HIT usage, *See*
        Organizational behavior characteristics,
        impact on HIT usage
  mergers and acquisitions of by for-profit institutions,
        42, *See also* Mergers and acquisitions
  mission of, 37–38
  organizational culture and HIT adoption, 15, *See
        also* Organizational culture differences, HIT
        adoption and
    achievement differences, 29
    cultural competence and, 25, 27
    incentives and compensation structure, 20–21

  missions and values, 18
  theoretical models, 17–18
  volunteers, 21–22
ownership characteristics and hospital performance,
      65–66
patient type selection behavior, 48
pay and performance issues, 45
stages of technology adoption and implementation,
      16
tax-exempt status, 19, 44, 83
top-down and bottom-up management, 43

O

Obstetrics, 99
Office of Civil Rights (OCR), 2
Organizational behavior characteristics, impact on HIT
      usage, 63–66
  billing issues, 83
  e-billing and electronic claims, 74–76, 82, 83
  e-prescribing, 76–78, 82
  examples of organizational behavior, 65
  HIT usage differences across providers and
        characteristics, 71–72
  interaction term, ownership and specialty practice,
        78–81
  literature, 65–66
  new or replacement EMR system installation,
        72–74
  policy analysis and implications, 82–84
  public health reporting, 79–81, 83
  short-term focus and lagged effects, 65
  study methods and statistics, 66–71
  training implications, 84
Organizational culture differences, HIT adoption and,
      15, 16, *See also specific types of hospitals*
  achievement differences, 29
  bond ratings and, 28–29
  collaboration, 30–31
  cultural competence, 25–28
  goal-oriented behavior, 28–31
  hospital size and, 29
  managerial incentives and compensation structure,
        20–23
  missions and values, 18–19
  policy implications, 31–33
  risk-based technology adoption, 20
  stages of technology adoption and implementation,
        16
  theory and models, 17–18
  training and impact on quality of care, 23–24
  volunteers, 21–22
Ownership characteristics, impact on HIT usage,
      64–66, *See also* Organizational behavior
      characteristics, impact on HIT usage
  interaction term, ownership and specialty practice,
        78–81

physician employment status, 65, 71
physician malpractice litigation perceptions and, 101–102, 107
public health reporting, 79–81
study methods and statistics, 66–71
Ozeran, L., 100

P

Parental access to medical records, 9
Patient-centered focus, 39
Patient-controlled health records (PHRs), 119–121
Patient directory information, 9
Patient fees, for electronic health records, 55–58, 61
Patient identification numbers, 3
Patient Protection and Affordable Care Act (PPACA), 1
    community outreach requirements for nonprofit hospitals, 19
    EMR system adoption requirement, 54
    HIPAA and privacy considerations, 2, *See also* Health Information Privacy and Accountability Act
Patients and healthcare consumers, HIPAA stakeholders, 9–10
Peggle, 128*t*
Performance measurement, 45–46
Performance reviews, 20
Pharmacy services, e-prescribing, 76–78
Philip's Telestation, 124*t*
Physician incentives, 47
    EMR system adoption requirement, 54
Physicians
    attitudes toward change, 22
    career satisfaction and perceived malpractice pressure, 106
    employment status and information technology usage, 65, 71
    health information technology and malpractice liability perceptions, 97–109, *See also* Medical malpractice
    HIPAA stakeholders, 7–8
    malpractice litigation history, 100
    public health reporting, 79–81, 83
    use of EMRs, 53
Pink, G., 45
Plagiarism, 11
Plague, 111
Pluralist theory, transition to public choice, 4
POCKET FIRST AID & CPR, 130*t*
Point of care (PoC), 124*t*
Policy analysis
    EMR system adoption financial issues, 54–55
    EMR systems and biosurveillance, 117–118
    HIPAA, 11–12
    hospital structures and financing mechanisms, 48–49

organizational characteristics and technology usage, 82–84
organizational culture and HIT adoption, 31–33
technology use and physician malpractice litigation perceptions, 108–109
Policy window, health care privacy, 3
Politics of healthcare reform, 53
Porter, Michael, 52
PPACA, *See* Patient Protection and Affordable Care Act
Preexisting conditions, 10
Prescriptions, electronic (e-prescribing), 76–78
Preyra, C., 45
Prince, T. R., 28
Principal-agent model, 44, 45, 46, 47
Privacilla.org, 6
Privacy of health records, *See* Health Information Privacy and Accountability Act
Privacy violations, malpractice issues, 8
Project Bioshield, 114
Psychotherapy confidentiality, 9
Public choice theory, 4–6
Public health awareness, 78
Public health reporting, 79–81, 83
Puffer, S. M., 22

Q

Quality Healthcare Alliance (QHA), 117
Quality improvement (QI), 28
Quality of care
    services for minorities, 86–87
    smaller versus larger hospitals, 43
    technology use and malpractice litigation risk, 103–104
    training impacts, 23–24
Quality of care, impacts of EMR systems, 85
    descriptive and inferential statistics
        computing discrete change, 90–93
        errors, time, and communication issues, 88–90
        minor versus major technology problems, 88–90, 93–94
        overall impact on quality of care, 88
    long-term implications, 93–95
    previous literature, 85–87
    study limitations, 93
    study methodology and variables, 87–88

R

Rational choice theory, 5
Referral networks, 41
Regression models, 66, 71, 85, 99, 100–101
Religious beliefs, 24, 26
Re-Mission, 129*t*
Reporting on public health issues, 79–81
Researchers, HIPAA and privacy considerations, 10–11

Return on investment, 44–45, 53
RevolutionHealth, 121
Roberts, B., 99
Robert Wood Johnson Foundation, 121
Roomkin, M. J., 20–21
Run Zombie Run, 128*t*
Rural areas
    bioterrorism risk and, 117
    e-prescribing and, 78
    healthcare provision differences, 37
    impacts of privacy regulations, 11
Rural hospitals, organizational characteristics and
        technology adoption, 23

S

Salmonella, 111
SARS (severe acute respiratory syndrome), 118
Saunders, W., 44–45
Schneider, A. L., 4–5, 11
Senior citizens, 71, 78, 82
Services, type of and HIT services usage, 65
    interaction term, ownership and specialty practice,
        78–81
Sexually transmitted disease (STD) screening, 9
Simon, Herbert, 4
Singh, H., 99
Sloan, F. A., 41, 65
Smart phones, 120
Snir, E. M., 46, 47
Specialty care services, 65
    e-billing and, 76
    interaction term, ownership and specialty practice,
        78–81
    malpractice premiums and, 99
    meaningful use and, 82
Stages of technology use, 16, 47, 100
Stakeholder analysis, HIPAA, 4, 6–11, *See also* Health
        Information Privacy and Accountability Act
Standardization, 54, 109
Stanford Hospital and Clinics, California, 29
State differences in hospital funding, 29–30
Sunk costs, 38, 41
Sunset Park Family Health Center, 25
Supply side healthcare economics, 37–38
Surgical care services, e-billing and, 76

T

Taborrak, A., 99
Tax-exempt status, 19, 44, 83
Teaching hospitals, 8
Technology adoption stage, 16
Technology implementation stage, 16
Technology use, stages of, 16

Third-party providers, HIPAA stakeholders, 10
Time management issues, EMR system use and, 88–90,
        93–94
Time with patients, malpractice litigation risk predictor,
        107
Trainees, medical errors and, 99
Training, 23–24
    cultural diversity and, 23–24
    HIPAA and privacy considerations, 8
    organizational characteristics and technology usage,
        84
    quality of care impacts, 23–24
Translation, 23–24, 87
TRICARE, 58
Tucker, C., 98

U

Uninsured patients, 39
United States, rank in world health systems, 113
U.S. Department of Defense, 58
U.S. Department of Health and Human Services
        (DHHS), 2, 6, 7, 18, 113, 114
U.S. Department of Veterans Affairs, 120

V

VensaHealth, 120, 122*t*
Vertical and horizontal integration, 46–47
Veterans Administration (VA) system, 65
Veterans Health Administration (VHA), 58
Vidanet, 120, 122*t*
VistA, 58
Volunteers, 21–22
Vraciu, R. A., 65

W

Walker, J., 60
Web-based cognitive behavioral therapy, 126*t*
Weber, Max, 17
Weisbrod, B. A., 20–21
Weltel application, 120
West, Timothy, 65
Wolff, N., 21
World Health Organization (WHO), 113

Y

Yersinia pestis, 111

Z

Zamzee, 128*t*
Zuger, A., 100

Trocaire Libraries

DATE DUE

MAY 1 3 2014

Brodart Co.   Cat. # 55 137 001   Printed in USA